Nicholson's

Access in London

A guide fo
problems getting around

Gordon Couch
William Forrester

ROBERT NICHOLSON PUBLICATIONS

This book is dedicated to Tony Milner, Old Hephaistian, remembering particularly his enthusiasm and determination

Gordon Couch is the organiser of Pauline Hephaistos Survey Projects (PHSP), 39 Bradley Gdns W13. This is an independent investigative group consisting of boys and old boys from the Hephaistos School near Reading and St Paul's School, Barnes. The group includes both able-bodied and disabled researchers, who have wide experience of travelling and of overcoming access problems.

William Forrester is a London Registered Guide and is himself in a wheelchair. He has extensive experience of organising trips and visits for disabled individuals and groups, both in London and throughout Britain and lectures on British heritage. He also has an adapted minibus available. He can be contacted at 1 Belvedere Clo, Guildford, Surrey (Guildford (0483) 575401).

First published 1984

Text researched by Pauline Hephaistos Survey Projects,
© **Pauline Hephaistos Survey Projects 1984**

Diagrams and itinerary maps kindly supplied by British Petroleum Co PLC,
© Pauline Hephaistos Survey Projects
Design criteria diagram reproduced from 'Designing for the Disabled' by
Selwyn Goldsmith with the kind permission of the publishers,
RIBA Publications Ltd
Other maps kindly supplied by British Petroleum Co PLC
to © design by Robert Nicholson Publications Ltd
Maps based upon the Ordnance Survey with the sanction of
the Controller of Her Majesty's Stationery Office.
Crown copyright reserved

Published by Robert Nicholson Publications Ltd
17 Conway St, London W1P 6JD

Great care has been taken throughout this book to be
accurate but the publishers cannot accept responsibility
for any errors which appear

Phototypeset in England by Tradespools Ltd, Frome, Somerset

Printed and bound in Great Britain by The Guernsey Press Co Ltd,
Guernsey, Channel Islands

ISBN 0 905522 79 6

Contents

Acknowledgements

The production of a guidebook like this one, researched and written during volunteers' spare time, depends on the help of a very considerable number of people. We are indebted to the many trusts, companies and individuals who have supported us. Without practical help the guide would never have been prepared and without financial help it would have been smaller or more expensive.

Pauline Hephaistos Survey Projects would particularly like to thank Freda Bruce Lockhart, who wrote the first 'London for the Disabled' in 1967 and thus inspired this new production, and who has given her full support; Robert Nicholson Publications, for agreeing to publish the guide on a non-profit-making basis; British Petroleum Co PLC, who prepared the artwork and maps; and the Queen's Silver Jubilee Trust for its sponsorship.

We would also like to thank all those involved with surveying, writing, typing and correcting the text; and the companies listed below, who have provided financial support for our projects. We hope that people will feel that their contributions have been well used.

Anderson Strathclyde
Augustine Trust
Barclays Bank
Benham Charitable Settlement
S & W Berisford
Blunt Trust
Cadbury Schweppes CT
Capper Neill
Carless Capel & Leonard
Central & Sherwood
Clothworkers Foundation
John S Cohen Foundation
Richard Costain
EDB Memorial CT
Esmée Fairbairn CT
Express Newspapers
Ferguson Benevolent Fund
Fitton Trust
Foster Wheeler
Godinton CT
H J Heinz
Hilden Charitable Fund
Robert Horne & Co
Imperial Brewing (Courage)
Imperial Continental Gas
ITT Executive Assn (UK) CT
Lilly Industries
Lloyds Bank

London Weekend Television
Lower Sapey Trustees
Derek McCulloch Fund for Hephaistos
Marks & Spencer
Mars (Pedigree Petfoods)
Martin the Newsagent
Mercers Co
Peter Minet Trust
Mobil Oil
Moorgate Trust Fund
National Westminster Bank
Petrofina (UK)
Joseph Rank (1942) Trust
Rayne Foundation
St Regis International
Coral Samuel CT
Sidlaw Group
Sketchley CT
Smith Kline & French
John Swire & Sons
3M UK
Tootal Group
Unigate
Wedd Durlacher Mordaunt & Co
M A Weinberg CT
Whesby Ltd
Wilkinson Sword
Sir Samuel Scott of Yews Trust

Introduction

People come to London for all kinds of reasons. There are the tourists who come to see the Changing of the Guard, the river and the big shops; those who come to visit relations in Neasden or Hackney; and those attracted by big sporting and national events, major exhibitions or places like Kew Gardens, for both interest and research. The reasons are varied, but most visitors take the opportunity of seeing some of the many interesting facets of London life and culture and of enjoying some of the enormous variety of things there are to do.

This guidebook has two purposes. The first is to help disabled visitors to get around more easily by providing specialised information; the second is to encourage change both in physical provisions and in attitudes, so as to make life easier for disabled people. Even after the International Year of the Disabled Person (IYDP) in 1981, an enormous amount remains to be done to make access—and therefore acceptance and integration—easier.

This guide is specifically an access guide. Its aim is to help visitors who have any kind of mobility problem, ranging from someone who has had a recent illness or accident to someone who has a chest or heart condition or is in a wheelchair. **We assume that people will use it in conjunction with conventional guidebooks and maps; it's most important to plan your visit so that you can get to the places of greatest interest to you.**

The research and survey work for the guide was carried out during 1982/83 by handicapped people, most of them in wheelchairs, together with a number of able-bodied helpers. Most of the information has been obtained at first hand and practically all the places included in the guide—public buildings, sights, hotels and so forth—have been walked into and wheeled over by one of our survey teams. The surveyors are part of a group called **Pauline Hephaistos Survey Projects** (PHSP) which has previously prepared access guides to places like Jersey, Paris, Brittany, Israel and the Channel ports. The group consists of pupils and ex-pupils from St Paul's School, Barnes SW13 and Hephaistos School, Farley Hill, near Reading, Berks. The 'we' used frequently in the text refers to PHSP. While we've tried very hard to be both accurate and objective, a few errors may have crept into the text either from a restricted survey or during the transfer of information from survey form to text. **All the views expressed are those of the survey teams and they relate to the place at the time of the visit.** We have tried to cross-check the information with those responsible for various buildings and facilities and have sent them a copy of the text for their comment but, of course, not everyone replied. However, readers must appreciate that accessibility will vary according to the time of day, the time of year and which officials are on duty (the lavatory attendant isn't there, so the loo is locked). Some people will be prepared to break or bend rules, while others will be more rigid. If particular features of access are especially important to you, check directly before setting off—we have included telephone numbers wherever possible. **A listing does not imply accessibility.** We've tried to describe the barriers as simply as possible and we do include some places that are inaccessible by most people's standards, simply so that you know what the problems are and don't waste time and effort.

"What's London like for disabled people?" you may ask. This is a question that is always hard to answer authoritatively. After all, what do you want to know? London is like anywhere else—it's good in parts; that doesn't mean it's like the curate's egg—that we're just being polite because it really stinks—but it does mean it can be a very mixed experience. Places where you would expect to be able to get in, like at the Tower to see the Crown Jewels, can turn out to be out of the question; yet you may discover somewhere quite small, like the Crafts Council Gallery, that has gone out of its way to be helpful. It depends on where you go, and who you meet. Two disabled people can come to London at the same time and go away with totally different impressions: one will say it's a 'no go' area, the other that it's magic—and they'll both be right.

There's much to see and do. It's best to plan, and perhaps even to stay near the places of greatest interest to you. There are enough places with relatively easy access to fill any holiday itinerary. Of course, there are other places where access is difficult or virtually impossible, but don't feel cheated if you only go to the sights or places with easier access. If you visit all, or even most, of these you'll be in London for several weeks and you'll have seen quite enough to make your trip memorable and worthwhile.

Emergencies

In the event of accident or emergency, the standard procedure is to telephone the Police, Fire Service or Ambulance by dialling **999**. That way you'll get the right help or advice, but remember that the first person you'll speak to is only the operator who will ask, "Which service do you want?". When you then get through you can explain what is needed. Note that normally both doctors and dentists are available only during working hours. If you have an accident or need emergency treatment, the following list of hospitals with a casualty department *open 24 hours a day* may be useful:

Middlesex Hospital Mortimer St W1 (636-8333).
New Charing Cross Hospital Fulham Palace Rd W6 (748-2040).
Royal Free Hospital Pond St NW3 (794-0500).
St Bartholomew's Hospital West Smithfield EC1 (600-9000).
St Stephen's Hospital 369 Fulham Rd SW10 (352-8161).
St Thomas's Hospital Lambeth Palace Rd SE1 (928-9292).
University College Hospital Gower St WC1 (387-9300).

University College Dental Hospital Mortimer Mkt, off Tottenham Court Rd WC1 (387-9300) is *open Mon–Fri 09.00–14.30, Sat 09.00–11.00, closed Sun*. At other times, if you have a genuine dental emergency you can go to any of the casualty departments listed above.

If you need to collect a prescription, your nearest police station keeps a list of local pharmacies and their opening times. Two chemists open late are:
Bliss 54 Willesden La NW6 (954-7373). *Open 24 hrs*.
Boots Piccadilly Circus W1 (734-6126). *Open 08.30–20.00, closed Sun*.

The Medicalert Foundation 11 Clifton Ter N4 (263-8597) provides a useful service for those with medical problems that could be compounded by treatment after an accident if the patient is unable to make known his or her particular condition. It is of special importance to those suffering from epilepsy, haemophilia, diabetes or allergies, and to those who need regular dosage of a particular drug. Life membership is available to anyone, for a nominal fee. Members wear a metal emblem engraved on one side with the name 'Medicalert', and bearing the telephone number of the Medicalert Emergency Service on the reverse side, where the immediate medical problems of the wearer are also noted—for example, 'Allergic to penicillin', 'Taking anti-coagulants', 'Wearing contact lenses', 'Under steroid treatment', 'Diabetic'. Additional medical information is filed at the Emergency Headquarters, where the telephone is manned 24 hours a day.

SOS Talisman Co Ltd 21 Gray's Corner, Ley St, Ilford, Essex (554-5579) operate a similar service, which works on the basis of including information in a small locket, which is worn permanently.

Wheelchair & equipment repair & hire

If one of your wheels drops off in Oxford Circus or if you need to hire special equipment for any reason, the following contact addresses should be useful. It's always a good idea to **carry a repair kit, including some simple tools**. It can pay to bring a few vital spares, too—especially if your chair isn't standard—and carrying one of the instant tyre-repair kits available from shops like Halfords may well be a sensible precaution.

The only official (DHSS agents) repairers are in Kingston and Harold Wood, both a long way out of the centre:
ALAC 53 High St, Kingston-upon-Thames (546-1011).
Harold Wood Hospital (ALAC) Gubbins La, Harold Wood, Romford (Inglebourne (04023) 74121).

For simple jobs it's probably best to go to a bicycle shop or a garage. There are a few suggestions here; otherwise try the Yellow Pages in the telephone book. If you have a DHSS chair, get a receipt for any repairs and remember that, in principle, repairs costing over £6.00 should be authorised by one of the ALAC centres listed above. If you ring for authorisation, make sure you note down the name of the person you speak to. In the following list, firms marked with an asterisk (*) also sell equipment. **London is a good place to come to buy a chair or other equipment**; you can get advice from the Disabled Living Foundation and also find agents for most of the main manufacturers.
*All Handling (Movability) Ltd The Old Mill, Old Malden La, Worcester Pk, Surrey (330-3360). Repair and rental of Newton Elan powered chairs and Batricars. Agents for Portascoot and Bec Scoota.
*Ashley Surgical Appliances 276 Stamford Hill N16 (800-2803). Zimmer and Carter chairs for sale or hire.
*Carters (J & A) Ltd 134 Brompton Rd SW3 (584-6416). Zimmer and Carter chairs for sale or hire.
*Cory Bros (Hospital Contracts Ltd) 166 High Rd N2 (444-9966). Zimmer and Carter chairs for sale or hire.
Hire Services shops About a dozen shops within the London postal area; a list can be obtained from their head office at 31 London Rd, Reigate, Surrey (Reigate (74) 49441). Hand-propelled folding chairs for hire.
*Porter Nash Pharmacy & Medical Equipment Ltd 116 Wigmore St W1 (486-1434). Everest & Jennings and Rolls Invacare chairs for sale or hire. Also other aids and equipment. Central location.
The Red Cross 9 Grosvenor Cres SW1 (235-5454). Chairs available for occasional temporary use. The central office may put you in touch with a local group if you're away from the centre. The type of chair depends on availability.

Reselco Ltd 262 King St W6 (748-5053). A couple of chairs for hire. Carter and Ormed chairs for sale.
Donald Rose Ltd 34 Margaret St W1 (629-6994). Central location and flat access to showroom. Days, Everest & Jennings, Vessa and McCarthy chairs for sale. There is a factory at Southend and they say that they can offer a fast service for repairs.
U Williams & Co 311 Brighton Rd, South Croydon, Surrey (688-2030). Newton and Carter chairs for sale or hire.

Other central stockists include:
Camp Ltd 116 Tower Bridge Rd SE1 (237-3195).
John Bell & Croydon 50 Wigmore St W1 (935-5555).
Raymond Ltd 69 Weymouth St W1 (935-8152).
Universal Hospital Supplies Ltd 58 Berners St W1 (636-3424).

Finally, here are the addresses of a few of the best bicycle shops. Most of them are some way from the centre, but in the event of damage to your wheelchair they may be able to help you out.
Bike Peddlers Ltd 50 Calthorpe St WC1 (278-0551).
F W Evans 77/79 The Cut SE1 (928-4785). *Closed Thur.*
Nash 155 Goldhawk Rd W12 (743-5133). *Closed Thur pm.*
B T Simpson (Cycles) 116 Maldon Rd NW5 (485-1706). *Closed Thur.*
Strattons 101 East Hill SW18 (854-2383). *Closed Wed.*

General information

The climate

Visitors to the capital must take into account the generally mild but unpredictable weather. There are, of course, hot spells in the summer and cold periods in the winter but the forecast of 'sunshine and showers' is all too common. When packing, you should allow for snow and ice in the winter (and often chilly winds) and for rain all year round. If you come in the summer, remember that relatively few buildings have air-conditioning. In general, the weather poses few problems for the disabled visitor, although there can be variations in temperature from 32°C/90°F right down to −11°C/10°F under extreme conditions. The average maximum daily temperatures are set out below.

	Jan	Feb	Mar	Apr	May	Jun	Jul	Aug	Sep	Oct	Nov	Dec
°F	45	45	50	55	63	68	70	70	66	61	50	45
°C	7	7	10	13	17	20	21	21	19	16	10	7

Information services & organisations

There are many sources of information and who you go to depends very much on what you want to know. If you need advice or help on any subject, you often have to be persistent and try different contacts if your first or second enquiry doesn't produce an answer to the questions you're asking. We list here a few of the general sources and major organisations for disabled people who both hold and publish a great deal of useful information. Note that if a telephone number or address has changed, you will almost certainly be able to get the new one from one of the other agencies listed, if not from the Telecom directory enquiries on **142**. You will find the telephone numbers of many places in the London telephone directory. In addition, the reference section of your local public library almost certainly has a good range of books and information. If you haven't ever been there, it's worth a visit sometime; you'll find lots of basic texts about disability and you may find useful contacts for solving problems.

There are numerous listings about what is happening in London, including pamphlets from LTB offices and the BTA office ('London Week'); 'The Standard', which is London's evening paper; the national dailies; and magazines like 'Time Out', 'What's On & Where to Go in London' and 'City Limits'. These will tell you about theatres, restaurants, sporting, musical and special events, and exhibitions. You'd best have a look on the bookstalls to decide which one covers what you are looking for. 'City Limits' has started to include brief access data, and we hope that other magazines will follow suit in due course.

Artsline 48 Boundary Rd NW8 (625-5666) provide an excellent telephone information service on access to the arts and entertainment. They have a lot of experience and knowledge for advising on what is possible and practicable. *Open Mon–Fri 10.00–16.00, Sat 10.00–14.00.*

The British Tourist Authority (BTA) 64 St James's St SW1 (629-9191) publish a number of useful booklets for visitors, including 'Britain for the Disabled Visitor', 'Invitation to Beautiful Britain' and 'A Traveller's Guide'. The latter is particularly useful for visitors from abroad, giving details of British entry conditions, duty-free allowances, coinage, rules of the road, licensing hours and so forth.

The Centre on Environment for the Handicapped (CEH) 126 Albert St NW1 (482-2247) aims to improve access to buildings and the environment generally, working with and through architects and others. It has a useful range of publications including design sheets and reading lists. The newly formed English Access Committee operates under the auspices of the CEH.

The Committee on Multi-handicapped Blind 55 Eton Av NW3 (586-5655) publishes a directory of services for visually and mentally handicapped people and for professionals working with them. It also gives advice on desirable provisions in buildings.

The Daily Telegraph Information Bureau (353-4242) gives a wide range of information about events and opening hours. Ask for 'Information'. *Open Mon–Fri 09.30–17.30.*

DIAL (UK) (National Association of Disablement Information and Advice Services) Dial House, 117 High St, Clay Cross, Derbs (Chesterfield (0246) 864498). DIAL is a growing organisation which co-ordinates local groups that offer free advice and information on all aspects of disability. This, naturally, includes access and, more generally, mobility. We include a list of the groups operating in the London area at the time of writing and you can check with the national HQ in Clay Cross as to whether more groups have been started, perhaps in your area.
Advice & Rights Centre for the Handicapped (ARCH) St John's Day Centre, 113 St John's Wy N19 (263-8622). Operates *Mon–Fri 10.30–15.30.*
Handicapped Help Line 88 High St South E6 (471-7188). Operates *Mon–Fri 21.00–23.00.*
Lambeth Disabled Advice Phone-in Service c/o A Higgins, 115 Clapham Rd SW9 (582-4352). Operates *Tue & Thur 13.00–15.00.*

Waltham Forest Social Services Pretoria Rd E17 (520-4111). Operates *Mon–Fri 10.00–16.00.*
Wandsworth Disablement Advice Service Atheldene Centre, 305 Garrett La SW18 (870-7437). Operates *Mon–Fri 10.00–16.00.*

The Disability Alliance (DA) 25 Denmark St WC2 (240-0806). The DA consists of many of the major voluntary groups and produces 'The Disability Rights Handbook' every year, updating in fairly straightforward language the various benefits to which disabled people are entitled. This handbook also contains a comprehensive list of virtually all the organisations of and for disabled people.

Disabled Living Foundation (DLF) 346 Kensington High St W14 (602-2491). The Foundation works to help disabled people in aspects of ordinary life which present difficulty. It offers a large showroom and comprehensive information service on aids and equipment of all kinds. Advice is given on visual impairment, incontinence, music, sport, clothing and skin care. Publication list available on application. **An appointment is necessary.** A proposal to move to larger premises is currently under discussion.

Disablement Income Group (DIG) & DIG Charitable Trust Attlee House, 28 Commercial St E1 (247-2128). DIG is a pressure group for legislative reform with branches throughout the country. The Trust publishes a journal, 'Progress', three times a year and 'Compass', which is an invaluable directory of information on a very wide range of subjects.

The Greater London Association for Disabled People (GLAD) 1 Thorpe Clo W1 (960-5799) is a voluntary organisation working through a network of borough associations to assist disabled people in London. It is thus uniquely suited to monitoring local authority activity and to encouraging the implementation of the Chronically Sick and Disabled Persons Act 1970 and its subsequent revisions. It provides a comprehensive information service to both residents and visitors and publications include a quarterly journal, a directory of clubs in the Greater London area and information sheets.

London Association for the Blind (LAB) 14 Verney Rd SE16 (732-8771). The LAB produces an excellent handbook of services for blind and partially sighted people, and is a source of both advice and information. Details are given in the handbook of a hostel for the partially sighted at Adams House, 2 Underhill Rd SE22 (693-7400).

The London Tourist Board (LTB) 26 Grosvenor Gdns SW1 (730-3488 *Mon–Fri 09.00–17.30*) is the main source of tourist information in London. In particular, they can tell you whether places will be open and give information about costs, and the Victoria station and Heathrow offices can also give help in finding accommodation. **The LTB desks are all accessible** to both (w) and (s), without steps, although those in Selfridges, Harrods and at Heathrow Central Underground station are a considerable distance from parking facilities. You can get updated information on the services available and a publications list from the head office. The LTB publishes a list of accessible and partly accessible hotels which, it is to be hoped, will be updated from time to time. In 1981 the LTB published 'London for the Disabled Visitor'. Enquiries in person should be made at one of the main desks:
Harrods department store Brompton Rd SW1, 4th floor. *Open shop hours.*
Heathrow Central Underground station Hounslow. *Open daily.*

National Tourist Information Centre Victoria station forecourt SW1, by the head of the taxi rank. Flat and ramped access. Rather cramped bookshop. *Open daily.*
Selfridges department store Oxford St W1, GF. *Open shop hours.*
Tower of London, EC3, west gate. *Open summer only.*

National Society for Mentally Handicapped Children & Adults (MENCAP) 123 Golden La EC1 (253-9433). Works to improve the facilities for the mentally handicapped and offers help to both parents and professionals. It publishes many books, pamphlets and leaflets and a quarterly magazine, 'Parents' Voice'.

Royal Association for Disability and Rehabilitation (RADAR) 25 Mortimer St W1 (637-5400). RADAR is the central co-ordinating body for all the voluntary groups concerned with disabled people. It can provide advice and information on a wide variety of subjects including access, housing, aids, benefits available and local authority responsibilities. It seeks both to investigate the causes and problems of disablement and to promote measures to eliminate or alleviate them. It is the co-ordinating group for preparing access guides throughout the country and keeps a list and a stock of all those currently available. It produces an extensive publications list; an annual guide, 'Holidays for the Physically Handicapped'; a quarterly magazine, 'Contact'; and a monthly bulletin. All contain useful information.

Royal National Institute for the Blind (RNIB) 224 Great Portland St W1 (388-1266). Promotes facilities for the rehabilitation, training and employment of blind people and provides a range of braille publications. The institute can advise on a wide range of issues and publishes a monthly magazine, 'New Beacon'.

Royal National Institute for the Deaf (RNID) 105 Gower St WC1 (387-8033). The RNID aims to promote and encourage both the alleviation and prevention of deafness. It provides a comprehensive information and counselling service for people of all ages with impaired hearing. It can provide technical advice to the owners of buildings and other facilities about the installation and use of induction loops, induction couplers and other aids.

There is, of course, an enormous number of other groups and societies and these are listed in some of the publications mentioned above and at the end of this chapter. We haven't attempted to include all the specialist groups here because there just isn't space, but we hope that enquirers will be persistent in seeking the right source of information and advice.

Tips for visitors

Escalators Elderly people and some (s) find escalators difficult, and they're obviously a problem for solo (w). Our own experience, however, is that they are a safe and easy way of changing levels for (w) with one or two sensible (ab) friends and most of our survey teams have learned how to cope with them. The pusher must be strong enough to control the chair safely and smoothly over a kerb. On an escalator the trick is simply to balance the wheelchair on the back wheels at the point of balance. The person behind pulls or pushes the chair on to the escalator, placing the wheels in the middle of a step as it opens up. The person in front simply pushes gently and horizontally against the chair and is only there to steady the chair if necessary. It's much easier than it sounds, though don't try it unless your (ab) friends are adequately strong.

Price concessions A number of places offer price reductions for (w) visitors and/or, sometimes, for a pusher. Reductions are not generally available for other disabled people except sometimes for the blind. The problem is that the system is highly capricious in that it can depend as much on who's on the door as it does on official policy. The offer of price concessions for entrance is, however, a well meant gesture, particularly in view of regulations which say that (w) may not enter many places without a friend or escort. Because of the unreliability of price concessions, we have tended not to mention them because we might be raising false hopes. Many museums and galleries have free entrance anyway. At a good number of other public buildings where an entrance fee is charged, either the (w) or the pusher is allowed in at a reduced rate; some, however, charge the full price. The same situation was found at theatres and cinemas. Some of the managements are both sympathetic and helpful, and a few will let both a (w) and a companion sit in the licensed spaces for the price of the cheaper seats.

If you want up-to-date information on entertainment venues, Artsline is the best source. Places where there are well established concessions include the South Bank (National Theatre and Festival Hall complex); the Barbican; the Fairfield Halls, Croydon; the Tower Bridge Walkway and the Tower of London.

Telephones The code for London is **01** and this is followed by seven numbers. However, when dialling from within London you don't need the 01 code, so central London numbers given here omit the code. Outside central London, different codes apply; we have given the exchange name, with the code from London in brackets. If you are dialling London from abroad, there will be a local code to replace the 0 (usually four figures). Dial this code, then the 1, followed by the seven internal figures. If in doubt, ask the operator for advice (dial **100**). British Telecom offer several useful services—here's a selection:

Emergency calls	999 (no charge)
Directory enquiries	142 for London addresses
	192 for addresses outside the London postal area
Children's London	246-8007
Motoring information	246-8021
Tourist information	246-8041
Weather forecast	246-8091

Note that normal public telephone boxes are inaccessible and the provision of a 'phone at the right height for (w) is rare. One recent innovation is the introduction of cardphones, which are operated by a special credit card and are particularly useful for those who find it difficult to push coins past the bar in the conventional coinbox. Also, an increasing number of telephones include an induction coupler, which is of great value to those using a hearing aid. Remember that telephone calls from a hotel room are frequently charged at a considerably higher rate than those from a public callbox.

NB Often, the management of hotels, restaurants and so forth request or even demand that disabled visitors telephone in advance. In our experience, this can be a very frustrating business if you're trying to dial into a busy line—a point frequently not appreciated by the receiver of the call. It sounds very helpful when someone says, "Do ring back in an hour's time when the person you want will be here", but given the difficulty of finding an accessible 'phone and the probability of encountering busy lines, it can be much harder than it sounds. We hope that managements will become more aware of the problems in future.

How the guide is arranged

We have tried to highlight particularly accessible sights and places and also small areas where there's a lot to see or do without too much walking or wheeling. These areas often form section headings but if you're unfamiliar with London you may find the index useful; we've tried to include all the variations on the names of buildings and sights.

There is a chapter on travel with a section on parking, and information on getting to specific places is given in the relevant text entry. It has been assumed that you will use this book in conjunction with a good map and conventional guide books which give the historical background and comment on items of interest. By and large, the chapters are arranged alphabetically, although several are sub-divided into inner and outer London. Inner London is defined broadly as the West End and the City. Where items of interest on the fringes of Greater London are included, they are grouped under the subheading 'Further afield'.

Metric units

We have given measurements in centimetres (cm), metres (m) and kilometres (km). Although these are the units increasingly being used internationally, many English people still think in Imperial measures. To convert Metric measurements to the more familiar Imperial units, use the following guidelines:

    10 centimetres is about 4 inches (2.5 centimetres = 1 inch)
    1 metre is about a yard
    3 kilometres is about 2 miles (1.6 kilometres = 1 mile)

Also,

    1 gallon is about 4.5 litres (US gallon, about 3.8 litres)
    1 kilo is about 2 pounds (weight)

The diagram in the 'Tailpiece' chapter gives the approximate dimensions of a standard wheelchair. This is a general guide, since chairs vary considerably in size; it would be worth checking the exact dimensions of yours.

Symbols

Some years ago the use of a symbol to denote facilities for disabled people was agreed internationally and everyone is now familiar with the 'wheelchair' sign. In principle, the sign is used in accordance with certain criteria—flat or ramped access, doors wider than x cm and so on—but unfortunately in practice it has been misused so widely that it has become virtually meaningless, particularly when used in general guide books and listings. The problem is that assessment of accessibility is made by so many different people with different perceptions of disability that some places listed as accessible have steps at the entrance or inside, or other barriers. If you think that's exaggerating, when the London Tourist Board (LTB) surveyed the 100 or so hotels with the international access symbol listed in the 1981 'Where to Stay' guide for London, *none* of them met the criteria set. This may be an argument for changing the criteria, but it certainly demonstrates that the use of the symbol in hotel, restaurant, theatre and other listings can be very misleading. Its use does, however, give you a bit of a lever when a place is listed with the symbol and you want to get in! The LTB, RADAR and other bodies are looking into the question.

Meanwhile, make further enquiries before you trust an access listing. An exception to the rule is the Society of West End Theatre (SWET) guide, where the sign is well used and gives accurate information.

Symbols have been used in this guide to highlight certain simplified data about access. We hope that a system such as this one will soon be used to summarise important access data in conventional guidebooks. While it's not perfect, it does at least form a basis for giving accurate information in sign form without, we hope, being over-elaborate. Comments on the system will be welcomed, as it can doubtless be improved.

The list of symbols and abbreviations given at the end of the book has been translated into French and German to enable it to be used by overseas visitors. Also, 'The Disabled Traveller's Phrase Book' lists useful words and phrases in six European languages; it is available for about £1.00 from Disability Press Ltd, 60 Greenhayes Av, Banstead, Surrey.

Suggested itineraries

We have tried to identify and suggest smallish areas where there are a number of varied sights within a relatively small area, where you will find a (w) loo en route and where the majority of the places to be seen are described in this guide. Obviously you must study the map, because only you know what sort of distance you can cope with. In each case we have suggested places to park. We have in mind the visitor who has only two or three days in which to see a bit of London. Obviously it's difficult to represent everyone's interests, and you'll have your own ideas about what you want to see. We hope that with the judicious use of a good map and of this and other guides that you can plan your own visit to make the most of your time and resources, doing the things of most interest to you.

The Barbican & St Paul's

One very varied group of sights is centred on the Barbican area. Parking is possible under the Barbican Arts Centre or in the MSCP in Aldersgate St, which has **lift access and −3 steps** from the lift to the pavement. Around the Barbican Centre are St Bartholomew-the-Great and St Giles Cripplegate churches and the Museum of London. There are **(w) loos** in the Barbican Arts Centre and in the Museum of London. Postman's Park offers a possible shady picnic spot, although a good number of office workers will probably have the same idea. A little further afield are the Guildhall, Clock Museum and St Paul's Cathedral (though note the possible **access problems at St Paul's**).

The City

At the east end of the City there's a compact area to see including the Tower (where **access is very limited** inside), the Tower Bridge walkway, St Katharine's Dock and All-Hallows-by-the-Tower Church. A possible extension of this visit could take in the London Dungeon and the London War Museum. Parking is possible by St Katharine's Dock or south of the river in Southwark, where the orange badge is valid. There are **(w) loos** at the Tower, in the Tower Hotel and in the Tower Bridge Museum. There's a detailed map of this area in Nicholson's 'London Streetfinder'.

The Barbican & St Pauls

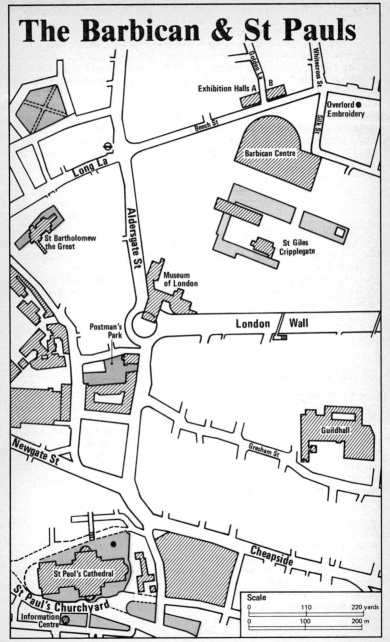

Exhibition Halls A B

Overlord ● Embroidery

Golden La

Whitecross St

Silk St

Beech St

Barbican Centre

Long La

Aldersgate St

St Bartholomew the Great

St Giles Cripplegate

Museum of London

Postman's Park

London Wall

Guildhall

Newgate St

Gresham St

Cheapside

St Paul's Cathedral

St Paul's Churchyard

Information Centre

Scale
| 0 | 110 | 220 yards |
| 0 | 100 | 200 m |

Kensington Museums

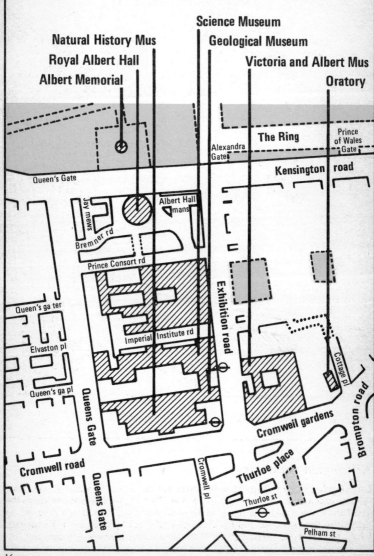

Natural History Mus

Royal Albert Hall

Albert Memorial

Science Museum

Geological Museum

Victoria and Albert Mus

Oratory

The Ring

Prince of Wales Gate

Alexandra Gate

Queen's Gate

Kensington road

Jay mews

Albert Hall mans

Bremner rd

Prince Consort rd

Queen's ga ter

Elvaston pl

Imperial Institute rd

Exhibition road

Queen's ga pl

Cottage pl

Queens Gate

Queen's ga pl

Cromwell gardens

Brompton road

Cromwell road

Queens Gate

Cromwell pl

Thurloe place

Thurloe st

Pelham st

Westminster to Piccadilly

KEY ● Car Parks ⊖ Underground Stations

Kensington museums

On the other side of central London there are the South Kensington museums, offering enormous variety. Most have (w) **loos**. Kensington Gardens are just to the north and if someone in the family wants to go shopping, Harrods is a little way to the east in Brompton Rd and Barkers and Marks and Spencer are in Kensington High St to the west. Parking can be arranged at some of the major museums.

Westminster to Piccadilly

The Westminster to Piccadilly map shows a somewhat larger area containing, again, a wide variety of sights. Parking is possible on the south side of the river round the Festival Hall complex (just off the map). There are a number of NCPs, for example those at the end of College Mews (near Westminster Abbey), in Artillery Row and in Whitcombe St. There's an Avis CP near Trafalgar Sq. However, it's a very congested area during the week and CPs are used mainly by season ticket holders and are often full up by 09.30.

If you decide to take in the whole area, St James's Park provides a good place for a rest or a picnic. Alternatively, you may find the distances involved too great and prefer to concentrate on, perhaps, the Westminster area. The Abbey is largely accessible and the Imperial Collection is nearby behind the Central Hall. Down Victoria St to the west are the Army and Navy stores and Westminster Cathedral. There are **(w) loos** past the Westminster Pier entrance, very near the bridge, and in the Army and Navy stores. Another possibility is to cross St James's Park to see Buckingham Palace, or to go north to Trafalgar Sq and Piccadilly Circus: accessible sights include the National Gallery, St-Martin's-in-the-Fields Church, the Royal Academy and Regent St—one of London's main shopping streets. About 300m from the Mall down Horse Guards Rd is the Cabinet War Room, which has lift access and a **(w) loo**. There are also **(w) loos** in the National Gallery.

Useful books

Maps & guides

There are an enormous number of publications about London which you will find in bookshops, on newspaper stands and at LTB information offices. The choice of good maps and guides is important and depends to some extent on what you want to do in London. **We assume that you will use this book in conjunction with conventional sources of information**; it is usually worth getting your maps and guides in advance in order to make the most of your visit.

Amongst the best maps are Nicholson's 'Streetfinder' and the Geographers' 'A–Z' series. The Geographia 'Greater London Street Atlas' covers an enormous area and is particularly useful if you are driving. The Nicholson 'Streetfinder' and 'London Map' contain much more information than most of their rivals, showing for example the location of CPs, hospitals and other services. Have a look at both and choose the one you find clearest and most suited to your needs.

As for guide books, the Nicholson series—including the 'London Guide', 'London Restaurant Guide', 'In London', 'Visitor's London' and 'London Night-life'—is pre-eminent. A full list of titles can be obtained from Robert Nicholson Publications, 17 Conway St W1 (387-2811) and the guides are widely available. The 'London Guide' is a very comprehensive listing of places and facilities, giving opening times and an indication of cost; it gives particularly good value but the print is small. There is larger print in Nicholson's 'In London', which is a unique area-by-area guide that could be used to identify useful itineraries. Three of the major guides which include a considerable amount of historical and architectural detail are published by Michelin, Penguin and Benn (the 'Blue Guide' series); all are widely available. In addition, there's 'Fodor's London' which is aimed particularly at visitors from North America but includes much useful information. The LTB publishes a number of booklets including 'This Is Your London' and 'London is for Children' which include basic access information, and the English Tourist Board (ETB) publishes a comprehensive hotels listing, 'Where to Stay', which is updated every year. There's an interesting series of guides from Shire Publications, Cromwell House, Church St, Princes Risborough, Bucks, called 'Discovering'. Titles include 'Statues and Monuments', 'Parks and Squares', 'Off-beat Walks in London' and 'London's Curiosities'. They are not expensive and the first two mentioned highlight ways of learning about London's history and architecture without any access problems at all. Write to the publisher's address given above if you want a complete list of titles. Finally, the GLC publishes a listing, 'What's On in GLC Parks and Historic Houses', which includes fairs, concerts, band performances and exhibitions. Send a large SAE to The Department for Recreation and the Arts, GLC County Hall, SE1 or telephone 633-1707.

Specialist books

Directory for the Disabled by Ann Darnbrough and Derek Kinrade has established itself as the main handbook for disabled and handicapped people, including sections on aids, employment, holidays, benefits and sports activities. It is regularly updated, and is published by Woodhead-Faulkner Ltd, 17 Market St, Cambridge.

Door to Door is a publication from the Department of Transport, which brings together basic information about transport for disabled people. It gives guidance on aids and financial benefits and goes in some detail into the various types of transport available; it also gives local contacts. Although general in nature, it is full of constructive ideas and includes useful sections on personal transport schemes, buses, trains, air and sea travel and so forth. Available from Department of Health and Social Security (DHSS) offices or direct from Department of Transport, Door to Door Guide, Freepost, Ruislip, Mddx HA4 0BR.

The Guide to the Social Services is published every year by the Family Welfare Association, 501 Kingsland Rd E8. It has details of what social services should be available locally, together with the addresses of all the local Councils of Voluntary Service throughout the country.

London Made Easy is available from the GLC and LTB. It is written for the over 60s and makes a number of useful suggestions. However, it was not researched by personal visit and you should beware of the list of loos which includes both proper (w) loos (as described in our guide) and small cubicles with rails which would help some (s) but would be totally unsuitable for (w).

Motoring and Mobility for Disabled People by Ann Darnbrough and Derek Kinrade cannot be too highly recommended. It is published by RADAR. The book covers a very wide range of subjects and is well researched and practical in its approach. There is information on cars, equipment and financing and there are also sections on wheelchairs, general publications, services available and 'On being caught short', with constructive suggestions about coping with incontinence and the general lack of accessible loos.

The Sunday Times Self-help Directory has an extensive list of voluntary organisations and of sources of help and advice on all kinds of problems. It really is surprising how many groups there are and how varied are the services available. The directory lists places like aids centres for the disabled, a firm called Anything Left-handed Ltd, and includes details of many organisations whose main function is helping and providing information for the disabled. It is published by Granada Publishing, 3 Upper St James St W1.

Travelling
& getting around

Travelling around London is probably the biggest problem for the disabled person who wants to be both independent and mobile. The area involved is very large, and because accommodation in the centre is expensive, most visitors stay some distance away from the main sights, just as most residents live out in the suburbs. For more seriously disabled people, undoubtedly the **best thing to do is to bring your own transport**, be it a car or an adapted minibus. Second best is the use of taxis or minicabs. Minicabs are in fact more accessible for some people, as they are conventional cars (although of various makes and sizes). Taxi drivers are usually helpful, however, and taxis are cheaper for short journeys.

London Transport has made virtually no provision for the seriously disabled passenger and disabled London residents are therefore very dependent on escort services provided by the Red Cross and on Dial-a-Ride schemes. Fortunately, the number of these schemes is currently growing. The co-ordinating group is **The Federation of London Dial-a-Rides**, The Portacabins, Ferdinand Street Estate NW1 (482-2325). The idea is excellent—you can ring up and they will organise a driver to take you shopping or to work or wherever, either alone or with a companion. The schemes operate from somewhat variable bases; each will have its own criteria for eligibility and its own area of operation, although most work within the boundary formed by the North and South Circular roads. The schemes currently operating are:

Brent Community Transport 105a Melville Rd NW10 (965-6439).
Camden Dial-a-Ride The Portacabins, Ferdinand Street Estate NW1 (267-2993).
Ealing Dial-a-Ride Bedford Hall, Bedford Rd W13 (840-3335).
Hammersmith Handicab Bishop Creighton House, 378 Lillie Rd SW6 (381-4446).
Islington Dial-a-Ride Albany Ct NW7 (607-8841).

Further Dial-a-Rides are planned for 1984 in Greenwich, Haringey, Lambeth, Tower Hamlets and Wandsworth. GLAD can give you up-to-date information on what schemes are operating and where. Following an experiment in Southwark, subsidised taxi fares for disabled people have been made available in Haringey, Hackney, Croydon and Camden, based on a Taxi Card issued by the GLC. Ask the disability association in your borough about the schemes in your area.

The British Rail (BR) network will be of interest to many since, although its coverage is limited and there are problems once you've reached the main line terminus, BR has gone to considerable lengths recently to improve facilities for both (s) and (w).

Also covered in this chapter are parking, vehicle hire and travel by coach, ferry and aeroplane. GLAD is currently conducting a two-year study to assess the transport needs of disabled people in London. This project is much needed; we hope that it will expose the gaps, highlight what is available, and ensure that facilities will be improved over the coming years for both residents and visitors.

Getting to London

British Rail

British Rail's provision for the disabled traveller has undergone something of a revolution during the last two or three years. Hassles still occur, but all in all things have got much easier. There is a Disabled Persons Railcard for UK citizens, which is available to the blind, partially sighted, deaf without speech and to those receiving certain disability benefits. You have to pay for the card, but the fee is soon recovered if you travel even once a month, as it allows half-price travel both for the disabled person and for a companion. Blind people travelling for certain specified purposes and (w)—both resident and foreign—can take a companion for free (ie one adult fare for two people) even without the card. Blind people travelling alone without the card must pay full fare, but guide dogs are carried free. Leaflets about these and other offers—such as the Senior Citizens Railcard—are readily available from BR. They will send them to you if you telephone 928-5100. There are also leaflets about the fares structure, including 'How to Choose Your Rail Ticket' and 'London Savers'.

On many Inter-City services—where BR is probably most useful—the new Mark III coaches have a removable seat in the 1st-class compartments for a wheelchair to slot in. Note too that in modern Inter-City 2nd-class coaches a table has been removed from the group of seats nearest to the entrance and the toilet, making access easier for (s). In addition, the new sleeper coaches now being introduced have an interconnecting door between certain compartments, which will be of particular value to some disabled travellers. In fact, you can travel in considerable comfort and at most major stations there is a portable ramp to get you up to carriage level. Doors into the carriages, however, are narrow; a 64cm chair will get in only with a bit of pushing. BR reckons the maximum chair width is about 62cm, although efforts are being made to increase this a little. At major stations a narrow, ambulance-type wheelchair is normally available to help you transfer if necessary. All this can be laid on with prior notice to the area manager's office. The BR leaflet, 'BR—A Guide for the Disabled Passenger' includes a map showing the routes on which these facilities are available. In the older coaches still operating on much of the network, including the routes to and from the Channel ports, doors are narrower and there is no removable seat. Most (s) can probably get in all right, although there are steps, but (w) may have to travel in the guard's van.

If you need help at stations and you know when you will be travelling, it's best to **let BR know a day or so in advance** by contacting the local area manager. This is obviously particularly important if you are travelling alone, or if you want to make complicated interchanges. The wider use of wheeled luggage trolleys also makes things much easier, and (s) who would find a journey difficult might consider using a wheelchair—you can make arrangements through the relevant area manager—which might ensure a much easier journey. Many disabled travellers are able and willing to give the prior notice of a journey requested by BR, but others are not; like everyone else, disabled people sometimes have to travel at short notice and some are just not good at pre-planning. Generally, if you travel from the main stations and take the precaution of arriving in good time, you should not have too many problems (unless you are really unlucky) and the worst that is likely to happen is that you will be in the luggage van, even on a 125, because the staff haven't had time to remove the 1st-class seat to make a space for you, or it may have been booked by another passenger. *See 'Getting around London' for further details.*

Coach travel

If you can overcome the minor hassles of coach travel and get up the **3 or 4 steep steps** into the average coach (a few tall coaches have more than that) it is a cheap and easy way to travel. Remember though that if you want or need to sit in the

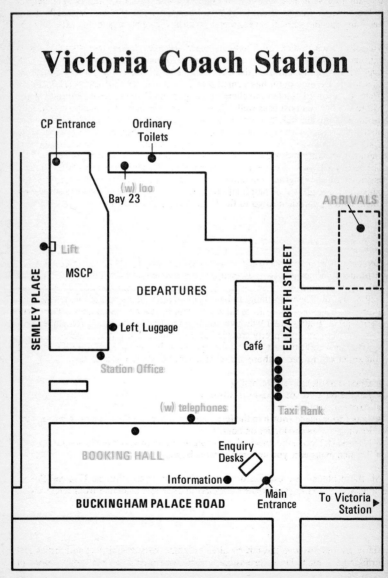

Victoria Coach Station

CP Entrance

Ordinary Toilets

(w) loo

Bay 23

ARRIVALS

Lift

SEMLEY PLACE

MSCP

ELIZABETH STREET

DEPARTURES

Left Luggage

Café

Station Office

(w) telephones

Taxi Rank

BOOKING HALL

Enquiry Desks

Information

Main Entrance

BUCKINGHAM PALACE ROAD

To Victoria Station ▶

front seats, which are easier to get to and have more leg-room, there may be a number of other people with the same idea! Seats behind the emergency door often have a little more leg-room, too. Note that the Alder Valley Bus Company, which operates from Aldershot, Hampshire, (some way out of London) has three standard buses modified for carrying (w) which are available for hire, and these are the only such vehicles available near London. Coach operators will try to be helpful but, as always, it is important to **let them know if you are disabled**, especially if you need any specific help. It is sensible to confirm verbal arrangements with a letter.

Victoria Coach Station Buckingham Palace Rd SW1 (enquiries 730-0202, reservations 730-3499). Arrival and departure point for most coach services for travel all over Britain and to and from the Continent. The coach station is some 500m from Victoria BR station but it has a small MSCP with adequate lift access (D 86cm, W 92cm, L 239cm). Disabled travellers should go straight to the station office (**1 step**), where the first aid post is as well. There are special toilets, but these are normally locked and the key held at the station office. The (**w**) **loo** is by bay 23 and there are plans for the provision of a second one. There's a **wheelchair available** for use. Note that there are kerbs around, although the main entrance is flat. The ticket office is cramped and the café is frequently crowded. There are (**w**) **telephones** by bay D. The Arrivals Hall is on the other side of Elizabeth St behind the Travellers' Tavern, as shown on the diagram. Generally, the station is flat and compact but busy and congested. People will be helpful if they can. The key is to **make your needs known when booking** and then to go to the station office in good time

Cross-Channel ferries

The crossings vary considerably in accessibility but generally, as newer ships are introduced and terminals are developed, access is improving. Your travel agent is unlikely to be able to give access details, so the Access guide mentioned below may well be useful. The main things to bear in mind are that it is preferable to travel on a ferry with a good-size lift from the car deck to the various other decks. The larger ferries (8000 tonnes plus) will give you a smoother crossing, but remember that most of the routes are pretty crowded at peak times during the summer.

The most difficult part of the journey is usually getting on and off the ferry; if you anticipate problems there are several sensible precautions to take:

● Choose a suitable ferry/crossing.
● Let the ferry company know in advance.
● Arrive in good time.
● Make your needs known to the ferry loading officer (ie the officer organising the loading of cars and lorries on board).
● Use the (w) loo in the terminal, particularly if the ship does not have one.
● Try and make sure you understand what is going on.

All the problems are explained in some detail in 'Access at the Channel Ports', published by PHSP (the present authors) in 1982 and available from RADAR.

Travelling by air

Many visitors arrive in the UK by air. For many years, the airport authorities and airlines have made better provisions for disabled travellers than organisations in charge of other forms of transport. Help is available at most airports for both (w) and (s), and if you find distances a problem you can either borrow a wheelchair or ride on one of those fancy new buggies. Access to aircraft loos remains the biggest problem, but there are plans to alleviate this in the next generation of aircraft.

Having said all that, air travel for the (w) who needs lifting can still be a somewhat problematic business. You may have to wait for a considerable time before getting off the 'plane and the system is frequently a bit bureaucratic. The procedures adopted vary from airline to airline, and even from day to day, so there is always a degree of uncertainty about what will happen. The major problem is that 'handling' is normally the responsibility of the airport, and not the airline staff, and there are sometimes strict procedures. Even if you are travelling with friends, they may not be allowed to lift you as it is, in principle, the responsibility of the airport. It's the old 'what happens if something goes wrong . . . we'd be responsible' syndrome, and sometimes people's wishes and even common sense go out of the window. It is, however, often possible for people who are totally reliant on their wheelchair to use their own chair to reach the cabin and to have it immediately accessible to them on disembarkation. Nowadays, more airlines are understanding about how difficult and uncomfortable it can be to use an airport chair instead of one designed for one's individual needs.

If you need help getting on or off the 'plane it is essential to tell the travel agent when booking and it is advisable to telephone the airline and check the arrangements a day or so before departure. The IATA has produced a standard medical information (MEDIF) form on which to define the help required. In some situations, for example if you have a chest condition or if you are recovering from an operation, medical clearance is required and your doctor will need to complete the form. Some airlines issue a standard Frequent Traveller's Medical Card (FREMEC) to people with a stable condition who travel by air. This does not make prior notification unnecessary, but it does reduce the administrative hassle.

Airports and airline operators are generally used to dealing with (w) and other handicapped travellers, but the procedures adopted vary from airline to airline and even from day to day so there is always a degree of uncertainty about what will happen. Rest assured that you *will* get on the 'plane, but be prepared for a few bumps and bruises en route and for the inevitable minor hassles. Airlines are generally more clued up in dealing with a group including several (w) rather than with an individual travelling alone or with a few (ab) friends.

With the advent of the wide-bodied jets carrying 300 or 400 people, physical access to the 'plane has improved, but aircraft loos are still cramped and inaccessible. The volume of air traffic is now so great that many airports cannot really cope; Heathrow and Gatwick, for example, get very congested during peak periods. Also any hiccup in the system, such as industrial action or air traffic control problems, causes disproportionate problems. In spite of all this, you will probably have a smooth flight without any real problems, and the worst that is likely to happen is that you may have to wait around a bit. Take a good book with you, or a game of chess or something. Here are a few hints which should help:

● When you book your flights, tell your travel agent what your disability is and what your needs are.
● Double-check with the airport shortly before departure that a wheelchair is available if you need it. Similarly, make sure that your airline has notified its personnel at your destination (and/or the airport) that you will need help in getting off.

- Carry a letter (and a couple of copies) from your doctor stating that you are fit to fly—particularly if you are travelling alone.
- Travel light, and take an absolute minimum of hand luggage. The ideal way to travel is with one's hands empty of everything except a good book and a newspaper, with a pocket full of small change, together with any necessary documents and medicines. Worrying about lots of Duty Free items is often not worth the effort but if you must buy them, the simplest thing is to get them on the 'plane.
- Put a label and luggage tag on your wheelchair, and remove anything that will come off (eg arms, footrests and cushions). Ideally, bring a soft, empty bag to put these in.
- Arrive in good time and make your needs known at the check-in desk. Ask what the procedure will be, and you have the chance to discuss things if you do not think they are satisfactory.
- Use a toilet at the airport before departure—make sure the airport staff give you time to do this. Unisex loos are available at most airports, so that your spouse or companion can help you.
- If you cannot walk far, arrange for an airport wheelchair to take you from the check-in to the final departure lounge. It can save a lot of trouble, and some airports are very big and you may have a long walk.
- Finally, leave as little as possible to chance. In particular, do not trust one-call telephone enquiries or verbal assurances. Get hold of your tickets in good time, and check them. Confirm and re-confirm any arrangements that are vital to you for getting on and off the 'plane and ensuring a smooth trip. Human errors do happen, messages don't always get remembered and acted upon and, while there is no point in being a nuisance, do *not* rely on messages left several weeks before your departure; make direct contact with both airport and airline to ensure that they know what is going on, confirming telephone calls with a brief letter.

Most airlines will not carry wet batteries from an electric wheelchair, although a few do. Enquire if necessary, otherwise you will have to arrange for batteries to be available at your destination. Check your wheelchair on arrival for any damage in the luggage handling system. British NHS chairs are not really built for this kind of handling and are liable to damage, and special light-weight chairs even more so. In our experience, a chair gets damaged on about one journey in ten. It is almost worth considering buying a stronger (and maybe narrower) chair for this sort of trip, both to last longer and to help you get in and out of places. If there is any damage, report it at the time and make sure that your complaint is registered.

Because of the time spent at the airport, especially if your flight happens to be delayed as well, it is worth eating something before you leave and maybe having a bar of chocolate or a sandwich with you, in case the airport catering facilities are crowded. On long flights, if you can manage without having to use the toilet, fine. If not, remember that the cabin staff have to handle food on the journey, and it is not part of their job to deal with toilet aids. Additionally, the staff cannot be expected to help lift anyone down the small aisles or into the cramped toilets. You can probably ensure that you and your travelling companions can sit near a toilet, but if the situation is likely to cause a problem then consult your doctor. There are obvious precautions like not drinking anything before or during the journey, but the doctor may also suggest the use of incontinence aids or of medical inhibitors. It is essential to get proper medical advice, and if your doctor wants further information, he or she can contact the **British Airways Medical Service**, Heathrow Airport (759-5511 ext 2378 or 750-5616).

Principal airports

Gatwick The British Airports Authority (BAA) issues an excellent booklet, 'Who looks after you at Gatwick Airport?', detailing facilities. If you want to know exactly where the (w) loos are and about other amenities, it is well worth getting hold of a copy. The airport can be reached by train from Victoria, which provides a fast and regular service. Normally, (w) would travel in the guard's van. There is a lift to take you from the platform at Gatwick up to the terminal concourse level, although a member of staff is required for its use. Access at Victoria is basically flat and so for a (w) not using a car this is a much easier journey than Heathrow. Parking arrangements are on the same principle as those at Heathrow. The **(w) loos** in the terminal are on the balcony adjacent to the passenger lounge. Access is by **lift**. There is another (w) loo at the other end of the building, inside Channel D at concourse level. The usual arrangements for (s) to use a wheelchair can be made if necessary.

Gatwick has special facilities for the hard of hearing, including an **induction loop** in the international departure lounge. Some public telephones have an **inductive coupler**. The BAA participates in the Sympathetic Hearing Scheme, and staff will try to give special consideration when shown the plastic card. The airport authorities have also tried to make signs and floor-level changes clear for those who are partially sighted, and the 3rd-floor restaurant and coffee shop have **braille menus**.

Heathrow Again, there is a BAA booklet, 'Who looks after you at Heathrow Airport?', detailing facilities. The Piccadilly line Underground goes direct to Heathrow from central London and if you can cope with this it is the cheapest way. Getting on and off the train, however, involves escalators and there is no luggage handling system to the Underground platform. There are airport buses direct from Euston, Paddington and Victoria main line stations, with some intermediate pick-up points; details from London Transport (222-1234). Alternatively, come by taxi or minicab.

If you arrive by car, you can stop right outside the terminal, but only for a few minutes. There are short-term car parks 100m to 200m from the terminals in the centre of the airport, but they are expensive if you want to park for more than a few hours. The long-term car parks are about 1km outside the main area, and are linked to the terminals by a minibus. There is room for a wheelchair in the back of the minibus since there is a seat removed for luggage, but it means a lift of about 70cm to get on. Intercontinental flights go to and from Terminal 3, internal flights Terminal 1. There is a ramped underground link to Terminal 3 with travolator moving pavements. European flights go either from Terminal 1 (British Airways) or Terminal 2 (other airlines). A fourth terminal is under construction, so the pattern will change in a few years time. There are **(w) loos** in every terminal. There are long distances to walk, but on request wheelchairs or other help are readily available for anyone who finds this difficult.

Useful books & leaflets

Access Travel: A Guide to the Accessibility of US and Other Airports Available from the Consumer Information Centre, Pueblo, CO 81009, USA.
Air Travel for the Handicapped (leaflet). Available from the TWA Sales Dept, 2 Penn Plaza, New York, NY 10010, USA.
Care in the Air Free leaflet available from the Airline Users Committee, Rm 600, 129 Kingsway WC2.

Free information leaflets about facilities for the handicapped at several major UK airports—such as Heathrow, Gatwick, Stansted and Edinburgh—are available from the British Airports Authority Publications Dept, Head Office, Gatwick Airport, Horley, West Sussex RH6 0HZ, or from RADAR, 25 Mortimer St W1. They are excellent.

Incapacitated Passengers' Air Travel Guide Published by the IATA, Francis House, Francis St SW1 (828-5841).

Travel Ability by Lois Reamy, published by Macmillan, 866 Third Av, New York, NY 10012, USA.

Getting around London

Boat trips

This is a highly recommended and restful way of seeing London. The piers at Westminster, Charing Cross and Greenwich are accessible by **ramp**. At the Tower, there is a ramp but then −3 steps to the level of most boats. The riverboats vary a lot and some are more suitable for (w) than others; some are totally unsuitable because there are steep steps immediately inside. During the summer the boats run about every 15 or 20 minutes, so it may be worth waiting until a good one comes along. A good boat, by our definition, is one which has a viewing area with flat access from the entrance. The area is usually right at the front or back of the boat, and will probably be somewhat congested with fixed seating, but it is easy for (s) and usually one or two (w) can be accommodated. The crew are generally helpful and competent, which is just as well since a certain amount of lifting may be necessary. **Loos on the boats are virtually impossible for access**, with steep steps and in most cases narrow cubicles.

British Rail

The rail network around London is of particular interest to disabled people because of the problems involved in using other forms of transport (ie buses and the Underground). North of the river, the lines are mainly radial, going out of London in various directions, with the exception of the line from Richmond through Hampstead to Broad St. South of the river there is a very extensive network. BR publishes a good map called 'BR Services in London and the South East Area'; there is also a larger scale map, 'London's Railways', which is published jointly by BR and London Transport and shows the links between the Underground and the main lines. The use of the Circle Underground line is possible without escalators (although there are steps) and this links several of the main termini. The only other way to get across is by bus (which is difficult) or by taxi. When the new taxi comes into wider use, the link between railway stations will be made a lot easier.

BR has an **induction loop** in use at one of the ticket windows at Waterloo and is also pioneering the use of the Sympathetic Hearing Scheme. **Guide dogs** accompanying blind people travel free and can generally be taken into buffets and restaurants.

Most of London's suburban network still operates with old-style coaches (*see* 'Getting to London'), with the exception of a few electrified lines, where the trains have sliding doors and 1 step. On Southern Region trains, amongst others, it is almost always necessary for (w) to travel in the guard's van, but this is a hardship only when the weather is really cold and at busy times can actually be an advantage.

It is important to note that **loos on trains are inaccessible to (w)**; access is flat but the doors are very narrow. An increasing number of the main stations have a (w) loo; details are in the RADAR guide, 'British Rail—A Guide for the Disabled Passenger'. This is a very useful publication, covering principal stations throughout the country. Southern Region publishes its own leaflet, too—'Southern Region and the Disabled Traveller'—with details of some 88 stations. **Most of the main line termini in London have flat access or lifts** to all the platforms; the one exception we found was Broad St, which is in any case due for closure. The flat route is not always signposted, however—notably at Euston.

We list here the major stations which have good access in the area up to about 60km from London; the information was kindly supplied by BR. Rail links are important since you may well be staying with relatives or friends a little way out of London and trains can provide an invaluable means of transport for the disabled person without a car. At many stations there are flights of steps to the platforms going under or over the lines. A few are equipped with service lifts (goods lifts) which can normally be used if needed. Parking facilities are indicated at a number of the stations listed. In central London these are very limited and are heavily used, so they are not always available. The same may apply at some out-of-town stations as well. Where mentioned, buffets and loos all have level access. At some stations it may only be the (w) loo which has flat access as the ordinary loos may be down steps. Also buffets sometimes have fixed seating which may cause difficulty for disabled people. This is not indicated here as we haven't visited all the stations involved.

Eastern Region

London Kings Cross 837-4200. CP. Level access everywhere; (w) loo and accessible buffet. Wheelchair available.

P ♿ ♿ wc ♿ ✕ U

London Liverpool Street 247-7600 ext 2494. CP. Avoid the Bishopsgate entrance where there are steps, otherwise there is level/ramped access everywhere. Buffet and (w) loo. Wheelchair available.

P A ♿ ♿ wc ♿ ✕ U

Stevenage Stevenage (0438) 316666. CP. Lifts available giving flat access to platforms. Buffet and (w) loo.

P ♿ 1↕ ♿ wc ♿ ✕

Midland Region

Bedford Midland Bedford (0234) 52061. CP. Flat access to platform 1 and (w) passengers can cross to platforms 2/3 via a sleeper crossing (ie across the lines). Unisex (w) loo on platform 1. Buffet. Wheelchair available.

P ♿ ♿ wc ♿ ✕ U

Hemel Hempstead Watford (0923) 45001. CP (400m). Entrance has 2 steps. Again, (w) passengers can use a sleeper crossing to avoid subway and stairs.

P (400m) ▣ E2 ▣

London Euston 387-9400 ext 3604. There is a flat route in (and out) via the bus stops off the Euston Rd but there are steps at both side exits and no signposting. Flat access everywhere. Unisex (w) loos. Buffet. Wheelchair available.

A ▣ ▣ wc ▣ X U

London Marylebone 387-9400 ext 4377. Flat access. Ordinary loos with level access to Ladies' but steps to Gents'. Buffet.

▣ ▣ X

London St Pancras 387-7070. Level access to all platforms and (w) loo on platform 7. Buffet. Wheelchair available.

▣ ▣ wc ▣ X U

Luton Luton (0582) 32922. CP, and (w) passengers can use a special street entrance to platform 5 and reach other platforms via sleeper crossings to avoid steps. Steps to ordinary loos. Buffet.

P A ▣ ▣ X

Milton Keynes Central Milton Keynes (0908) 70883. CP. Lifts available giving level access everywhere; (w) loo on platform 3. Buffet.

P ▣ ↑↓ ▣ wc ▣ X

St Albans City Luton (0582) 452589. CP. Access to all platforms ramped. Unisex (w) loo.

P ▣ ▣ wc

Watford Junction Watford (0923) 44311. CP with ramped access to station opened on special request, otherwise some 250m round to ticket office via the access roadway. Lift available giving level access everywhere.

P A ▣ ↑↓

Southern Region

(For more details see BR leaflet, 'Southern Region and the Disabled Traveller'.)

Basingstoke Basingstoke (0256) 21980. CP. Lift available to reach platforms. Wheelchair available. Ordinary loos only. Buffet.

P ▣ ↑↓ ▣ X U

East Croydon 686-8821. Ramped access to all platforms. Ordinary loos only. Buffet.

[♿] [♿ ✕]

Epsom Epsom (78) 23520. Lift available giving flat access everywhere. Ordinary loos.

[♿] [⑪]

Gatwick Airport Gatwick (0293) 20000. There is a lift available to and from the airport terminal concourse. There are parking and restaurant facilities associated with the airport, and (w) loos.

[⑪] Terminal [♿] [♿ wc] [♿ ✕] U

Guildford Guildford (0483) 72483. CP. Ramped access to platforms. Ordinary loos. Buffet.

P [♿] [♿ ✕]

London Blackfriars 928-5151 ext 2260. Normal access by escalator or stairs. Lift available to platforms except for trains to and from Holborn Viaduct. There's a (w) loo.

[A] [♿] [⑪] [♿ wc]

London Bridge 928-5151 ext 2251. Flat or ramped access everywhere, and (w) loo. Buffet. Wheelchair available.

[♿] [♿ wc] [♿ ✕] U

London Charing Cross 928-5151 ext 2301. Flat access everywhere and (w) loo. Buffet. Wheelchair available.

[♿] [♿ wc] [♿ ✕] U

London Holborn Viaduct 928-5151 ext 2246. Flat access everywhere. Ordinary loos (level to Ladies', stairs to Gents').

[♿]

London Victoria 928-5151 ext 7373. Flat access everywhere, and (w) loo. Buffet. Wheelchair available. Can get very congested. National Tourist Office just outside with flat access.

[♿] [♿ wc] [♿ ✕] U

London Waterloo 928-5151 ext 3356. Limited parking facility. Flat access everywhere and (w) loo. Buffet. Wheelchair available.

P [♿] [♿ wc] [♿ ✕] U

Mottingham 928-5151 ext 8712. CP. Flat access everywhere. Ordinary loos.

P 🚾

Redhill Redhill (91) 42017. CP. Flat access everywhere. Lift available. Buffet. Ordinary loos.

P 🚾 ⑪ 🚾✕

Reigate Reigate (74) 42017. CP. Flat access everywhere. Ordinary loos.

P 🚾

Richmond 940-1951. CP. Steps to booking office. Lift available on request to give flat access to platforms. Ordinary loos. Buffet.

P ◣ E2 🚾 ⑪ 🚾✕

Sevenoaks Sevenoaks (0732) 452231. CP. Ramps and steps to the booking office. Lift available to platforms on request. There's a (w) loo. Buffet.

P 🚾 ⑪ 🚾 wc 🚾✕

Surbiton 399-0132. CP. Lift available on request. Ordinary loos. Buffet. Wheelchair available.

P 🚾 ⑪ 🚾✕ U

Sutton 642-8161. CP. Lift available on request. Ordinary loos. Buffet.

P 🚾 ⑪ 🚾✕

Swanley 650-4858 ext 2300. CP. Lift available on request. Ordinary loos (can be reached by lift).

P 🚾 ⑪

Tonbridge Tonbridge (0732) 353882. Lift available on request. Ordinary loos. Buffet. Wheelchair available.

🚾 ⑪ 🚾✕ U

Tunbridge Wells Central Tunbridge Wells (0892) 31275. CP. Level to trains for London, lift available to other platform. Ordinary loos. Buffet. Wheelchair available.

P 🚾 ⑪ 🚾✕ U

Windsor & Eton Riverside Windsor (95) 61244. CP. Level access everywhere. Ordinary loos. Buffet.

P 🚾 🚾✕

Western Region

London Paddington 723-7000 ext 2222. Limited parking facilities. Main line platforms all with level access. For flat/lift access to suburban platforms 13/14 ask station staff at first aid post, where the (w) loo is. Buffet.

[♿]   [♿ wc]   [♿ ✕]

Reading Reading (0734) 595911. CP 100m. Level access to platforms 1/4; others can be reached via station lifts. Buffet on platforms 4 and 5. Unisex (w) loo.

P [♿]   [❙❙]   [♿ wc]   [♿ ✕]

Slough Slough (75) 21271. CP 50m. Flat to platforms 1 and 2 and lift access elsewhere. Adapted loo on platform 2. Buffet on platform 5.

P [♿]   [❙❙]   [♿ wc]   [♿ ✕]

By car

For many disabled people, getting around by car or in a special minibus is the only practical way, since most if not all public transport is inaccessible to them. In a few boroughs there are Dial-a-Ride schemes or special taxi rates, and the number of such schemes is slowly growing. In other areas there are voluntary service councils and community transport schemes which may be of help. *See the introduction to this chapter for details of Dial-a-Ride and taxi schemes* currently in operation; we hope that other boroughs will soon adopt the idea.

Car drivers have to face severe congestion, especially during the rush hours, and a fairly aggressive driving style. There are also severe parking problems. Driving is much easier at weekends, as is parking, which is also easier in the evenings except in the West End. For daytime use, there are numerous multi-storey NCPs, and if you are sharing the cost between three or four people, they are not really expensive. Your reaction to driving in London will depend very much on your experience as well as your driving skills and temperament. The locals tend to be very positive and to go quite fast, but most people get used to it quite quickly. It may be sensible to avoid large junctions like Marble Arch and Hyde Park Corner until you've mastered some of the smaller ones. Other problems are one-way streets and no-right-turns, which seem to crop up everywhere. The secret is not to panic but just press on and to make sure you've got a good map in the car, so that you can stop and sort yourself out and work out another route when necessary.

Parking

Parking is a subject on which it is extremely difficult to give good advice. It depends on what your needs are, on local conditions, on the time of day and even on which traffic warden is on duty. It also depends on how long you want to stay. There are, however, certain general points. It is difficult to park in central London during the week and most of the area has a parking meter system for short stays; there is, of course, no guarantee of finding a meter available. There are a good number of off-street CPs, mostly operated by **National Car Parks (NCP)**, 60 Charlotte St W1 (637-9191). Although they may appear expensive, they offer quite good value if you can choose a well placed CP enabling you to visit several places; if the cost is shared between three or four people, it can be much the same as using public transport. NCP can supply you with an up-to-date list which shows whether they are surface, UG or MSCPs. Also, CPs are marked on Nicholson's 'Streetfinder'. Most CPs are either multi-storey or are buried deep underground, so that getting out can be quite a hassle. Friendly CP attendants may be willing to keep a place near the exit if you 'phone in advance.

The Orange Badge is not valid in Westminster, Kensington and Chelsea, the City or Camden south of the Marylebone Rd, although special permits and spaces may be made available for those who live or work in these areas. Our survey teams with cars used the technique of parking somewhere where they were clearly not causing an obstruction and leaving an explanatory note on the windscreen. We also made a point of not parking for too long, and we didn't have any problems. You may be unlucky and catch a traffic warden or policeman on an off-day but that's life—we can't guide you around that one! Remember that **the Orange Badge** *is* **valid in Lambeth, Southwark and Islington**, all of which contain and border on interesting parts of London. The police have introduced a system of wheel clamps to tie down illegally parked cars in the London area, but it has yet to be seen how this will be applied to cars with disabled drivers or passengers. The worst areas for parking are the City (where there are few off-street facilities) and the West End. We have tried to indicate in the guide if there are parking facilities attached to any place of interest or if there is an NCP or equivalent nearby. In the evenings and particularly on *Sun*, parking is generally much easier, although theatreland gets crowded in the evenings.

Readers will understand that it is not always possible to be precise, and sometimes advice or information about parking near a particular building is not very useful—it's no good knowing that there are parking meters nearby if they are all full when you want to use them. With NCPs it may be worth giving them a ring first if it's important and you know where you want to park. Surprisingly, there are useful ones near important spots which are not always full, such as the one behind Debenhams in Oxford St and the one in Aldersgate St near the Museum of London. Some places of major interest can make special arrangements for disabled people if there is a real need. The facilities are usually limited, but prior negotiation may secure a spot near the museum or site of your choice. We have indicated where such arrangements are possible in the text.

Taxis & minicabs

London taxi drivers are usually helpful, although obviously not always. They are licensed by the police and every vehicle carries its licence number prominently displayed. They operate a meter on which the fare is recorded. Taxis are not obliged to accept a hiring for over six miles (about 10km). Traditional taxis are, unfortunately, of a unique and difficult design, adapted from the old-fashioned hackney (horse-drawn) carriage. They're particularly difficult for (w) since, unlike in a conventional car, the main seats are set back from the door and about 40cm above the floor. Due to lack of headroom and narrow doors it's difficult to lift someone in but if the chair is narrow enough and the door sufficiently wide, the wheelchair can be tilted so that the front wheels are resting on the floor and the chair can be lifted into the taxi, probably needing a couple of (ab) helpers. Older taxis tend to have slightly wider doors. Active (w) may be able to transfer to the tip-up seats which face backwards. A new design of taxi is due to be introduced during

1985 and access should be a great deal easier. It is planned to provide a ramp, wider doors and more headroom. There probably won't be many new taxis around for some time as taxis have a long life, but if schemes to subsidise fares for those in receipt of Mobility Allowance become more widespread, some mobility problems will be eased.

The problems posed by taxis mean that minicabs or hired cars can be of particular importance. Both are ordinary cars but must be ordered by telephone or from an office, since they are not allowed to ply for hire. Your hotel or hostel can almost certainly give you the names of local firms, and the Telecom Yellow Pages are full of them. Most will be willing to carry disabled passengers, but remember that the cars involved vary a lot and even if you have removable footplates and a folding back to your chair, it may not fit in the boot. Check when booking that the car you need is the car you'll get.

If it's rush hour or if it's raining, it's ten times more difficult to get a taxi (or minicab) because everyone wants one. One tip for getting a taxi is to go to one of the major ranks, eg at a main line station, and/or to find a feeder road leading empty taxis back to a rank. You can book a minicab to collect you from a theatre, shop or gallery if you wish, but of course if you do you've then got to keep to time; also make sure the arrangements are absolutely clear about where you'll be and how you'll be recognised. In negotiating with a minicab or car hire firm it is important to agree the cost of the journey before you set off. Most of them, of course, are not rogues—but a few are, and most do not use taxi meters.

Vehicle hire

There are a few possibilities for vehicle hire, either of vehicles adapted for (w) or of hand-controlled cars. This is an area where the situation changes quite quickly, and GLAD or RADAR may be able to provide up-to-date advice if you draw a blank. Vehicle hire is one way of making a visit possible and you may be able to hire or borrow a suitable vehicle from near where you live, also using it to get to and from London. Some possibilities in and around London for cars, vans and minibuses follow.

Chalfont Line 4 Medway Pde, Perivale, Mddx (998-6516) operate minibuses with tail lifts, and supply drivers.

Gastonia Coaches The Common, Cranleigh, Surrey (Cranleigh (0483) 273757) operate a number of Transit vans with ramps.

The John Grooms Association 10 Gloucester Dr N4 (802-7272) have a motor caravan at Edgware fitted with tail lift, cooker and adapted loo, which is suitable for one (w) plus friends or family.

Kenning Car Hire 478 Green Lanes N13 (882-3576) have hand-controlled saloons and hatchbacks, but there are only a very limited number. They do, however, have agencies and a back-up service throughout the country.

Mobile Access Services PO Box 213, Winslow, Bucks (Winslow (029671) 3169) operate self-drive welfare coaches with tail lift, with space for several (w). They will deliver and collect the vans in central London, but require reasonable notice of your needs since the vehicles are often on contract hire to the DHSS.

The Possum Users Association 160 De la Warr Rd, Bexhill-on-Sea, Sussex (Bexhill (0424) 217093) operate a variety of converted vans **for members only**.

Trevor Pollitt 1 Johnston Grn, Guildford, Surrey (Guildford (0483) 233640) has a self-drive Datsun E20 van with windows and tail lift, which can take two (w) and six other passengers. Very reasonably priced.

Wheels on Wheels Taxi Service Station House, Hollingbourne, Maidstone, Kent

(Hollingbourne (062780) 308) operate a small Bedford van with ramps and a raised roof, which can take one (w) and one (ab). Driver provided.
William Forrester 1 Belvedere Clo, Guildford, Surrey (Guildford (0483) 575401) has an adapted minibus available with a driver and can organise trips.

The big international car hire companies such as Hertz, Europcar, Avis etc all operate throughout the UK; Godfrey Davis have offices at many main line railway stations. Hertz have many branches and offer a Vauxhall Astra 1.3 automatic with Alfred Bekker hand controls; reservations should, if possible, be made seven days in advance. These companies advertise widely and have plenty of branches, but they offer a service and charge rates that are perhaps more appropriate to the business client. We list here a few companies which offer a more modest service but also, generally, charge a more modest price. **These are for the hire of cars with conventional controls.**

Auto Rent International Ltd Bath Rd, Harlington High St, Hayes, Mddx (759-0056/7).
Car Hire Centre 23 Swallow St W1 (734-7661).
Cartel (Self-Drive) Ltd 18 Rosebery Av EC1 (278-6001).
Central Rent A Car 48/56 Ebury Bridge Rd SW1 (730-9138/9130).
Connaught Car Hire (Belgravia) Ltd 202 Carlisle La SE1 (633-9410).
E & P Self-Drive Ltd Sloane Avenue Mansions Garage, Sloane Av SW3 (581-2255/6).
H F Edwards 11/13 Adam & Eve Mews, Kensington High St W8 (937-0802/3751).
The Motorhome Centre Ltd Elborough Rd SE25 (656-7615).
Strawberry Hill Car Rental 6/14 Hampton Rd, Twickenham, Mddx (894-9309).
Team Cars Ltd 327 King St W6 (748-8465).
Two Horse Hire 4 Farnham Royal, Kennington La SE11 (735-6079).
Wilsons Motor Caravan Centre Nonsuch Estate, East St, Epsom, Surrey (Epsom (78) 28391).

London Transport

Head office 55 Broadway SW1 (222-1234). London Transport (LT) runs both the tubes (Underground trains) and the buses, and together with British Rail controls virtually all public transport services in the Greater London area. Its principal function is to provide a fast mass transport system which best meets the needs of the majority, and there are basically no provisions for (w) even with new facilities in the system. In spite of the fact that LT has recently taken a positive interest in the ambulant disabled passenger, neither the bus nor tube system is usable without help by anyone who is seriously disabled. Having said that, blind people travel regularly and our survey teams including disabled members reckon to go anywhere, including the tube, with appropriate help from (ab) friends. LT has designated certain seats on both the buses and Underground as being for elderly and disabled people and there's a sign requesting (ab) passengers to give up those seats if they see someone in need. LT has also gone to considerable lengths in the layout and design of new vehicles, and also with staff training, to help (s).

The bus

There are steps both on entry and on exit from a bus but LT is providing more bus shelters and is currently retaining some crew-operated services. Financial pressures, however, favour the introduction of more one-man buses. If you can use them, buses provide a convenient and cheap method of transport, and LT provides good bus maps and other information. We feel that many users of this guide will be unable to get on and off a bus easily, and we have written other sections on that assumption. It may, however, be quite feasible for (s) and for (w) with (ab) friends to use the seats just inside the platform of a bus. The airport buses and the London sightseeing tours use vehicles with relatively easy access, although it is not possible for (w) to stay in their chairs on any service.

The Underground

The Underground (tube) system has its own access guide, 'Access to the Underground', which is the result of a very thorough and impressive survey by the Richard Cloudesley School and is available from LT or from RADAR. Unfortunately, because the system is old and there are steps and escalators at the vast majority of the stations, the guide is, in practice, a statement of inaccessibility. At interchange stations there are often long distances to walk, and both steps and escalators to negotiate. At the few stations where there are lifts there are nearly always stairs as well, although the lifts do help to reduce the effort needed. A few cross-platform transfers are possible. At certain times of the day, and also at the time of big events, such as the Cup Final and major rallies, the trains get extremely crowded. In our travels on the Underground when surveying, we discovered just how useful the Circle line can be. The (w) needs two strong (ab) helpers to get down the 40 or 50 steps to be found at each station, but for (s) there are no escalators to contend with. The Circle line links most main line stations, and also places like Westminster, Kensington, the Tower and the Barbican. If you can get on it, it really is remarkably useful.

LT's official policy is that (w) are allowed only at off-peak hours and by prior arrangement, and even then only on the surface and near-surface sections of the system (although where these are is not clear from the Underground maps). The near-surface sections include all of the Circle, District and Metropolitan lines; the surface sections of most of the other lines are away from the centre of the city. The deep sections are, theoretically, out of bounds for (w), mainly because of possible evacuation problems in an emergency. Our survey teams (which include (w)) have not had difficulty in using any part of the system, however, with adequate (ab) help. It is to be hoped that LT will lift the formal ban on (w) using escalators and the deep-tunnel sections of the system, since the possibility of serious problems is so remote. Discussions with LT are currently in progress.

LT Underground stations with lifts and/or easier access Frequently there are steps even at stations with a lift, and if the existence of the lift is vital to you it's an idea to ring LT first and check that it's working, because most of the lifts are fairly elderly installations. Also some stations have flat access to one platform only with a subway or footbridge to the other side, so easy access then depends on which direction you want to go or come from.

Aldwych Ticket office E−4 steps from Surrey St. Lift then −21 steps to platform. (**NB** It is only on a branch line.)
Amersham E0 from Chiltern Av. Flat access for southbound trains.
Angel E0. Lift then −22 steps.
Bank King William St to northern booking office −25 steps. Lift then −21 to Northern line.
Belsize Park E−4 steps. Lift then −20.

Borough E0. Lift and flat access for northbound or −18 steps for southbound.

Caledonian Road E1 or exit −2 steps. Lift and then flat access.

Carpender's Park E0 (ramp to and from subway). Flat access to all platforms.

Chalfont & Latimer E0. Flat access to both platforms, one from Bedford Av, the other from Station Approach.

Chalk Farm E0. Lift then −20−2 steps.

Chesham E0. Flat access to southbound platform (all the trains go south).

Chorleywood E0. Ramped subway to platforms.

Covent Garden E−2 steps. Lift then −19 steps.

Dagenham Heathway E0. Ramped access to platforms.

Debden E0. Flat access to eastbound platform.

Edgware Road Bakerloo line −3 steps. Lift then −19 steps.

Elephant & Castle E0. Bakerloo line: lift then −20 steps. Northern line: lift then −20 to southbound platform or 18+15 to northbound platform.

Elm Park E0. Ramped access to platforms.

Gloucester Road To Piccadilly line E0. Lift then −12−15 to platform.

Goodge Street E0. Lift then −20 steps.

Hammersmith Metropolitan line E0. Flat access to platforms.

Hampstead From Hampstead High St 2 steps. Lift then −20.

Hatch End E0. Flat access for northbound trains.

Holland Park E1. Lift then −21 steps to platforms.

Holloway Road E1. Lift then −19 steps to platforms.

Kennington E0. Lift then −19 for northbound trains, lift then −16−18 for southbound trains.

Kensington Olympia E0. Flat access. (**NB** This is an exhibition service only.)

Kew Gardens E0 from Station Approach. Flat access to eastbound platform.

Lambeth North E0. Lift then −20 steps.

Lancaster Gate E1 or exit 2 steps. Lift then −13−13 steps to platforms.

Mornington Crescent E0. Lift then −16−20 steps to platforms.

New Cross E0. Flat access to platform.

North Weald E1. Flat access to platform.

Ongar E0. Flat access to platform.

Pinner E0. Flat access to southbound platform.

Queensway E2 or exit 1 step. Lift then −21 steps.

Regent's Park E−20−15. Lift then −20−8 to westbound platform; lift then −15 to eastbound platform.

Rickmansworth E0. Flat access to southbound platform.

Roding Valley E0 from Station Wy. Flat access to westbound platform.

Ruislip E0. Flat access to eastbound platform.

Russell Square E1. Lift then −14 steps.

Shadwell E1. Lift then −8−15 steps.

Snaresbrook E0. Flat access to eastbound platform.

South Woodford E0 from George La West. Flat access to westbound platform.

Sudbury Town E0. Flat or ramped access to platforms.

Theydon Bois E0. Flat access to eastbound platform.

Tufnell Park E1 from Brecknock Rd. Lift then −11 to platform.

Upney E0. Ramped access to platforms.

Uxbridge E0 from Uxbridge High St. Flat access to platforms.

Wapping E0. Then 2+2 steps, lift, then −4−2 steps.

West Finchley E0 from Nether St. Flat access to northbound platform.

Woodford E1 from The Broadway, then flat access to eastbound platform; or E0 from Snakes La/Madeira Gro, then flat access to westbound platform.

Accommodation

Accommodation in London tends to be expensive, partly because many of the bigger hotels cater primarily for the business visitor on an expense account. There is a shortage of good, cheap accommodation in general and an even greater dearth of reasonably priced accommodation that is accessible. In the survey, we've covered hotels in various price ranges and also campsites, self-catering accommodation and youth hostels. We are indebted to a very detailed hotel survey carried out by the LTB in conjunction with **Holidaycare Service**, 2 Old Bank Chambers, Station Rd, Horley, Surrey (Horley (02934) 74535). Holidaycare Service is a clearing house for information and advice about holidays and accommodation. They hold more detailed information than we have room for here, and if you want to make use of their services we suggest that you contact them at the above address.

In view of the sheer physical size of London and of the difficulties you may encounter getting about, the location of your hotel may be very important—so we've included a hotel map. It may be worth considering staying at one hotel for two or three nights, using it as a base for visiting one part of London, and then moving to another hotel in order to visit another area—especially if you don't have a car and taxis are difficult for you. Sometimes it may be worth considering a central hotel with less than ideal access, in order to save yourself travelling long distances.

An important facility is provided at the Tara Hotel in Kensington (no 46 on the map) where there are **ten superbly adapted rooms** for disabled guests. These can be booked at reduced rates through the Visitors Club, Juxton House, 94 St Paul's Churchyard EC4 (248-9155 ext 3172) to whom a nominal membership fee is payable. The rooms cater for many different needs. The door can be opened by pushing a card into the lock rather than having to mess around with a key, there are low level wardrobes and loos have been designed for either **left- or right-hand transfer to the WC**. Two rooms have overhead **tracked and motorised hoists** to ease transfer from bed to bathroom. There is an **entryphone** by the bed, so you can let someone in without struggling to get up. Blind visitors will find **raised letters and braille inscriptions** in the lift and on room numbers. For the deaf there are **strobe light alarms, induction couplers on the 'phone** and a vibrator fitted to the bed to alert you should an alarm go off at night. The provisions are superb and it is hoped that the instigators, The London Hotel for Disabled People Ltd, will be successful in their aim of providing a wider choice of both price and location of accommodation for disabled people during the next few years. **The facilities provided at the Tara set a high standard and will be particularly useful to many seriously disabled visitors.**

Camping & caravan sites

Perhaps camping is not the most obvious occupation for disabled people and camping in or around London sounds unlikely for anybody. Many disabled people do go camping, however, and have a great time—and a campsite can provide a cheap and adequate base for a holiday. The LTB publishes a list each year of camping and caravan sites in and near London which gives the up-to-date position and prices. In 1982 it cost around £4 per night for two people, a tent and a car.

At peak time it is sensible to reserve a place in advance, although this is not always necessary. It's also advisable to have a good road map with you for finding your way around. One site at Edmonton has really excellent facilities:

Picketts Lock Sports and Leisure Centre Picketts Lock La N9 (803-4756). Level grass site. Sheltered, and open all the year round. The washroom block has **ramped access and two specially adapted cubicles with a (w) loo and (w) showers** with a seat and hand-rails etc. There are a number of disabled groups using the facilities in the Leisure Centre who might be interested in meeting disabled visitors, and if visiting groups require special facilities—eg breakfast or packed lunches—contact Mr Phillips, the recreation manager, and he will help if he can.

Hotels

The information in the following tables is divided into three sections: Inner London, Outer London–north and Outer London–south. The hotels in the central area are subdivided by postal district and numbered to correspond to the hotel map accompanying this chapter; those marked with an asterisk are just outside the map area. The hotels in the other two sections are listed alphabetically. **It is very important to check the location of any hotel in the Outer London sections**, as some are quite central but others are as much as 25km from the centre of the city.

Access to hotels varies and is usually better in the more expensive ones, where there is also more help available. The main problem is nearly always access to the bathroom and loo. Sometimes the geography of the bathroom is such as to defeat even the most determined (w), and **the listing of an hotel does not imply that the bedrooms, dining room(s) and bars are all accessible.** We have tried, however, to provide basic descriptive data.

Price brackets are based on the cost for two people of a twin-bedded room, including breakfast and VAT, at the time of going to press:

£—under £25 **££**—£25–£40 **£££**—£40–£60 **££££**—over £60

You will see that there is very little accommodation available at less than £25 per night. Obviously some hotels are on the borderline of these brackets; you can get exact, up-to-date prices from the current English Tourist Board (ETB) 'Where to Stay' list or direct from the hotel. Use the brackets given here for purposes of comparison and remember that you may be able to get a better deal by booking your hotel through a package holiday operator.

We've tried to find some accessible hotels in the cheaper range and there are several which, although they do not have ideal access, would be possible for some people to use. We've particularly looked for hotels with bedrooms on the ground floor (GFBs), but it hasn't been easy. We managed to find five hotels in W1 that are under £40 per night and have minimal access problems, in that they have either GFBs or a lift, We would also draw your attention to The Nayland, The Averard and The Allandale in W2, Baden-Powell House in SW7 and The George in SW3. Two of the more expensive hotels also have a particular reputation for catering for disabled guests: they are The Berners and The London Tara. Note that in a few cases we only quote the door width of the lift; if the other dimensions are critical for you—for example, if you cannot remove the footplate of your chair—we suggest that you check direct with the hotel. Lift dimensions are not always given where there are GFBs, since in such hotels the lift is irrelevant to the best access. In almost all cases where the door measurement is given, our survey teams reported the lift to be 'adequate for (w)'. Also note that we haven't included details of fire doors, which can prove a considerable hazard. You may want to make enquiries about how many there are en route to your room, and whether they incorporate glass panels (so that you can see through them).

You may well need to make further enquiries to the hotelier. If so, make sure that your letter is clear and brief. What you need to know will depend on your particular needs, but here are a few examples of the sort of question you might ask:

● Is there parking space or a garage at the hotel?
● Can you please confirm the following details about access—eg steps, split levels, size of lift?
● Is there flat access from the pavement to reception, and then to the bedroom, toilet, bathroom and dining room?
● My wheelchair is 62cm wide; can I get from the bedroom to the toilet? (A rough sketch may be helpful to illustrate a possible route and any potential problems.)
● How far would I have to walk from the reception desk to the bedroom, and from the bedroom to the dining room?

It may also be useful to mention that you already have some knowledge of the hotel, quoting the details given here, before asking specific questions relating to your own particular needs. Other points you may need to clarify include whether or not the hotel can cater for a special diet, or whether they will accept a guide dog. Remember that the **door widths given in the tables may not apply to all the rooms in the hotel**—check when you book. **In making enquiries, explain clearly what you need and why, and above all be brief.** People will get confused if you ask too many questions or give too much detail.

Hotelspace Group Services 10 Lower Belgrave St SW1 (730-7148). Hotelspace offer an economical service for booking groups of ten or more. Substantial price reductions are available.

Self-catering

If you're thinking of a longish stay in London, if you don't like hotels or if you're travelling with a small group of people, self-catering offers particular attractions. Unfortunately it too tends to be expensive, but there are some 50 companies offering such accommodation in the ETB's 'Where to Stay', so you have plenty of choice. The information given here is based mainly on survey by questionnaire so, unlike most of the rest of the guide, it's what the management told us. However, we have only included information which looked as though some care had been taken over it and we are therefore fairly confident of its accuracy.

Dolphin Square Furnished Apartments Dolphin Square Trust Ltd, Dolphin Sq SW1 (934-9134). They have 144 apartments centrally sited in Pimlico near the Thames, about 4km from Westminster. There is a NCP in the building. At the main entrance there is flat access to Rodney House. Good size lift (D 77cm, W 129cm, L 121cm). Doors generally over 73cm. The company say that they have a number of disabled guests who seem to cope very well. There are also a number of other facilities in the building such as a restaurant, shops and a swimming pool. Although not cheap, the cost compares quite favourably with many hotels at £100–120 per person per week. In addition, separate guest rooms can be hired at about £11 per night (prices correct at time of going to press).

Gloucester Lodge (C B Ward Ltd 262-5771) 131 Gloucester Ter W2. GF flats up 4 steps. Bathroom doors 61cm.

Kensbridge Apartments 64 Eccleston Sq SW1 (834-0985). Two GF units up 5 steps. Bathroom doors 62cm.

Youth hostels

There are five youth hostels in London and they provide inexpensive accommodation for both individuals and groups. Accommodation is mainly in dormitories, commonly using double-tier bunks. They are **open only to members**, but membership is available to callers at the hostels. Hostel opening times and charges are given in a leaflet available from the Youth Hostel Association (YHA). Hostels are mainly for young people but there is, in fact, no age limit and some hostels have family rooms. **Booking is essential**, especially if you have particular requirements. Enquiries should be addressed to the YHA at Trevelyan House, 8 St Stephens Hill, St Albans, Herts.

Hampstead Heath YH 4 Wellgarth Rd NW11 (458-9054 or 458-7196). The **best hostel in London for access**, it has been acquired by the YHA fairly recently and has accommodation for 220. The dormitories are closed during the day. The main entrance is ramped and there is flat access to the dining room, a ten-bed dormitory, two washrooms and a shower cubicle—all specially arranged and adapted for (w) visitors. There is parking space in the road.

Carter Lane YH 36 Carter La EC4 (236-4965). An old building with awkward access to all dormitories, toilets and washrooms via stairways. Small groups of (w) have used it, with a high ratio of (ab) friends. The warden is very happy to help.

Earls Court YH 38 Bolton Gdns SW5 (373-7083). Less accessible, but still sometimes used by disabled visitors. There are about 10 steps at the entrance. There are no further steps to the dining room, men's dormitories and washrooms. There are 3 steps to the women's dormitories and about 20 to the women's washrooms. The doors into the dormitories are narrow. The warden is very happy to discuss the problems with group leaders before a visit, to give further information and to help if he can.

Highgate YH 84 Highgate West Hill N6 (340-1831). A small hostel for 60 people. Not particularly accessible. The road outside is a steepish hill. There are 8 steps at the entrance and steps inside to all the main facilities.

King George VI Memorial YH Holland House, Holland Pk W8 (937-0748). Disappointingly inaccessible. The route avoiding steps to the GF is through the kitchen. There is only one GF dormitory and other facilities are upstairs. Doors to dormitories, toilets and washrooms are all narrow.

University of London Accommodation Office

Another possible source of accommodation. Their office is in the Union building, Malet St WC1 (636-2818). They will supply anyone with a list of Halls of Residence, many of which are open to all *from Jul–Sep*. An example is Hanover Lodge in Regents Pk, which is often used by groups. There are portable ramps available for the front, (w) loo on the GF and several bedrooms with flat access.

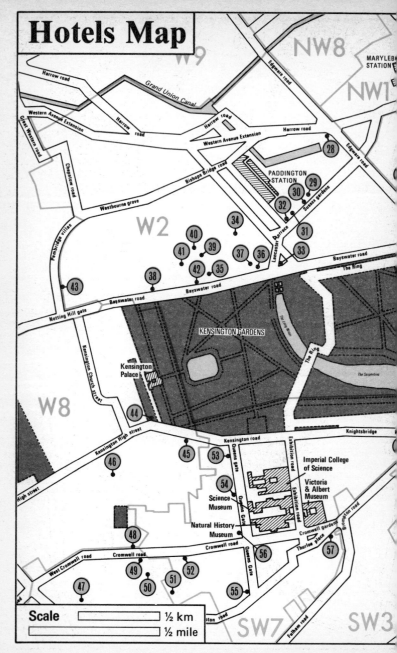

Hotels Map

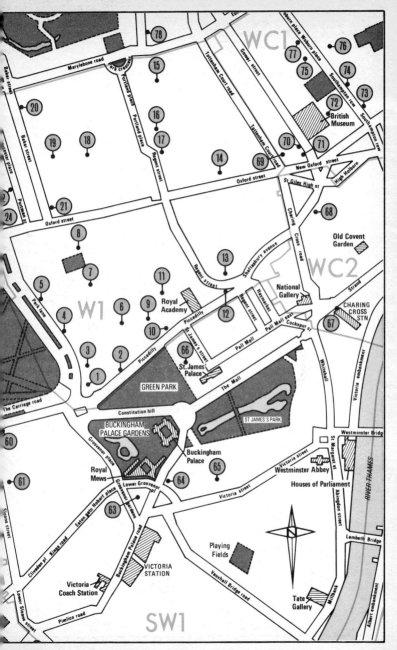

WC1

78

76

77
75
74
73

72

British
Museum

70
71

Marylebone road

Park crescent

15

20

16

19
18

17

14

69

Oxford street

St Giles High st

New Oxford street

High Holborn

68

21

Oxford street

24

Old Covent
Garden

WC2

8

13

7

11
Royal
Academy

National
Gallery

5

6

9

12

CHARING
CROSS
STN

67

4

10

Piccadilly

Regent street

Haymarket

Pall Mall east

Cockspur st

Strand

Shaftesbury avenue

Charing Cross road

Tottenham Court road

St Giles High st

W1

3

2

Piccadilly

St James's street

66

St.James
Palace

Pall Mall

The Mall

Whitehall

Victoria embankment

1

GREEN PARK

The Carriage road

Constitution hill

ST JAMES'S PARK

Westminster Bridge

60

BUCKINGHAM
PALACE GARDENS

Grosvenor place

Buckingham
Palace

65

Victoria street

St Margaret st

Westminster Abbey

Houses of Parliament

61

Royal
Mews

Lower Grosvenor

64

Victoria street

RIVER THAMES

Abingdon street

63

Eaton gate Hobart place

Grosvenor gardens

Buckingham Palace road

Lambeth Bridge

Cliveden pl

King's road

Sloane street

Victoria
Coach Station

VICTORIA
STATION

Playing
Fields

Tate
Gallery

Millbank

Albert embankment

Lower Sloane street

Pimlico road

Vauxhall Bridge road

SW1

Inner London
W1

Name, address tel & price	Steps at entrance	Lift size (cm)		Bedrooms	Remarks
1 Inn on the Park Hamilton Pl, Park La 499-0888. **££££**	0	D	80	Doors 77cm, some with 71cm bathrm door. Front rooms have larger bathrms	CP. Lounge on GF. Restaurant on 1st floor
2 Athenaeum 116 Piccadilly 499-3464. **££££**	3	D W L	80 114 126	Doors 75cm, bathrm doors 64cm	CP. Restaurant & lounge on GF
3 Hilton International London 22 Park La 493-8000. **££££**	3	D W L	80 90 122	Two specially adapted rooms, doors 77cm, bathrm doors 63cm	UGCP with lift access. 5 steps in lounge. (w) loos on 1st floor. Fine view from Roof Bar & Restaurant
4 Dorchester Park La 629-8888. **££££**	3	D W L	80 91 122	Doors & bathrm doors both 77cm	Grill Room accessible. 3 steps to Terrace Restaurant Bar split-level
5 Grosvenor House Park La 499-6363. **££££**	4 Alt flat access	D W L	80 91 122	Doors 77cm, bathrm doors 71.5cm	CP. Split levels: 5 steps to lounge; 4 steps to main restaurant. Flashing lights on bedrm 'phones
6 Chesterfield 35 Charles St 491-2622. **££££**	1	D W L	72 130 111	Doors 69cm, bathrm doors 63cm	Restaurant on 1st floor
7 Connaught Carlos Pl 499-7070. **££££**	3	D W L	90 128 139	Doors & bathrm doors both 77.5cm	CP. Valet parking
8 Europa Grosvenor Sq 493-1232. **££££**	0	D W L	80 91 132	Doors 77cm, bathrm doors 63cm	12 steps to lounge & restaurant

#	Hotel	Parking/Steps	Dimensions	Doors	Notes
9	**May Fair** Berkeley St 629-7777. **££££**	1	D 92 W 153 L 164	Four specially adapted rooms, near lifts	Nearest NCP is five mins' walk. Flat access to restaurant; 3 steps to coffee lounge
10	**Bristol** Berkeley St 493-8282. **££££**	0	D 80 L 90	Doors 75cm, bathrm doors 61cm	Parking
11	**Browns** 21-24 Dover St 493-6020. **££££**	1	—	Two GFBs, doors & bathrm doors both over 77cm	Steps in reception. Restaurant on GF
12	**Piccadilly** Piccadilly 734-8000. **££££**	0	D 80 W 180 L 106	Large rooms, bathrm doors 77cm	Restaurant & lounge both accessible
13	**Regent Palace** 12 Sherwood St 734-7000. **££**	0	D 85 W 118 L 125	Doors 77cm, wash basin. Public bathrm doors 77cm. Public loo doors 65cm	Very central. 2 steps to restaurant & lounge
14	**Berners** 10 Berners St 636-1629. **££££**	0	D 76 W 129 L 153	12 specially adapted rooms, doors 76cm. Handrails etc in bathrm. Lateral transfer to loo	No parking. (w) loo on lwr GF
15	**Regent Crest** Carburton St 388-2300. **£££**	Steep kerb. Temporary ramp	D 80 W 91 L 122	Doors 70cm, bathrm doors 63cm. Some improvements planned	CP with lift access. Restaurant accessible on 1st floor
16	**Astor Court** 20 Hallam St 636-4133. **££**	2+2	—	Three GFBs, bathrm doors 64 & 69cm	Breakfast in room on request
17	**St George's** Langham Pl 580-0111. **££££**	1	D 80 W 84 L 113	Doors 70cm, bathrm doors 62cm	Parking for two cars at front, ten at rear. GF reception. Rooms start on 9th floor. Restaurant on 14th floor
18	**Clifton-Ford** Welbeck St 486-6600. **£££**	2	D 80 W 91 L 122	Doors 74cm but bathrm doors only 60cm max	CP. Restaurant & lounge on GF

Name, address tel & price	Steps at entrance	Lift size (cm)	Bedrooms	Remarks
19 Durrants George St 935-8131. **£££**	2	D 76 L 94	GFB, bathrm doors 62cm	1 step to bar. Flat access to restaurant. Lift access to lwr GF breakfast room. GF loos, cub doors 62cm
20 Sherlock Holmes 108 Baker St 486-6161. **£££**	2	D 80 W 91 L 122	Doors 71cm, but bathrm doors only 58cm	
21 Selfridge Orchard St 408-2080. **££££**	0	D 80 W 91 L 122	Doors 75cm, some bathrm doors 64cm	NCP attached. 4 steps to restaurant. Lounge on 1st floor
22 Portman Intercontinental 22 Portman Sq 486-5844. **££££**	0	D 80 W 91 L 122	Doors 77cm, bathrm doors 68.5cm	(w) loos on 1st floor. Restaurant mostly accessible
23 Portman Court 30 Seymour St 402-5401. **£/££**	2	—	Two GFBs. Separate bathrm has large outward-opening door	Breakfast in room or lounge
24 Cumberland Marble Arch 262-1234. **££££**	1 from Oxford St	D 80 W 144 L 121	Doors 77cm, bathrm doors 68cm	NCP adjacent. 3 steps to restaurant. Provision of unisex (w) loo planned
25 Bryanston Court 56 Gt Cumberland Pl 262-3141. **££**	2	D 57 W 75 L 75	Two GFBs, doors 70cm, bathrm doors 63cm	CP 50m. Flat access to restaurant & lounge
26 Concorde 50 Gt Cumberland Pl 402-6169. **££**	2	D 66	Two GFBs, doors 69cm, bathrm doors 62.5cm	CP 50m
27 Holiday Inn Marble Arch 134 George St 723-1277. **££££**	0	D 80	One specially adapted room; other bathrm doors 62cm	GF lounge. Partial access to restaurant & coffee lounge

No.	Hotel		D	W	L		
28	**London Metropole** 225 Edgware Rd 402-4141. ££££	0	76			Doors 77cm, bathrm doors 66cm	(w) loo, coffee shop & grill on GF. 2 steps to lounge. NCP nearby
29	**Norfolk Plaza** 29 Norfolk Sq 723-0792. £	2	80	91	122	Three GFBs, doors 75cm, bathrm doors 64.5cm. Some narrow passages	Lift access to basement restaurant
30	**Nayland** 134 Sussex Gdns 723-3380. £	1+1	—			Two specially adapted GFBs, doors 70cm; common loo, door 71.5cm	Free parking. (w) loo with lateral transfer. Lounge & breakfast room −18 steps, but breakfast served in room
31	**Garden** 10 Talbot Sq 723-5676. £	3	—			Two GFBs. Separate bathrm/loo off corridor, fairly wide door	Flat access to all main facilities
32	**Mitre House** 180 Sussex Gdns 262-0653. £	+4−1	—			Four GFBs, doors 76cm, bathrms cramped but manageable for many	Parking for 15 cars. Flat access to all main facilities
33	**Royal Lancaster** Lancaster Ter 262-6737. £££/££££	0	80	91	122	Doors 72cm, bathrm doors 60cm. Separate bathrms, door 77cm	UGCP. (w) loos on 1st floor
34	**Allandale** 3 Devonshire Ter 723-8311. £	2	—			Two GFBs, doors 71cm, bathrm doors 73cm	Long flight of steps to breakfast room & lounge so inaccessible. Limited room service & 'phone to reception provided on request
35	**Charles Dickens** 66 Lancaster Gate 262-5090. ££	4	85	120	180	Some GFBs with flat access; doors 75cm, bathrm doors 62cm	4 steps to restaurant. Split levels on upper floors. Only a few rooms with flat access from lift
36	**Park Plaza** Lancaster Gate 262-5022. ££	3	—			Some GFBs with flat access but bathrm doors only 45cm	Flat access to bar & restaurant

Name, address tel & price	Steps at entrance	Lift size (cm)	Bedrooms	Remarks
37 Averard 10 Lancaster Gate 723-8877. **£/££**	5	D 72	One GFB. Other bedrms with bath have relatively good access	Flat access to GF bar, restaurant & lounge
38 Coburg 129 Bayswater Rd 229-3654. **££**	0	Main lift D 68; –4 steps to D 79 W 84 L 116	Several (w)-suitable rooms, doors & bathrm doors both 76cm	NCP nearby. 4 steps to lounge, 6 to restaurant, both GF
39 Craven Gardens 16 Leinster Ter 262-3167. **££**	1	—	Four GFBs along 64cm-wide passage, bathrm doors 67cm	Flat access to restaurant
40 Henry VIII 19 Leinster Gdns 262-0177. **££**	0	1 step D 66 W 94 L 109	Doors 69cm, bathrm doors 65cm. Some 1st-floor rooms fairly spacious	Lift access to basement restaurant. 6 steps to heated indoor pool
41 Central Park 49 Queensborough Ter 229-2424. **££**	0	D 80 W 91 L 94	Doors 74cm, bathrm doors 61cm	UGCP with direct access to lift. Lwr GF loos, outer door 77cm, cub doors 64cm
42 Hospitality Inn 104 Bayswater Rd 262-4461. **£££/££££**	2 or ramped side entrance	D 80 W 89 L 122	Doors 71cm, bathrm doors 68cm	Parking. Restaurant accessible by back lift
43 Pembridge Court 34 Pembridge Gdns 229-9977. **££/£££**	7 or 1+3	—	Two GFBs	Parking for two cars. Restaurant inaccessible but meals served in rooms

#	Name & Address	Access	Doors	D/W/L	Notes
44	**Royal Garden** Kensington High St 937-8000. **££££**	5	Doors 77cm, bathrm doors 66cm	D 80 W 91 L 122	UGCP, ramped access via garage & lift. Lift access to 10th-floor roof restaurant. Few steps to GF bar & coffee shop
45	**De Vere** 1 De Vere Gdns 584-0051. **£££**	1	Doors & bathrm doors both 77cm. Rooms 60 & 62 especially good	D 78 W 91 L 122	No parking. Restaurant accessible
46	**London Tara** Scarsdale Pl, Wrights La 937-7211. **£££**	0	Doors 77cm, bathrm doors 67cm. Some rooms specially adapted	D 80 W 91 L 122	CP. (w) loos on mezzanine. Some reduced price & specially adapted rooms available under London Hotel Project. *See chapter introduction*

#	Name & Address	Access	Doors	D/W/L	Notes
*	**Hilton International Kensington** 179 Holland Park Av 603-3355. **££££**	4 or flat access at side	Two specially adapted rooms; doors 70.5cm, bathrm doors 75cm	D 80	Parking, 1 step to conference rooms. Grill & coffee shops mostly accessible

#	Name & Address	Access	Doors	D/W/L	Notes
47	**George** Templeton Pl 370-1092. **£/££**	5	Five GFBs, doors 75cm, bathrm doors 72cm	D 76 W 91 L 122	Access fairly good except at entrance
48	**Elizabetta** 162 Cromwell Rd 370-4282. **££**	2	Doors 75cm, bathrm doors 64.5cm	D 70 W 91 L 108	UGCP, lift to reception. Flat access to lounge, 7 steps to restaurant
49	**London International** 147 Cromwell Rd 370-4200. **£££**	3 Ramp available	Doors 77cm, bathrm doors 64cm	D 80 W 91 L 122	GF restaurant & coffee shop; −7 steps to lounge

Name, address tel & price	Steps at entrance	Lift size (cm)	Bedrooms	Remarks
50 Manor Court 35 Courtfield Gdns 373-8585. **£/££**	5 Ramp available	D 70 W 100 L 100	Two GFBs, doors 75cm, bathrm doors 72cm	No parking
SW6				
* West Centre Lillie Rd 385-1255. **£££**	0	Adequate	Doors 77cm, bathrm doors 67cm	CP. Adapted loos on GF. Lift access to 1st-floor restaurant
SW7				
51 Edwardian 40 Harrington Gdns 370-4444. **££**	6	D 76	Doors 71cm but bathrm doors only 50cm	Restaurant & bar on lwr GF
52 Forum 97 Cromwell Rd 370-5757. **£££**	High kerb	D 80 W 91 L 122	Doors 77cm, bathrm doors 67cm. Detachable doors on 2nd-floor bathrms	CP & garage. Hotel entrance in Ashburn Pl 3 steps, but can be bypassed. Accessible 1st-floor restaurant. Lift access to adapted loos on mezzanine
53 John Howard 4 Queen's Gate 581-3011. **££££**	5	D 106 W 80 L 200	Doors 75cm, bathrm doors 71cm	Lift access to Japanese restaurant in basement
54 Embassy House 31 Queen's Gate 584-7222. **£££**	4	D 78 W 91 L 122	Rooms 314 & 212 specially adapted, doors & bathrm doors both 77 cm	Lift access to basement restaurant
55 Regency 100 Queen's Gate 370-4595. **££**	5	D 80 W 91 L 122	GFBs, doors 74cm but bathrm doors only 56cm	Public loos, cub doors only 60cm. GF lounge, 6 steps to restaurant

No.	Name / Address / Phone / Price	Ramp		D/W/L	Individual rooms / bathrm doors	Notes
56	**Baden-Powell House** Queen's Gate 584-7030. **£**		D W L	80 91 122	Individual rooms, doors 77cm; dormitories, doors 71.5cm	UGCP. Adapted public loos, cub doors 70cm but no lateral transfer
57	**Rembrandt** 11 Thurloe Pl 589-8100. **£££**	4	D W L	71 114 86	Doors 77cm, bathrm doors 76cm	GF restaurant

SW3

No.	Name / Address / Phone / Price	Ramp		D/W/L	Individual rooms / bathrm doors	Notes
58	**Capital** 22 Basil St 589-5171. **££££**	4	D W L	80 91 84	Doors 77cm, bathrm doors 63cm	UGCP but no lift access. GF restaurant

SW1

No.	Name / Address / Phone / Price	Ramp		D/W/L	Individual rooms / bathrm doors	Notes
59	**Knightsbridge Green** 159 Knightsbridge 584-6274. **£££**	1	D	74	Some rooms with flat access from lift. Bathrm doors 66cm & over. Fairly spacious rooms	No restaurant or public rooms. Breakfast served in room
60	**Sheraton Park Tower** 101 Knightsbridge 235-8050. **££££**	0	D W L	80 91 122	Doors 77cm, bathrm doors 66cm	UGCP with lift access
61	**Hyatt Carlton Tower** 2 Cadogan Pl 235-5411. **££££**	0	D W L	80 91 122	Doors 74cm, bathrm doors 60cm	UGCP. Restaurant −3 steps from foyer, flat from street. Hotel being refurbished when surveyed
62	**Holiday Inn Chelsea** 17 Sloane St 235-4377. **££££**	0	D W L	80 91 122	Doors 77cm, bathrm doors 61cm. Rooms rather cramped	Steps to lift. Flat access to indoor pool
63	**Goring** 15 Beeston Pl 834-8211. **££££**	5	D W L	80 91 163	Doors 75cm, bathrm doors 66cm	Parking for 16 cars. GF restaurant
64	**Rubens** 39 Buckingham Palace Rd 834-6600. **£££**	3	D W L	67 126 80	Doors 77cm, bathrm doors 75cm. Narrow corridors. Some rooms with adequately spacious bathrms & loos	Convenient for Victoria, The Mall, Buckingham Palace etc. Flat access to dining rm

Name, address tel & price	Steps at entrance	Lift size (cm)	Bedrooms	Remarks
65 St James Buckingham Gate 834-2360. **££/£££**	Ramp	D 80 W 91 L 122	Doors 77cm, bathrm doors 67cm. 1 step to some rooms	CP for 120 cars. Restaurant & coffee shop in separate building with steps
66 Stafford 16 St James' Pl 493-0111. **££££**	3	D 70 W 96 L 132	Doors 77cm, bathrm doors 69cm	Parking for three cars
WC2				
67 Charing Cross PO Box 99, The Strand 839-7282. **£££**	Ramp	D 80 W 91 L 122	Three specially adapted rooms; doors 70cm, bathrm doors 68cm, turning space for (w) & rails by loo & bath	Limited parking at front. 1st-floor restaurant and loos, cub doors 72cm Ladies', 70cm Gents'
68 Shaftesbury 20 Monmouth St 836-4422. **£**	0	D 80 W 96 L 176	Doors 70cm, bathrm doors 73cm	NCP 120m. GF lounge. Access to lwr GF restaurant by small lift: D 68cm, W 102cm, L 62cm
* Howard Temple Pl 836-3555. **££££**	−3	D 80 W 180 L 115	Doors 69cm, bathrm doors 67cm	UGCP for 24 cars. Access to lift via baggage door (ask porter)
WC1				
69 YMCA 112 Gt Russell St 636-3576. **££**	Steps or ramp via Y Club	D 78	Doors 76cm, but bathrm doors only 56cm. Bathrms cramped	UGCP. Y Club has many facilities including indoor pool
70 Kenilworth 97 Gt Russell St 636-3283. **££**	1	D 77 W 116 L 119	Flat access to some 1st- & 4th-floor rooms, bathrms small. 1st-floor public bathrms, doors 77cm	Flat access to GF restaurant & lounge. Public loo, 74cm door

		Steps	Dimensions	Bathroom	Access
	Bloomsbury St 636-5601. ££/£££			65cm. Some rooms have wash basin	to restaurant & bar
72	**Montague** Montague St 637-1001. ££	4	D 78 W 91 L 122	Four GFBs, doors 70cm but bathrm doors only 54cm	GF restaurant
73	**Bonnington** 92 Southampton Row 242-2828. £££	0	Adequate for (w)	Doors 77cm. Public bathrm, door 63.5cm	Specially adapted unisex (w) loo on 1st floor
74	**Imperial** Russell Sq 837-3655. ££/£££	0	D 80 W 91 L 122	Doors 68cm, but bathrm doors only 56cm	UGCP with lift access. 1st-floor restaurant. 1st-floor Gents' loo, cub door 66cm
75	**Royal National** Bedford Way 637-2488. ££	1	D 76 W 129 L 153	Some specially adapted rooms; doors & bathrm doors both 77cm, rails etc in bathrm	UGCP with lift access. Specially adapted GF loos, cub doors 77cm
76	**Bloomsbury Crest** Coram St 837-1200. £££	0	D 80 W 91 L 122	Doors & bathrm doors both 69cm	UGCP with lift access. Specially adapted loo in GF Ladies', cub door 77cm
77	**Tavistock** Tavistock Sq 636-8383. ££	1	D 80 W 99 L 190	Doors 77cm but bathrm doors only 53cm	UGCP but no lift access. Basement loos but cub doors only 56cm. GF wine bar, 1st-floor restaurant
*	**London Ryan** 6 Gwynne Pl 278-2480. £££	0	D 80 W 175 L 109	Doors 77cm but bathrm doors only 58cm	CP for 60 cars. Close to King's Cross station (BR & tube). GF restaurant; 2 steps to lounge
*	**Mount Pleasant** 53 Calthorpe St 837-9781. £	−4 −3	Adequate	GFBs, doors 70cm but bathrm doors only 56cm	−3 steps from lift to restaurant

N1

		Steps	Dimensions	Bathroom	Access
*	**Great Northern** King's Cross station 837-5454. £££	6	D 61 W 91 L 122	Two rooms with 77cm doors, 71cm bathrm doors	Lounge & restaurant accessible

Name, address tel & price	Steps at entrance	Lift size (cm)	Bedrooms	Remarks
NW1				
78 White House Albany St 387-1200. **£££/££££**	−3–3 Hydraulic ramp available	D 91 W 114 L 203	1 specially adapted bedrm with bathrm; other bathrm doors 65cm	Specially adapted unisex loo on GF. 7 steps to GF bar. 3 steps to restaurant, −3 steps to Garden Café (coffee lounge)
* **Kennedy** Cardington St 387-4400. **££**	1	D 80 W 115 L 194	Doors 70cm but bathrm doors only 57cm	UGCP for ten cars. Loos with 62cm cub doors. Close to King's Cross station (BR & tube)
Outer London—north				
Acton Park 116 The Vale Acton W3 743-9417. **££**	Ramp	Small	2 GFBs with bathrm	CP. Flat access to restaurant
Blenheim 2 Blenheim Av Gants Hill, Ilford 554-4138. **£/££**	2	—	2 double GFBs, 1 single GFB with bathrm & loo next door	CP. Flat access to restaurant
Carnarvon Ealing Common W5 992-5399. **£££**	1 Ramp at rear	D 80 W 85 L 123	Doors 69cm, bathrm doors 63cm	Large CP. GF restaurant & lounge. GF loos, but cub doors only 53cm
Chiswick 73 High Rd W4 994-1712. **££**	2+1	—	Four double GFBs & three single GFBs, all with shower & loo	CP. Flat access to breakfast room & other facilities. Turnham Green & Stamford Brook tube stations (District line) 400m
Cottage Royal Zone, Hillingdon	1	—	One GFB with bathrm & loo	CP. Flat access to bar & restaurant

Hotel	Steps	Door (cm)	Bathroom	Notes
Cranford 22 Argyle Rd, Ilford 478-8403. £		—	One GFB with adequate separate bathrm	station (BR) 300m
Cumberland St John's Rd, Harrow 863-4111. ££	3 at rear	—	Two GFBs with bathrm & loo	CP. 2 steps to restaurant
Cunard International Shortlands W6 741-1555. £££	0	D 80 W 91 L 122	Doors 77cm but bathrm doors only 56cm (some to be widened)	Special parking arrangements on request. (w) loo with rails etc on 1st floor
Garth 72 Hendon Way NW2 455-4742. ££	2	—	Two GFBs with bathrm	CP. Flat access to restaurant
Heathrow Crest Bath Rd, Longford West Drayton 897-1055. £££	10cm threshold	—	Several GFBs with bathrm & loo	CP. Flat access to breakfast room but not to restaurant
Hindes 8 Hindes Rd, Harrow 427-7468. £	Small threshold	—	One GFB with bathrm & loo	CP. Flat access to dining room. Harrow-on-the-Hill station (BR & Metropolitan line) 300m
Holiday Inn Swiss Cottage King Henry's Rd NW3 722-7711. ££££	Ramp	D 80	One specially adapted room	CP. (w) loo on 1st floor. Easy access to GF restaurant & coffee shop
Kempsford House 21 St John's Rd, Harrow 427-4983. £	2	—	One GFB with shower & loo	CP. Flat access to restaurant. Harrow-on-the-Hill station (BR & Metropolitan line) 200m
Osterley Comfort Gt West Rd, Isleworth 568-9981. ££	6	—	16 GFBs (outside main hotel) with bathrm & loo	CP. Flat access to restaurant
Park 327 Cranbrook Rd, Ilford 554-9616. £	1	—	One GFB with bathrm	CP. Flat access to breakfast room

Name, address tel & price	Steps at entrance	Lift size (cm)	Bedrooms	Remarks
Post House 215 Haverstock Hill NW3 794-8121. **£££**	0	D 80 W 91 L 122	Doors 77cm but bathrm doors only 56cm	UGCP. Public loos, cub doors 65cm
17th Century Barn West End Rd, Ruislip Ruislip (0895) 636057. **££/£££**	0	—	One GFB with bathrm & loo in outbuilding with ramped access	CP. Flat access to restaurant
Tower St Katherine's Wy E1 481-2575. **£££/££££**	2 or ramped baggage entrance	D 107 W 191 L 155	Doors 78cm, bathrm doors 66cm	UGCP but no lift access. (w) loos on 1st floor. Lift access to upr GF restaurants
Travelodge Scratchwood Service Area M1 Motorway NW7 906-0611. **££**	0	—	GFBs, doors 70cm, bathrm doors 63cm	Parking. GF lounge & bar
Wembley Crest Empire Way, Wembley 903-3564. **£££**	0	D 79 W 91 L 97	Doors 77.5cm, bathrm doors 65cm	CP. Flat access to restaurant
West Lodge Park Ferny Hill, nr Barnet, Enfield. 440-8311. **£££**	+2–3	D 76 W 80 L 107	Doors 76cm, bathrm doors 71.5cm	GF restaurant

Bexley Crest Black Prince Interchange Southwold Rd, Bexley	Ramp	—	Two specially adapted GFBs, bathrm doors 77cm	Flat access to GF restaurant & coffee shop. (w) loos in GF Ladies' & Gents'

		Large	Best rooms with bathrms on upt floor of new wing	
Bromley Court Bromley Hill, Bromley 464-5011. ££	3	—		
Central 3 South Park Hill, Croydon 688-0840. £/££	3	—	Two GFBs with good-sized bathrm doors	Flat access to restaurant. South Croydon station (BR) 150m
Clarendon 8 Montpelier Row SE3 318-4321. ££	4 Ramp	D 80 W 91 L 91	Two GFBs, doors 72cm, bathrm doors 64cm	Large CP. GF restaurant & lounge. Lift stops between floors, so steps to all non-GF rooms. Blackheath station (BR) 200m
Hatherley 85 Worple Rd SW19 946-5917. £/££	1	—	One GFB with bathrm & loo	CP. Flat access to restaurant. Wimbledon station (BR & District line) 700m
London Park Longville Rd SE11 735-9191. ££	1	D 80	Doors only 62cm, bathrm doors only 56cm	CP. Flat access throughout. Lift access to lwr GF restaurant
Norfolk Court 315 Beulah Hill SE19 670-3744. ££	0	—	Two GFBs (nos 2 & 6), doors & bathrm doors both 70cm	CP in front. 1 step to lounge & restaurant
Quendale Lodge 70 St Augustine's Av South Croydon 688-2839. £	0	—	Specially adapted bungalow with 2 small steps	CP
Windmill Inn Clapham Common Southside SW4 673-4578. ££	3	—	One GFB with bathrm & loo	CP. Meals can be served in room. Bar crowded & noisy in evening
Worcester House 36 Alwyne Rd SW19 946-1300. ££	3	—	Two GFBs with shower & loo	Flat access to restaurant. Wimbledon station (BR & District line) 200m

Historic buildings & areas of interest

This chapter covers many of London's main attractions; a great deal can be seen and is accessible without much hassle. Obviously, there are problems in some places, and we have tried to give details where relevant. Entries are divided into inner and outer London, and then listed alphabetically by area.

Good places for views over London are very limited. They include the Tower Bridge Walkway, Waterloo Br, Primrose Hill, the bridge over the lake in St James's Pk and Westminster Cathedral Tower (*but see entry in 'Churches' chapter for snags*). The re-opening of the viewing platform of the Telecom Tower (formerly the Post Office Tower) is currently under discussion, but this would require substantial engineering for additional lifts and won't happen for a year or two.

Inner London

The City

The so-called 'Square Mile' is an area of highly concentrated commercial buildings where millions of pounds change hands every hour. Parking is particularly difficult here so, if possible, it's an area to go to and from by taxi or minicab. Pavements are narrow and during the week they're crowded. Eating is expensive. However, it's a fascinating area and there are many old and famous buildings and churches. We have outlined two itineraries—one around the Barbican Centre and the other around the Tower—in the introductory chapter, and there are surveys of many of the major sights here and in the 'Churches' chapter. Much can be seen and enjoyed from outside the buildings. The City of London Corporation PR Office produces an access guide to the area, available from the City Information Centre on the south side of St Paul's Cathedral (606-3030 ext 2456/7). If you come by car it is worth visiting the Stock Exchange and negotiating to leave the car there for a couple of hours; you could then transfer it to the Aldersgate St NCP or to a parking area near the Tower to see other parts of the City.

The Barbican is a sizeable area bounded by London Wall, Moorgate and Aldersgate St; it has been redeveloped on two levels as a residential area. There are historical sites, tower blocks of flats, offices, pubs and shops, both at ground level and on the high-level walkway which covers much of the development. The most interesting places are the Barbican Arts Centre in one corner alongside the artificial lake; St Giles's Church, restored after extensive bomb damage; and the Museum of London. **Access to the Barbican area is generally good but signposting is poor,** nor are there adequate maps or layout plans. No (w) routes are signposted, ramps are not marked and pub loos are inaccessible. Access to the Arts Centre and to the Museum of London is excellent, however. *For further details, see 'Arts complexes' chapter.*

Dr Johnson's House 17 Gough Sq EC4. Contains many Johnson relics. Entrance has **5+1 steps**. High bellpush (150cm from the ground). The GF is accessible and a first edition of the famous dictionary is in a room on the left. A visit to other parts of the house involves up to three flights of stairs which spiral on the bend: 19+18+18 steps in total.

 E6N55 25%

The Guildhall Off Gresham St EC2 (606-3030). The city is governed from this 15thC building, and you can see the Great Hall unless there's a council meeting. Main entrance has **3 steps** but for an **alternative entrance with flat access** ask one of the attendants.

E3 A

HMS Belfast is moored opposite the Tower and is the largest cruiser ever built for the Royal Navy. Sadly, it is **not the place for a disabled visitor**. Basically all you'll be able to do is to see a bit of the deck. Getting inside involves narrow doors, tiny hatches, vertical ladders, narrow gangways and so on. It's one of the few sights (like the Monument) which we'd advise both (w) and (s) to leave alone. There are good views of the ship from the riverside and from Tower Br.

The Monument Monument St EC3. This giant Doric column commemorates the Great Fire of London and is 62m high—it lies the same distance from the supposed site of the outbreak of the fire, in Pudding La. There are 311 steps and it can hardly be described as accessible!

E311

The Old Bailey (Central Criminal Court) EC4 (248-3277). On the site of the old Newgate prison. You have to queue outside to get into the public galleries and there are **many steps**. The building has not been fully surveyed but we were told that there are about 20 steps to court 18; 20 more to other courts in the new wing; and many more to those in the older part of the building. Advisable to ring first.

The Royal Exchange On the corner of Threadneedle St and Cornhill EC3. Attractive and distinctive exterior. It is now occupied by the International Financial Futures Exchange. There is a viewing gallery reached by **9+4+11+7 steps**.

E31

St Katharine's Dock This area has been reopened for visitors and includes the Historic Ships Collection, the World Trade Centre, a variety of small shops, a restaurant and a large pub. There is a CP entered from Thomas More St. Parking is not allowed on the internal roads. The area is generally flat and there is a road around most of it. There are cobbled sections and the odd kerb or step to get over at the dock gates etc. Altogether, it's a fairly attractive area, if a bit touristy.

The historic ships are basically inaccessible with steps and narrow companionways etc but (w) can go down on the pontoons running around the dock to get a closer look (without charge).

The Dickens pub is inaccessible, although it is possible to sit outside in good weather: entrance 10 steps, 17 to 1st-floor restaurant and then 19 to the fish restaurant.

The Warehouse restaurant (481-3356) is near the river and has flat access but is expensive. Signposting is quite good.

P ⊟ ⧑ 50%

The Stock Exchange Throgmorton St EC2 (588-2355). Well worth seeing but somewhat isolated from other accessible City sights, although the Guildhall is not too far away. In this area the main sights are buildings which can be seen only from outside, such as the Bank of England and the Natwest Tower, although the City is still a fascinating area during the week. More money changes hands on the floor of the London Stock Exchange than anywhere else in the world except Wall St. The best time for a visit is normally *14.00–15.00*, as there are often school parties in the mornings. A 'phone call in advance may ease your path and also ensure that the movable (w) viewing platform is there. There are no public CPs nearby, but if you 'phone there are limited facilities for (w) and (s) visitors to park. Normal entrance from Old Broad St has **3+29 steps**. There is, however, an **alternative way in** from Throgmorton St and there is a large lift up to the Gallery without steps. The small cinema with an introductory film is somewhat cramped and without formal (w) spaces. There are ordinary loos with smallish cubicles: Ladies' flat, Gents' up 3 steps.

◪ E32 Ⓐ ⧑ ⎕⎕

Tower Bridge Walkway & Museum Tower Br SE1 (407-0922).

The overhead walkway, giving fine views over London and the Thames, was reopened in 1982. **Access by large lifts** and no charge for (w). There are exhibitions on both sides showing how the structure and mechanism were designed and how it operates. You may have to ask the lift operator to let you out to see these displays. Out on the walkways, the balustrades are unfortunately just about the height of a (w) eyeline. There are two small platforms with very steep ramps by which (w) can get a view. It's not a very good arrangement and suggestions have been made about improving it. The staff are generally helpful.

E0 ⧑ ⎕⎕

The museum is on the south side and entrance is included in the admission price. The normal route to get there is down a flight of about 20 steps but by taking a longish detour of about 300m **the steps can be bypassed**. There is a high kerb outside the museum. Inside it is accessible and there is a **(w) loo**.

◪ E1 ⧑ ⧑ wc

Tower of London Tower Hill EC3 (709-0765). One of London's prime tourist attractions. Wheelchair pushers are normally admitted without charge. There is some parking space outside as well as the meters on the street. There may be long queues to get in on popular days such as bank holidays and summer weekends; during the tourist season it's generally fairly chaotic. The Tower consists of a group of buildings with two surrounding walls. The area is roughly 200m square and many of the paths and courtyards are cobbled and sloping, making progress bumpy and difficult for (w). Since the buildings are several hundred years old, access to many of them is difficult and although it's possible to see quite a lot from outside, this is not much help if it's raining. It's sad that even if you are with friends who can get you safely down the 50 steps, regulations prevent (w) from seeing the Crown Jewels. The most accessible buildings are the Oriental Gallery, the Bowyer Tower and the GF of the Jewel House, although none have absolutely flat access. Also, there are plans to build a ramp into the History Gallery, in which the story of the Tower is told in words and pictures. Once inside, there is flat access and shelter.

Bloody Tower Very narrow spiral staircase. Easiest access by the exit stairway of 19 steps. The History Gallery has flat access from the entrance. The tower is cobbled inside.

Bowyer Tower 1 step at entrance.

Cafeteria At the east end of the wharf.

Jewel House The easiest way in to the GF is through the exit, where (w) are admitted. Have a word with the yeoman warder, as they're usually pretty helpful. There is frequently a long queue in the summer. Crown Jewels −50 steps.

Loos Provision is better than at most tourist spots—(w) loos near the Bowyer Tower, near the main entrance and in the Tower Hill underpass.

Oriental Gallery 3 steps at entrance. Spacious inside.

Royal Fusiliers Museum 12 steps at entrance.

Tower shop On the wharf near the main gate. Enter via exit door (1 step).

White Tower 12+20+10 steps at the entrance, but only 24 if you use the exit (76cm door). Basement −15 steps from GF.

 E0 N 25%

The Ceremony of the Keys, which is the ritual of locking up the great fortress, takes place every day *between 21.30 and 22.05* and has done every night for some 700 years. Apparently, it was a little late one night in 1941 when a bomb blew the escort off their feet. Admission is by ticket only from the Resident Governor, Tower of London, Tower Hill EC3 (709-0765) and disabled visitors should mention their disability when applying. There is flat access but (w) need to get a door specially unlocked afterwards in order to get out! Book well in advance, and give alternative dates if possible.

 E0

Covent Garden & Piccadilly

Covent Garden is the area behind the Royal Opera House in Bow St, running north and west to Shaftesbury Av. It's a pleasant place on a sunny day but is often crowded, especially in the evening, and has generally poor access. It is a recent development on the site of the old Covent Garden fruit and vegetable market. There are lots of small shops and stalls and there is frequently open-air entertainment from buskers, small music groups and Punch and Judy shows. It's generally a very animated scene. The shops are mostly small and up 1 or 2 steps; much of the shopping area is under cover, so it's a good place to go if the weather is uncertain. There's an open-air crafts market (that is, open at the ends but roofed over) on the south side. Parking is difficult, although there are a few meters in surrounding streets. There are NCPs at the bottom end of Museum St, just by the junction with High Holborn, and in St Martin's La, just past Litchfield St. Generally very little thought has been given to the needs of (w) and (s). Surfaces are rough and consist of cobbles or paved flagstones with poor joints.

London Transport Museum Flat entry and (w) loos. Café and lecture hall have flat access and 90% of the museum is accessible.

Loos There are two (w) **loos** nearby, one in the London Transport Museum, where admission is free for (w), and another in the National Jazz Centre in Floral St.

Moss Bros, the famous clothes hire shop, is one the corner of New Rd and Bedford St. There are 2+2 steps to the lift, which gives access to most departments.

The Punch & Judy is the main pub and must rate as the most inaccessible in London, with bars involving either 30 or −30 steps (mind you, this didn't deter one of our more intrepid survey teams!).

St Paul's Church is up several steps, and features a classic (w) loo nearby, reached—would you believe—by −19 spiral steps. The church does, however, offer a garden and seats, some shaded, providing a quiet spot for a rest or a picnic; entry from Henrietta St, 4 steps or from Bedford St, flat.

Piccadilly Circus is one of London's famous landmarks, but it is small and crowded with heavy traffic and is not particularly attractive. The pavements are narrow and you won't miss much if you drive around it in a taxi or even just buy a postcard of it.

Piccadilly Circus (Trocadero) Development On the north side of Coventry St is a massive new development which will house the Guinness Book of Records Exhibition and the London Experience, among other things. We are told that there will be flat access (via lifts to all levels) and a unisex (w) loo. As the building will be open both in the daytime and evenings this is potentially a very valuable facility.

E0

Holborn & The Strand

Central Registry Office *See entry on Somerset House.*

Dickens' House 48 Doughty St WC1 (405-2127). This was Dickens's first real home in London. Entrance: 1+1 steps. Bell 150cm high. There's a small room at the end of the hall −1 step for postcards etc, but the main part of the house is −14 steps to the basement (kitchen and wine cellar) or 19+20 steps up to the other floors. Exhibits in showcases are difficult for (w) to see as they are 104cm high. **Altogether not an accessible site.**

E2N39/14 20%

Inner & Middle Temple The area between the Law Courts and the river. It is an interesting place to wander around. There are 4+3 steps into the Middle Temple Hall and 1 into Temple Church via the south door. The area is slightly hilly but if you use Inner Temple La or Middle Temple La, access is mostly ramped. The way through Mitre Ct involves 5 steps.

Land Registry Lincoln's Inn Fields WC2 (405-3488 and ask for 'Enquiries'). There are 8+5 steps to the enquiries office, but security staff are always willing to help. Documents and deeds are widely dispersed throughout the country. London documents are normally held at Harrow and Croydon district land registries, for example, so a telephone enquiry first explaining what you want might save wasted effort.

E13

Law Courts The Strand WC2 (405-7641). This elaborately fronted building at the east end of the Strand houses the Royal Courts of Justice. Access to GF (main hall) is via **3+4 steps** at the main entrance, or alternatively you can get to the 1st floor via the Carey St entrance up 6+2 steps. Inside there is a lift, but it doesn't help access much as it goes to intermediate levels. From the main hall there are 2 steps to an exhibition of robes and paintings, and to the Citizens Bureau. Also 2 steps to a Ladies' (w) loo and a Gents' with 62cm door and to low-level telephones. Courts 1–19 are on the 1st floor, 20–25 and 51–52 are in the basement and 39–50 are in the Queens Building, which is a separate new building up near Carey St, with **lifts and flat access** from the CP entrance by St Clement Danes Church. Courts 31–38 are in the West Green Building, access by 3 steps from the CP entrance; 31–36 are on the 1st floor, 37 and 38 are on the GF.

Lincoln's Inn WC2. Another lawyers' area behind the Law Courts. Interesting and attractive, especially Lincoln's Inn Fields. Fairly flat. Access to the New Hall and library off New Sq is difficult, as there are a total of nearly 40 steps and we couldn't see any way round these. Sir John Soane's Museum is on the north side of the Fields.

Public Record Office Chancery La WC2 (405-0741) & Ruskin Av, Kew, Surrey (876-3444). The principal repository of public archives, documents and state papers and also of some aspects of family histories (*see also entry on Somerset House*). There are useful leaflets outlining which records are held where and a telephone call or two might save a lot of wasted effort. The records are split between Chancery La, Portugal St (nearby) and Kew near the south end of the bridge. The office in Chancery La poses considerable access problems: 4 steps to the enquiries office and then considerably more to most sections. The staff will try and help wherever possible. The Kew office is more modern and has ramped/lift access to most parts.

Chancery La E4   Kew

Public Record Office Museum at Chancery La, which includes historical documents such as the Domesday Book, is entered via +14−7 steps.

E21

Somerset House & other registry offices The registry offices are all close to each other. If you are seeking particular information it may be useful to write or telephone in advance, but if you just turn up the staff are usually quite helpful.

Alexandra House Kingsway WC2 (242-0262) holds the Register of Deaths. It is on the west side of Kingsway near St Catherine's. The entrance has **1 step**.

E1

St Catherine's House 10 Kingsway WC2 (242-0262) holds the Registers of Births and Marriages. It is on the south corner of Kingsway where it meets the Aldwych.

There are **1+2 steps** from the entrance to the reception desk, but the staff will bring information to the entrance for (w). It is advisable to ring first.

▟ E3

Somerset House Strand WC2 (438-6622) holds the Registers of Divorce and of Wills and Probate. The main pedestrian entrance from the Strand is cobbled and involves **+2−1 steps**. Alternatively you can come in with the cars, but the road is bumpy too. Once inside, there are 1+3+1 steps to the enquiries desk.

▟ E5

Kensington & Chelsea

Chelsea Royal Hospital Royal Hospital Rd SW3 (730-6161, ext 44 for RSM). In this unique retirement home for soldiers, the Chelsea Pensioners wear the famous and distinctive scarlet coats and black tricorns on high days and holidays. It may be possible for (w) or (s) to park inside, if you ring first and ask. Otherwise the nearest CP (excluding meters) is in the Kings Rd. Entrance hall is 100m from gateway, then 10 steps up to both the chapel and Great Hall. Some movable seats at the front of the chapel. Hospital museum up 2 steps.

P E0 ▟ N10 🚻

Disabled Living Foundation 246 Kensington High St W14 (602-2491). A very useful advice agency on all kinds of subjects, which has a permanent exhibition of aids and equipment for disabled people. **An appointment is necessary. Flat access.** There is a **(w) loo**.

E0 🚻 🚻 wc

Kensington Palace State Apartments (937-9561). The Palace is at the side of Kensington Gardens and some considerable distance from the roads. Queen Victoria spent her early years here. Entrance **3+1 steps**. Inside: there were no exhibits on the GF when the survey was made, but there are plans for a dress collection to be sited there. Other exhibits are on the 1st floor, up 13+9+9 steps with handrails on both sides. Staff will normally be willing to help individual disabled visitors. The whole circuit would take you some 300m in about half an hour. There are plans to provide a (w) loo during 1984.

▟ E4N31 🚻 30%

Regent's Park

London Zoo Regent's Pk NW1 (722-3333). London Zoo is situated on the north side of Regent's Pk and contains the country's biggest collection of animals. **Access around the zoo is generally good**, although some of the older houses are more difficult to visit. Specific provisions have been made in all the modern buildings (eg ramps into the elephant house). It is a big place however, and there is plenty that can be seen. **Paths are tarmac'd throughout and the ground is fairly flat.** There are slopes in the tunnels under the outer circle and some of the enclosures (eg lions and bears) are terraced, involving a considerable number of steps for the best view. The zoo is roughly triangular in shape with sides 500m×500m×800m. The main entrance is roughly in the middle. Guide books are available at the main entrance and there are plenty of plans placed prominently on walls. It is worth sending for a zoo guide before you visit. **Pushchairs and wheelchairs can be hired** near the main entrance. These will be of value to (s) and to those who do not want to do too much walking.

Cars and taxis can stop outside the main gate and there is one official Orange Badge space there. There are dotted yellow lines along most of the Outer Circle starting 18m from the main gate. Cars may park here *after 11.00* or use the CP 300m away. Getting there by public transport is not so easy. It is 1km to the nearest Underground station, at Camden Town. Buses pass the northern edge of the zoo. If you arrive by waterbus (from Little Venice) there are about 40 steps up from the canal, or a long sloping path which is too steep for many (w). There is a telephone which can be used to call a taxi or minicab at the main gate. This is the best exit for (w) and (s), as most of the other pedestrian exits have turnstiles. The zoo makes special arrangements for parties of (w), including admitting helpers free of charge under certain conditions. If in doubt, telephone before your visit.

Aquarium Usually (w) are not admitted for insurance reasons and there are 5 steps and a very narrow entrance, 50cm wide. Our survey team went in through the exit, up 7 steps, but we had to be careful because we were going against the flow of visitors. Also, it took a minute or two to get used to the low level of lighting.
Bird houses Entrance has 1 shallow step.
Children's zoo Flat access.
Clore Pavilion for small mammals. Flat access to the GF, with easily viewed exhibits; −21 steps to the Moonlight World exhibition of nocturnal animals.
Cotton Terraces for camels, zebras, giraffes and antelopes. There are some steps if you want to use them but most of the animals are viewable from ground level, accessed by ramps.
Elephant & rhino house Ramped access from the side nearest the penguins.
Insect house Up 13 steps.
Loos **The (w) loos near the main entrance are clearly marked on the map in the 'Zoo Guide'**. The Gents' is just past the aquarium entrance and the Ladies' is just past the giant pandas. There is also a (w) loo in the first aid post near the new lion terraces. A number of other loos are clearly marked on the map.
Mappin Terraces for bears, goats and sheep. To go right round the terraces involves 10−8+10+15+15 steps up and a similar number to get down again. Not recommended for (w). There's a good viewing area outside the Mappin Café, up only 10 steps.
New lion terraces Although going around these involves quite a few steps, most of the big cats can be seen adequately from ground level.
Reptile house After 2 steps to get in, the inside is 90% viewable.
Restaurants, kiosks etc Ramped access to the cafeteria, Tavern Room and Pavilion Bar, as well as to the Zoo Study Centre. The main restaurant is up 34 steps. The shop has 1 step at the entrance.
Sealions & seals Viewing over the barrier is difficult for (w).
Snowdon Aviary Ramps make this easily seen.
Sobell Pavilion for apes & monkeys. All the animals can be seen either outside or through glass viewing windows. A low hedge can restrict some (w) views outside.
Stork & ostrich house Flat access.

D E0 ⬆ 75% ♿ wc U

Telecom Tower Cleveland St W1. Discussions have been going on for some time about re-opening the public viewing gallery and obviously for the disabled visitor this would be of enormous value. British Telecom are unfortunately particularly sensitive about security and even if it is opened, the possibility of a (w) smuggling explosives past their airport-type checks seems to worry them. They are concerned about the potential number of visitors and say there is a problem even in providing 'sterile' chairs for a (w) to transfer into for a visit. It is hoped that a practical way round all this will be found so that everyone can enjoy the spectacular views if the tower is re-opened.

Westminster & St James's

Buckingham Palace The palace itself is, naturally, not open to the public as it is the Queen's London home and is lived in by many members of the royal staff. On special occasions and for distinguished foreign visitors, there are processions and there is pageantry. When the Queen is in residence, the Royal Standard is flown. *The Changing of the Guard* both at Buckingham Palace and at Horse Guards Pde, Whitehall, is a regular attraction for visitors. Mounted Life Guards pass the palace regularly at *10.50 & 11.35*, except on *Sun* when they're an hour earlier, and the Changing of the Guard takes place between *11.15 & 12.10* in the palace forecourt, every day in summer and alternate days in winter. It is possible for disabled people to get permission to watch from inside the railings since there is often a considerable crowd outside, particularly in the summer. If you are inside, remember that you're there for about one and a half hours, and there's no loo. To get permission you should contact the Master of the Household, Buckingham Palace SW1 (930-4832). For other information, eg about the times of events, contact 930-4466 and ask for the public information office (ext 2357).

Cabinet War Room Horse Guards Rd W1. This is where Churchill held many of his vital cabinet meetings during World War II. The site comes under the auspices of the Imperial War Museum (to whom any queries may be directed) and opened in April 1984. It's not an easy area for parking but there are one of two CPs round Trafalgar Sq. There are about **15 steps but there's a lift to bypass these** for (w) or (s) visitors, available on request. Once at the bottom there's **flat access** everywhere and just one door which might be a problem for some electric wheelchairs. **A wheelchair is available** for you to transfer into to get into this room if you need it. It sounds really good and should be an interesting place to visit. Best approach 300m from the Mall to the corner of King Charles St.

Houses of Parliament & Westminster Hall St Margaret St SW1 (219-3000). For security reasons the Palace of Westminster is no longer open to the public except at the invitation of a Member of Parliament, for an official lobby or to gain access to the public galleries. Although normal access to the Central Lobby or the Strangers' Gallery involves a substantial number of stairs, there is an **alternative route** via the Chancellor's Gate and King's Lift to the principal floor level. Generally the police on duty will be very helpful. There are **(w) spaces** at the back of the Strangers' Gallery in the Commons (the public gallery) which is steeply stepped; access is by a ramp from the lift. There's a **(w) loo** off the Lower Waiting Hall. To get to the

Committee Rooms, there is a lift from the Lower Waiting Hall to the main or upper Committee corridors. Mass lobbies involving disabled people normally take place in the Westminster Hall.

 E A [&] [¶] [& wc]

Parliament Square & Westminster Bridge Another tourist magnet with Big Ben, Churchill's statue and the bridge itself (*see also entries on Westminster Abbey and St Margaret's Church in 'Churches' chapter, and entry on Imperial Collection in 'Museums' chapter*). There's a **(w) loo** at Westminster Pier, which is also a good starting point for river trips as the pier is ramped.

Passport Office Petty France SW1 (213-3434). Meter parking area and no nearby MSCPs. Access via **+1−6 steps** with a central handrail. There is a back door giving **ramped access** from Vanden Pl which can be opened on request and there are security officers on hand who would always get some help for (w) if asked. The waiting rooms have seats, and there are adapted loos on the 1st floor with lift access, although (w) would need a spot of help to negotiate the fire doors en route.

 E7 A [&] [& wc]

Whitehall SW1. Whitehall runs from Westminster to Trafalgar Sq and is a wide street flanked by government offices. Partway along is the Cenotaph, which is the principal memorial to those who died in the two World Wars; the annual national ceremony of remembrance is held here in *Nov*. Horseguards Pde, with its daily Changing of the Guard ceremony (*see entry on Buckingham Palace*) is just beyond the Cenotaph as you go towards Trafalgar Sq.
The Banqueting Hall (opposite Horseguards Pde) is the only bit of the Palace of Whitehall left. Charles I was beheaded here in 1649. There are magnificent Rubens paintings on the ceilings. There's **1 step at the entrance, then 17+6** inside. Seats around the walls. The loos are 3 steps from the entrance; both Ladies' and Gents' have a large cubicle with a 63.5cm door opening outwards.

 E1N23

Downing Street with its well known resident at no 10 is halfway up Whitehall on the left. It is sometimes possible to go down it and see the outside of the house; otherwise you must view it from the end of the road.

Outer London

Brentford & Chiswick

Brentford Steam Museum (Kew Bridge Engine Museum) Green Dragon La, Brentford, Mddx (568-4757). Just at the north end of Kew Bridge. Partly accessible: 2 steps to rooms 4−5, flat access to rooms 6−7; 12 steps to main 90-inch (2.3m) engine, the longest steam engine in the world. An interesting visit if you can manage the steps, although it's worth ringing first to check that the engines are running. Both Ladies' and Gents' loos on the flat; Ladies' has one very large cubicle, almost a (w) loo.

E2N12 [&]

Chiswick House Burlington La W4 (995-0508). Smallish 18thC house, set in its own grounds, about 150m from the road. Parking inside is possible for (w) and (s) with prior arrangement. **Entrance and GF mostly flat**, with 2 steps into one room. There's a spiral staircase inside to the 1st floor; alternatively 7+6+7 ordinary steps round at the front of the house, but this route must be opened specially. Ordinary loos (63cm cub door) and refreshments in the grounds about 100m from the house.

E0 ⬛ N20 ⚿

Hogarth House Hogarth La W4 (994-6757). Small house where Hogarth lived, containing copperplate prints from 'The Rakes Progress' etc. **Entrance −3 steps. GF flat,** but 13 steps with tricky 90° turn to 1st floor. For loos (ordinary ones) and refreshments, go to Chiswick House about 300m away.

⬛ E3N13 ⚿ 50%

Syon House & Park Park Rd, Brentford, Mddx (560-0884). The house is fairly well signposted and there is adequate parking inside. There are reserved spaces for disabled people by the house itself and also near the garden centre. There's a **(w) loo** about 200m from the main CP area, near the Motor Museum. Access generally good apart from some steps if you tour the house.
Butterfly House 20m from main CP. Ticket area cramped. Path inside rough in parts (gravel and paving). Most showcases and exhibits visible. Surface OK in main exhibition room.
Garden Centre Centre large, approximately 100m×60m. All flat and well paved.
Motor Museum About 250m from CP. Flat easy access.
Syon House CP spaces for disabled people right outside. 100m to main CP. 1 step, then −5 and then a ramp. There are six rooms with furniture and exhibits.

P ⬛ E6 ⚿ ⚿ wc

Enfield

Forty Hall Museum Forty Hill, Enfield, Mddx (363-8196). A small museum of fine art and local history set in pleasant grounds complete with duck pond. CP 150m, but disabled visitors may park outside the front door. Main entrance 2 steps, **side entrance 1 step**, and then about half the house is accessible. The GF is flat, including the tea-room and ordinary loos. There are plans for providing a (w) loo.

⬛ E2/1 ⚿ 50% ⚿ X

Greenwich

An interesting and varied area with plenty to see and do, but (w) will need to take a firm attitude in some places. The most attractive way of getting to Greenwich is by riverbus from Westminster or the Tower. There is ramped access at most of the piers and although the boats vary considerably in accessibility, the crews are generally used to accommodating (w) passengers (*see entry on boat trips in 'Travelling' chapter*). Alternatively you can go by BR train to either Greenwich or Maze Hill or by car, parking at the bottom of Crooms Hill or in the centre of Greenwich Pk (via the Blackheath gate). The underground (pedestrian) tunnel under the Thames shown on the maps is a feasible route from the north side of the river (Canaletto painted Greenwich from the north bank). The tunnel is about 300m long with steepish slopes in places (about 10%) and huge lifts at each end, and is an interesting sight in its own right.

'Cutty Sark' King William Wlk SE10 (858-3445). The area round this old tea-clipper is cobbled and there's a wooden bridge leading to the dry dock. There's ramped access to the middle deck, but the other decks are only accessible up or down very steep staircases. Nearby is Gipsy Moth IV but the tiny yacht is, not surprisingly, inaccessible.

Flamstead House (858-1167) is very near the Observatory in the park. Our survey team was refused entrance, although the GF exhibition is accessible by 4 steps through an exit. The normal route involves climbing to the 1st floor up a difficult stairway, and descending first to the GF and then to the basement. Many many steps.

Greenwich Park with Blackheath behind provides a large area for walks. Tarmac paths throughout. If you're lucky, you'll find squirrels so tame that they will eat out of your hand. There's a (w) loo near the gate to Blackheath.

Greenwich Pier SE10 (858-3996). Ramped access to river boats. The large **(w) loo** is normally locked, but the key is available from the attendant on the pontoon. It is possible to park nearby with permission from the person on the gate.

National Maritime Museum Park Rw SE10 (858-4422). This is a very large museum, over 200m long with exhibits on two floors and a mezzanine. A full visit to the museum involves quite a number of steps because of split levels. The museum publishes an information sheet including a plan and it is helpful to read this entry in conjunction with that plan, as we have used the same numbering system. The museum has also prepared a note on 'Facilities for the Disabled', but our survey teams found this somewhat confusing. We met typical 'Does he take sugar?' attitudes, and suggestions that we made about the possible provisions of stair-lifts at key places were the subject of a certain amount of buck-passing. A 'phone call beforehand would no doubt help if there's something particular you want to see. Special parking facilities can be made available near the entrance to the Neptune Hall.

The front entrance is via the Trafalgar gate and involves a 150m walk and 6+7 steps. The best entrance for (w) is either through the exit from the Neptune Hall, giving access to part of the museum, or via the Park Row gate, going some 150m and gaining flat access to the colonnade area past the Queen's House and thence to the West Wing (ii on the plan). The entrance to the café is via 8 steps from outside. Inside, if you want to see particular sections, it is worth studying the plan of the museum and working out the easiest route. Otherwise use one of our 'best' entrances, accept the steps, and see whatever you can. From the entrance by the West Wing there is a **large lift** giving access to galleries 3–5 on the 1st floor. There is a **(w) loo** in the Ladies' in the West Wing (GF). There are 9 steps up to the mezzanine for galleries 6–10. To avoid steps you can go out and around the building and see the Neptune Hall, with **flat access** at the entrance and 3 steps to see galleries B–F which are all on one level.

The Queen's House involves either getting the Orangery door opened (it is normally locked) or 4 steps in the middle of the colonnade. There are −4 steps towards the East Wing, where there are **(w) loos** near the information desk. There is **flat access** to galleries 12–16 and the wing can be reached on the flat from the entrance in the colonnade.

A		N		30%			

Old Royal Observatory Greenwich Pk SE10 (858-1167). CP in the middle of the park only 50m away. There's quite a hill and some steps if you walk up from the river. Equally, because of the high ground there's a good view over East London. There's a refreshment kiosk near the CP. A good part of the observatory is accessible by going through the main entrance. There is a very narrow passage to the rest of the buildings, which can be bypassed by going round through an exit. The staff are generally very helpful. Part of this second section is on a split level, 14 steps. Loos: cub doors 62cm, door opens out (nearest **(w) loos** in the East Wing of the National Maritime Museum or by Blackheath gate).

E0 | | 70%

Royal Naval College King William Wlk SE10 (858-2154). A little way to the east of the 'Cutty Sark', about 100m from the road. The halls inside contain some magnificent painted ceilings. The entrance has 3+15 steps to the Lower Hall, then 8 steps to the Upper Hall. Across the path outside, access to the Chapel is via 1+3+14 steps, and again the ceiling is beautifully decorated.

E18N8

The Thames Barrier is a little further down the river from Greenwich and is an impressive sight. The Riverside Wlk gives superb views of the structure, and there is a CP nearby. The small complex includes a viewing gallery with audio-visual displays and a working model, a small shop and refreshment facilities, and is situated in a 4m-deep well behind the flood wall. At the time of writing, it was not clear whether a lift or a ramp would be included. The suggested ramp would be stepped, with one 10cm step every 1.5m—it would be like going up a whole succession of kerbs. The ramp would lead to the top of the flood wall for views. It is planned to site a unisex **(w)** loo just outside, which would be available even when the building is shut.

Hampstead

Hampstead Heath and Hampstead Village should be high on the list of 'musts' for anyone wanting to see the pleasanter side of London. However, a lot of the charm of the area stems from the fact that it is situated on the slopes of a steep hill, the highest point in London, from which there are superb views. Hampstead proper, meaning the area around Hampstead High Street, is full of good (but expensive) shops and restaurants of all kinds. Unfortunately, it is not ideal for **(w)** owing to the steep slopes and often quite narrow pavements; it is, however, by no means impossible with a reasonably fit helper and deserves investigation.

The Heath is best approached from its lower reaches in the area of Parliament Hill. There is a reasonably sized free CP in East Heath Rd at the South End Green end, from where it is possible to enjoy a very pleasant wander across the Heath without encountering over-severe slopes. Another recommended access point is at the end of the road called Parliament Hill: from here one can either climb to the top of Parliament Hill itself, which is the Mecca of kite-flying enthusiasts and also commands probably the best view there is of London; or, if feeling faint-hearted, one should take the path to the left and enjoy a less exacting amble towards Highgate Ponds.

Kenwood House is situated at the northernmost end of the Heath—a handsome period house with a fine picture collection. Open-air concerts are held in the grounds and concerts and poetry readings are held in the Orangery on the GF. Access is from Hampstead La and cars can be parked in front of the house. The entrance is flat and the GF presents no problems. The exhibition area on the 1st floor, however, is basically inaccessible to (w) as there is no lift and quite a number of stairs. Cafeteria and adapted loos reached by a small step from GF.

P E0 60%

Pubs

The Flask Flask Wlk NW3 (ex-directory)—*the* Hampstead pub, serving Young's beer. Rather cramped inside.

Jack Straw's Castle North End Wy NW3 (435-8374, restaurant 435-8885). At the junction of North End Wy and Spaniards Rd, the highest point in London. This well known pub is a good lunchtime stopping place. There is a large CP at the side and rear; ramped pavement to front entrance, 3 steps to wide double doors. Inside GF, several bars in an open-plan layout with plenty of space. There is a garden terrace accessible through a wide door with a small raised doorstep. A food bar runs throughout the year and a barbeque in summer. **NB: the loos are inaccessible,** upstairs in the restaurant reached by a small lift (D 76cm, W 130cm, L 76cm).

P E3

The Nag's Head 79 Heath St NW3 (435-4108). Free house with a wide variety of real ales, and food. Spacious saloon bar with movable tables and chairs. Air-conditioned. Access: 3 steps to both bars; flat access to ordinary loos with narrow cubicles.

The Old Bull & Bush North End Rd NW3 (458-4535)—the pub of the song, of the book, of the film. Large CP and easy access to several bars. 'Pub-plush' decor detracts slightly.

Spaniards Inn Spaniards Rd NW3 (455-3276). The other Hampstead show-pub. The inside is really not on for (w) but there is flat access from the CP to the pretty garden.

Isleworth, Richmond & Twickenham

Ham House Ham St, Richmond, Surrey (940-5070). Attractive setting and free access to the grounds. Rooms furnished from various periods. CP some 300m from the house, but it is possible for passengers to be set down near the house if the car is taken back to the CP. There are **4+5+1 steps** at the entrance and 1 inside. Then it's virtually all flat via a **small lift** (D 61cm, W 91cm, L 93cm). Most (w) would have to consider the lift size fairly carefully as it's really only suitable for smallish chairs with removable footplates. Alternatively 9+9+9 steps to the 1st floor. There are (w) loos outside +4−1 steps from the path.

■ E11 [&] [¶¶] [& WC] ■ 5

Marble Hill House Richmond Rd, Twickenham, Surrey (892-5115). A white villa built in the early 1700s for Mrs Howard, the mistress of George II. A stately home on a manageable, homely scale. CP 100m. BR station (St Margaret's) about 1km. The grounds round the house are mostly flat. House has **1 step** at the entrance and then the GF, with changing exhibitions, is flat. The main collection of period furniture is up some 20 steps on the 1st floor. There is a **(w) loo** near the main entrance and a tea room with flat access about 50m away. Note that Orleans House is nearby and both might be visited in an afternoon.

P ■ E1N20 [&] 40% [& WC] [& X]

Osterley Park House Jersey Rd, Isleworth, Mddx (560-3918). Neo-classical house set in huge grounds with period furnishings. CP about 300m. Entrance **10+10+1 steps, then flat access**. There is a video film on the architecture of the house. Refreshments available in the stables and **(w) loos** nearby with flat access.

P ■ E21 [& WC]

Kew

Kew Gardens & Kew Palace The Royal Botanic Gardens are world famous as a research centre, and offer an interesting day out. They are attractively laid out and have generally good facilities. Signposting of facilities for the disabled is virtually non-existent, however, although ramps are marked on the newer maps. An excellent guide book is available from the Orangery bookshop (940-1171 ext 4113) or from Her Majesty's Stationery Office (HMSO), 49 High Holborn WC1 (postal orders to PO Box 569, London SE1). The book includes a map and a table showing which plants are in bloom at different times of year. This may determine which of the four entrances you use. Parking is particularly difficult on *Sun*. There are parking spaces around Kew Grn for the main gate, including three reserved for Orange Badge holders. By the Brentford Ferry gate there is a CP with a small charge (well worth it to avoid hassle) but if you use the Victoria or Lion gates you have to park in the surrounding residential streets. In the winter the Ferry gate CP is open but is approached through a narrow gap between two posts—designed to prevent gipsy visitors from setting up camp! You could also come by riverboat from Westminster; there is ramped access from the pier to Kew Br. **Wheelchairs are available** for hire at the main gate and can be reserved by telephoning 940-1171 ext 4143.

The Gardens are basically **flat** with tarmac paths to most parts. They are also large, covering over 120 hectares. There is flat access at all the entrances; the turnstiles can be bypassed by (w). It is best to decide what you want to visit and part-plan a route, bearing in mind that, for example, the Palace is in one corner and the main refreshment pavilion in another about 1km away. If you have particular interests, check opening times on 940-1171 ext 4113.

Kew Palace is approached by bumpy and part-cobbled paths, and there are steps: 2+1 to the GF, 11+3+11 to the 1st floor. There is a tea bar up 2+2 steps nearby.

Loos are marked on the map, but (w) loos are not specifically indicated. There is a Gents' **(w) loo** by the Orangery, a Ladies' 50m away towards the Palace, and (w) loos for both sexes by the Pavilion gate and by the Water Lily Pond (Ladies' closed in winter, for some reason).

The plant houses and museums nearly all have ramped access, although there are some narrow doors which are kept closed because it's important to keep a constant temperature. The Wood Museum has ramped access, as has the Palm House and the Water Lily House. Museum 1 has 1+1 steps at the entrance and the Marianne North Museum, with a unique collection of paintings of plants and insects, has 6+5+1 steps. The Temperate House is ramped on the north side. Ramps are marked on the newer maps with an R.

Queen Charlotte's Cottage has 1+2 steps at the entrance, then 23 steps to the 1st floor.

Refreshments are available *in summer* at the Pavilion, with tables both inside and out. The self-service counter has narrow (70cm) clearance and a 90° turn at the end, and is difficult for (w). There is a kiosk open in winter, and a tea bar between Kew Palace and the Brentford gate for snacks. There are plans for another refreshment area near the Wood Museum.

A new tropical conservatory is under construction which will give visitors a unique glimpse of tropical flora in a house divided into ten different habitats. It will be sited near the main entrance (from Kew Grn) and is due to open in 1985. The basic route around the building is ramped although because of differences in floor level some parts of the house are only accessible by stepped ramp. Where there are steps, good handrails will be provided. Our impression is that considerable thought has been given to ensure good access and that (w) will find it an interesting and reasonably easy place to visit.

P D E0 [&] 90% [& wc] [& X] U

Kew Green is an attractive spot near the Gardens, where cricket is played in the summer. There are a number of pubs around the Green with gardens or outside drinking areas, such as the Rose & Crown and the Coach & Horses.

St Anne's Church on the edge of the Green is both interesting and unusual, with **flat access**. Its decoration is mostly Baroque.

E0 [&]

Maids of Honour tea rooms/restaurant is just opposite the Gardens in Kew Rd. It gets crowded and is somewhat congested but it has **flat access** and is a popular eating place.

E0 [&]

Churches

London has an enormous number of historic and important churches, of which we have surveyed only a selection. Most were built with architectural barriers of one kind or another, and our experience has been that the ecclesiastical authorities have been generally slow in providing ramps or stair-lifts to bypass these. Most churches have steps at the entrance, although All-Hallows-by-the-Tower is a welcome exception with good access, and the provision of a stair-lift at St Paul's Cathedral is of enormous value. Westminster Abbey, Westminster Cathedral and St Bartholomew-the-Great are to be recommended, since all three have good access and are of exceptional interest. If churches are your special interest, it would be worth getting 'A Guide to London's Churches' by Mervyn Blatch, available from Constable, 10 Orange St WC2.

Abbeys & cathedrals

St George's RC Cathedral Lambeth Rd SE1 (Cathedral House 928-5256). This cathedral was rebuilt after destruction by bombing in World War II. **There are 2 small steps, but access is otherwise flat.** There is plenty of space for (w) at the sides and front. **An induction loop** has been installed. The nearest (w) loo is 200m away in the gardens around the Imperial War Museum.

 E2

St Paul's Cathedral Ludgate Hill EC4 (248-4619). This is Sir Christopher Wren's masterpiece and it dominates the London skyline. The dome is the second largest in the world and contains the famous Whispering Gallery. Parking is not easy, although there is a NCP in Ave Maria La. Access is also not very straightforward. There are **10+14 steps at the main entrance** with revolving doors at the top. However, **there are two alternatives**; both involve getting an (ab) to ask for help from the cathedral staff. You can ring first if you are in doubt, or if you want to make advance arrangements. The principal route is on the south side of the cathedral, opposite the Information Centre, via 1+2 steps and a platform stair-lift measuring 66cm×83cm. The stair-lift takes one chair at a time and is rather slow, so allow plenty of time if you are coming with a group. The other route, which might be used if the stair-lift is out of action, involves a longish walk and will have to be opened by a staff member.

Most of the Nave and the Crypt are accessible by the service lift described above, and ramps have been put in the Crypt. The various galleries are up literally hundreds of steps: 259 to the Whispering Gallery, 375 to the Stone Gallery and 530 to the Golden Gallery. Even we would reckon this a bit adventurous, but the service lift gets near the Whispering Gallery. There are then a further 23 steps and the corridor is too narrow for an adult wheelchair. The nearest (w) loos are in the Museum of London but there are plans to build one in St Paul's.

 E24/3

Southwark Cathedral Borough High St SE1 (407-2939). Though much restored, this building retains its traditional Gothic style. Access is via a flight of about 25 steps from Borough High St, or on the level via Beadle St, or Tooley St and Montague Clo. There is a big kerb down from the Borough Market CP. The easiest entrance is through the door about half-way down the length of the church, by the south transept. **The entrance is −3+1−1 steps** at the west door, giving access to the Nave, and 1+3−2 if you go right round to the chapel behind the high altar. Parking is very difficult during the day, but much easier during the evenings and on *Sun*. There may be parking space round the Borough Market if you're lucky.

 E5/6

Westminster Abbey Broad Sanctuary SW1 (222-5152). This is the church used for most national occasions and royal events. It contains the tomb of the Unknown Warrior and those of many famous people. Parking in the immediate area is

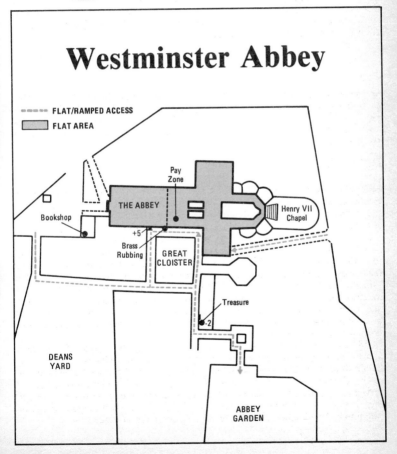

difficult during the week. (*See suggested itinerary in introductory chapter.*) Access via the main west entrance, **bumpy surface and 1+2 steps**. After that, all the area shown in tint on the plan is flat, apart from the odd step into side-chapels. You can see into most of them anyway. **Alternative flat/ramped ways in are shown on the plan,** but strictly speaking they are exits from the area in which normally you have to pay. If you can use the main entrance, then do.

There is a lot to see. Henry VII's Chapel is inaccessible because of 15 steps to negotiate. The Confessors' Chapel is also on this level; it contains the famous Coronation Chair and Stone, but is reached through a very narrow door 52cm wide. The Brass Rubbing area is accessible but somewhat congested (if you're interested in brass rubbing, *see also entry on All-Hallows-by-the-Tower*). There are −2 steps to the Abbey Treasures exhibition, which includes a reproduction of the Coronation regalia. The Abbey gardens, which are open *on Thur only*, are the oldest gardens in England, with seats and shade, and the access is flat though slightly bumpy. Atmospheric and highly **recommended**. There are band concerts *in summer*. The Chapter House, which was the original meeting place of the House of Commons, is up 10 steps.

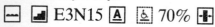 E3N15 [A] [&] 70% [+]

Westminster RC Cathedral Ashley Pl SW1 (834-7452). This is of striking 1880s design with a wide square in front opening on to Victoria St, where you'll find the Army & Navy stores and many smaller shops. For parking, there are meters in the adjacent street or a NCP in Artillery Row (get there early to be sure of a space). The entrance has 3+2 steps, but there is a **ramped entrance to the right** near the cathedral bookshop, although it is neither obvious nor well signed. **Inside, access is flat** to all the main areas. There are 1 or 2 steps into some side-chapels, and −3 steps to the book and souvenir shop. For access to the Tower, there is a **lift** (D 68cm, L 110cm), adequate for most (w). There are interesting though not brilliant views from the top, but there are access problems because of a 23cm threshold blocking the narrow balconies. It is not easy for (w). A little bit of thought about access at the top of the Tower would make an enormous difference. The main cathedral bookshop is to the right of the main entrance and has ramped access but is fairly cramped inside. There's another (though smaller) religious bookshop with flat access in the square in front of the cathedral. The Conference Centre alongside the bookshop has ramped access and **(w) loos**.

 E5 [A] [&] 80% [!!]

Churches

All Hallows London Wall EC2 (588-3388). This 18thC church is used as the reference library for the Council for the Care of Churches, and so is normally locked. The interior is very pretty, however, and access may be obtained via the Council office at 83 London Wall EC2 (638-0971/2), although even then access is by **3+8 narrow steps**.

[■] E11

All-Hallows-by-the-Tower Byward St EC3 (481-2928). This is an interesting church and there are facilities for brass rubbing. Pepys watched the Great Fire from the tower. **Access is good.** There are 3 steps at the main entrance neatly bypassed by a

ramp. This is steep in parts, though much easier than the steps, and most (w) will need just a bit of a push. **Once in, the whole place is flat** and there's a variety of things to see. The Brass Rubbing Centre is a friendly spot and the tables are at a suitable height for most (w) to do this if they want; some of the brasses are quite small and are mounted on mobile plinths (you could even do them on your knees). On the south side by the font there are 2 steps. The church contains a museum about London's history and there's even a Roman pavement, but both are in the Crypt, involving more steps and an awkward turn. **Recommended.**

E0 ⎣⚹⎦ ⎣⚹ X⎦

All Souls Langham Pl W1 (580-3522). A very appealing church. Recently the foundations were relaid on rubber buffers to absorb the vibrations of the tube lines! There is **ramped access** on the north side and an entryphone to summon help. Lift inside (D 80cm, W 80cm, L 150cm) which goes up to the Nave and bookstall and down to the basement for the Church Hall, tape library and (w) **loo**.

⎣A⎦ ⎣⚹⎦ ⎣‖‖⎦ ⎣⚹ wc⎦

Brompton Oratory Brompton Rd SW7 (589-4811). A quiet and attractive church, well worth a visit. There are **6+2 steps** at the entrance, and access is **flat inside**.

▣ E8 ⎣⚹⎦

Central Hall Storey's Gate SW1 (222-8553). The 'cathedral' of Methodism. Used on *Sun* for worship and at other times for meetings and exhibitions. There are **4+14 steps** to main hall level, and further steps to other parts of the building. It is possible to bypass most of this by the use of lifts. We met a fairly unusual attitude here, and were told that apart from church services and special visits before exhibitions are generally open, **(w) would not be admitted**. The management said that they would review the matter with the GLC.

▣ E18N ⎣⚹⎦ 30% ⎣‖‖⎦

City Temple Holborn Viaduct EC1 (583-5532). This is the City's main Free Church. Being relatively modern, it is not of special historical interest. **Hearing aids are available.** Access is via **3 steps** at the entrance, but a door can be opened to make a **ramped bypass** available.

▣ E3/0 ⎣⚹⎦ ⎣⟨?⟩⎦

Holy Sepulchre without Newgate Junction of Holborn Viaduct & Faringdon St (248-1660). A church with strong musical traditions. The garden is dedicated to the Royal Fusiliers, London Regiment. The entrance is in Holborn with **1+2 steps** to swing doors, and then two further sets of doors after 90° turns. **Access inside is flat.**

▣ E3 ⎣⚹⎦

St Andrew's Holborn Circus EC1. Wren's largest parish church, restored with a simple, modern interior. Access is by **−6−7+3 steps** to swing doors then a 90° left turn through an inside door. **Flat access from there.**

▣ E16 ⎣⚹⎦

St Bartholomew-the-Great West Smithfield EC1 (606-5171). Apart from the Tower Chapel, this is the oldest London church, and is very atmospheric. The entrance is at the corner of West Smithfield and Little Britain, where there are **rough surfaces and a small step, then flat access**. NCP nearby. **Recommended.**

⬛ 🚻 **90%**

St Bartholomew-the-Less West Smithfield EC1 (606-7777). Serves as the hospital's chapel. Entrance is through the porter's lodge opposite the market, **5 steps**.

🔳 **E5** 🚻

St Botolph's Bishopsgate Bishopsgate EC2 (588-1053). A stately church dedicated to the patron saint of travellers. Entrance is via **2+2+3 steps** with two sets of quite tricky swing doors.

🔳 **E7** 🚻

St Bride's Fleet St EC4 (353-1301). Another Wren church, the tower of which is reputed to be the model for tiered wedding cakes. Access **2+1 steps** from Fleet St. There is a museum of printing in the Crypt but access involves steps.

🔳 **E3** 🚻

St Clement Danes Strand WC2 (242-8282). This is the 'Oranges and Lemons' church. It was blitzed during World War II and has now become the RAF church. Entrance via **1 easy step** at the west end, but the church is on an island surrounded by busy roads.

🔳 **E1** 🚻

St Dunstan in the West Fleet St EC4 (242-6027). Here are housed a 17thC clock with two 'striking jacks' which ring the bell each hour, and the only known contemporary statue of Queen Elizabeth I. Entrance has **4 steps**.

🔳 **E4** 🚻

St Ethelburga the Virgin within Bishopsgate Bishopsgate EC2 (588-3596). An inscription on the floor reads 'Bonus intra. Melior exi'—that is, you go in good and come out better! Entrance **1 step**.

🔳 **E1** 🚻

St Giles Cripplegate Fore St EC2 (606-3630). In the middle of the Barbican development, this church was restored after bombing in the 40s. Milton is buried here. The entrance has **3 shallow steps**.

🔳 **E3** 🚻

St James's Piccadilly W1 (734-5244, London Brass Rubbing Centre 437-6023). An outstanding Wren church set in a peaceful garden. Entrance is **−3+2 steps** from Piccadilly or **2+3** from Jermyn St. There is a small coffee house with movable tables and chairs up 1 step from the courtyard. Sometimes there's an open-air market in the courtyard, −3 steps from Piccadilly.

■ E5 🚶

St Lawrence Jewry Gresham St EC2 (600-9478). The church of the Corporation of London. Entrance: **1 large step** at the west end.

■ E1 🚶

St Magnus Martyr Lower Thames St EC3 (626-4481). Noted for its fine steeple and baroque interior. **Flat access.**

E0 🚶

St Margaret Lothbury Lothbury EC2 (606-8330). Here are housed some beautiful fittings from other demolished Wren churches. There is a particularly fine courtyard. Entrance is **1 step**, best access being by the centre door.

■ E1 🚶

St Margaret's Parliament Sq SW1 (222-6382). The parish church of the House of Commons. Sir Winston Churchill was married here. There are **2+1 steps** at the entrance.

■ E3 🚶

St Martin-in-the-Fields St Martin's Pl WC2 (930-1862). Has been called 'the parish church of London'. Entrance is via **5 steps** in front, **then flat access** to the Nave and Chancel. Alternatively, there is a **ramp** on the north side of the church giving access to the Chancel. About 30 steps up to the Gallery and steps down to the Crypt.

■ E5 **A** 🚶

St Mary Abchurch Abchurch Yd EC4 (626-0306). Unexpectedly beautiful inside. Entrance **1+4 steps**, then right turn through another door. There are seats in the courtyard.

■ E5 🚶

St Mary-le-Bow Cheapside EC2 (248-5139). There are **5 steep steps** at the entrance, **then flat access**. The Court of Arches, which decides Ecclesiastical Law cases and confirms the election of bishops, is held in the Crypt down more than 20 steps.

■ E5 🚶

St Mary Woolnoth Junction of Lombard St & King William St EC3 (626-9701). Sumptuous interior. Entrance via **4+1+3 steps** and two sets of swing doors.

■ E8 🚶

St Peter-upon-Cornhill Junction of Cornhill & Gracechurch St EC3 (626-9483). Supposedly, built on the City's oldest church site. Frequent music recitals. Enter on the south side via a back alley—a little exploration will get you there. Entrance is via **1+1 steps.**

 E2

St Stephen Walbrook Walbrook EC4 (283-3400). The headquarters of The Samaritans. Its dome was possibly the prototype for St Paul's. Entrance: **+1−6 steps**.

 E7

St Vedast Foster Lane Cheapside EC2 (606-3998). Easy to overlook with St Paul's and St Mary-le-Bow so close by, but the skilful restoration of this Wren church, blending old and new, makes it worth a visit. Entrance involves **4+1 steps**, then a right turn through swing doors.

 E5

University Church of Christ the King Gordon Sq WC1 (387-0670). A fine Victorian church. Entry is via the west end, where there is just **1 tiny step**. Not all of the church is accessible, but it is well worth a visit.

 E1

Wesley's Chapel City Rd EC1 (253-2262). The founding church of Methodism, where Margaret Thatcher was married. Entrance is **3 steps but there is a permanent ramp**. Wesley's house has now re-opened next door, where two downstairs rooms are accessible.

 E3/0

Theatres

Gaining access to entertainment in London isn't always easy, and one of the problems highlighted by our survey of entertainment places was inconsistency in the information given about them. There are many places where the access is good and where the needs of disabled people have been considered, and our survey teams were frequently given a friendly welcome. There are other places where our enquiries were not welcomed and where, for whatever reasons, the needs and sensibilities of disabled people do not seem to have been taken into account. Of course, many of the buildings are old and were built long before access was even thought of, and public safety (that is, of the majority public) is of great importance. But the requirements for access have been shown to be achievable at a considerable number of venues, including old buildings, while not compromising safety (in other words, the various regulations mentioned below are satisfied). Also, a balanced view of safety requirements is essential. It is to be hoped that recent positive developments such as those at the Coliseum, the Duke of York's, and the Mermaid will be copied wherever possible.

One thing that ought to be stressed is that for (w) it really is necessary to negotiate about the access with the box office or manager before setting out. Many managements will try and help those who are hard of hearing, the blind or partially sighted and both (w) and (s) who may want either an accessible seat or one with extra leg-room. It is essential, however, that they are told what is needed. It is frequently a good idea to speak to the house manager in order to get reliable information since, as we discovered, people in box offices sometimes know neither the geography nor the regulations of their own theatre. **The other basic condition covering (w) access to nearly all places of entertainment is that (w) shall be accompanied.** Since both requirements—prior negotiation and having a friend to go with you—apply everywhere, they are not mentioned elsewhere in the text.

One of the reasons for this guide is to provide people with some authoritative data from which to negotiate. It is important not only to understand what the regulations are, but also to know what is possible and to hope for a friendly and helpful reception, which you will find in many places. If you meet with negative attitudes, we hope that you will negotiate with confidence, and pursue your objective with unruffled politeness and persistence.

The GLC produce a rather formal-looking document called 'Just the Ticket', specially for disabled people; although we thought that it had a somewhat bureaucratic style, each new edition will include some useful updated information about access. You will understand that the situation does change from year to year, and hence the information from Artsline (*see below*) is particularly valuable. There are GLC regulations governing the admission of wheelchairs, and these seem sometimes to have been formulated perhaps a little too officiously and specifically. Accessibility depends on the attitude of managers, whether the auditorium is full or not, and on all kinds of other things, as well as on the formal regulations. Of course, the rules are important and the manager always has the right to refuse admission. We found many anomalies, but fortunately laws and rules in Britain are rarely quite as rigid as they may seem. On the other hand, a manager who breaks or bends his licence conditions may risk losing that licence, and even his job—so don't be too hard on the individual who won't allow you in.

There is no problem in the admission of (s) to auditoria, as regulations are written round (w). **In categorising the various venues, we have used the GLC lettering system**, described here:

A is for the (s), or (w) who can walk a little (that is, into the auditorium).

B is for the (w) who cannot transfer into an ordinary seat, and who therefore needs to stay in the chair during the performance.

C is for the (w) who can transfer, or be transferred, to an ordinary seat, so that the wheelchair can be taken out of the auditorium.

What the survey has shown is that many theatres have facilities for at least one B category patron, although sometimes in a box with a restricted view. It is particularly difficult for institutions or clubs with a number of (w) members to organise outings because very very few places can accommodate more than two or three (w). However, the new and relatively good facilities at the National Theatre, the Mermaid and the Barbican give hope for the future.

One thing we did not expect to find was the high cost of going to the theatre in a wheelchair. Normally, (w) have to sit in the most expensive part of the auditorium and must have a companion; the situation is similar for (s) who cannot manage steps. It all makes a visit quite pricey. Some theatre managers have realised this, and there is sometimes latitude for negotiation.

Many, if not most, theatres are prepared to allow blind patrons to come with a guide dog and, with prior arrangement, will normally provide a dog-sitting service since it is usually impractical to have a dog amongst the seats—there just isn't room. We have not listed all the places that allow guide dogs, since our survey wasn't sufficiently comprehensive, but Artsline will be able to advise you.

Helpful organisations

Artsline (625-5666) is an excellent telephone information service giving up-to-date access data on a wide range of entertainment venues and events. The staff have lots of experience and are interesting people to talk to. *Open Mon–Fri 10.00–16.00, Sat 10.00–14.00.*

The Society of West End Theatre (SWET), Bedford Chambers WC2 (836-3193) publishes a fortnightly 'London Theatre Guide', indicating the venues with the best access and those with sound amplification systems. It is available at most theatres and ticket agencies.

Central London

Adelphi Strand WC2 (836-7611). Entrance **1 step**. Flat access to Stalls. Dress and Upper Circles up 30/50 steps. **Each of the four boxes can accommodate (w)** but the view is somewhat restricted, and only two have flat access, via the stage door. One box is near a private loo which can be made available. Other loos: Ladies', flat from Stalls; Gents', 6 steps. Helpful management.

 E1 A 🚹 (A/B/C)

Albery St Martin's La WC2 (836-3878). Entrance **3 steps. Two (w) spaces** in box M (door 65cm), reached from a side door in St Martin's Ct, and then 3 steps. Easiest seats for transfer are in row H of the Royal Circle, reached by the same route. Over 30 steps to Stalls (down), and Grand Circle and Balcony (up). Ordinary loos by the side entrance. **Sennheiser system used with special hearing aids,** available for a nominal charge.

■ E3 ⬛ ⬛ (A/B/C)

Aldwych Aldwych WC2 (BO 836-6404, M 379-6721). Entrance **5 steps.** No (w) spaces and (w) who can transfer would normally sit at the side of the Dress Circle, reached from an exit into Drury La and then −2 steps. There are −26 steps to the Stalls, or 24 to the Upper Circle. Loos: Ladies', off the foyer; Gents', about 25 steps from the Dress Circle.

■ E5/2 ⬛ (A/C)

Ambassadors West St WC2 (836-1171). Entrance **1 step.** No (w) spaces. The best place for (w) who can transfer is the Dress Circle with 5 steps; −30 steps to the Stalls. Loos: Ladies', off the foyer, 1 step; Gents', 3 from the Dress Circle.

■ E1 ⬛ (A/C)

Apollo Shaftesbury Av W1 (437-2663). **Entrance flat.** No (w) spaces. Up to four (w) who can transfer can be admitted to Dress Circle, with 12 steps.

E0 ■ N12 ⬛ (A/C)

Apollo Victoria Wilton Rd SW1 (828-8665). Entrances: Wilton Rd **4 steps**, Vauxhall Bridge Rd 9 steps. **One (w) space** in the front row of the Dress Circle, reached through exit at street level in Wilton Rd. Those (w) who can transfer should also use this entrance. All parts of the theatre are up or down steps from the Dress Circle, including the foyer and loos.

■ E4/9 Ⓐ ⬛ (A/B/C)

Arts 6 Great Newport St WC2 (BO 836-3334, M 379-3280). Also houses the *Unicorn Theatre* for children. Very friendly. They have tried to provide access and have plans for improving things, including the provision of a ramped side entrance. Entrance via **1 step** into the main foyer, then 5 steps to the Circle and −1 step per row inside. The Stalls are −4−13 steps from the foyer and then gently sloped. There are **three (w) spaces** at the back of the Circle, where there are a small number of removable seats which are normally sold last. This is one of the best possible solutions to access problems, and we hope other theatres will follow suit. There is a small **adapted loo** and a low-level telephone on Circle level. The loo has handrails but it's not quite large enough for sideways transfer. The restaurant is on Stalls level with −4−13 steps. There is an **induction loop** for both Stalls and Circle, and the management would be willing to look after a guide dog during the performance. As always, a telephone call helps if you have particular needs.

■ E1N5 ⬛ ⬛) ⬛ (A/B/C)

Astoria 157 Charing Cross Rd WC2 (437-6565). Entrance **7 steps**; 9 steps to Stalls bar, then 12 steps to Stalls. A total of 50 steps to the Circle.

■ E7N21 (A/C)

Barbican *See 'Arts complexes' chapter.*

Cambridge Earlham St WC2 (BO 836-6056, M 836-7183). Entrance **1 step**, then −4 steps to Stalls. **One (w) space** and the possibility of two or three more by prior arrangement. Loos flat from Stalls, but narrow cubs.

■ E1N4 ⬚ (A/B/C)

Coliseum (London Coliseum) St Martin's La WC2 (836-3161). Entrance has 3 steps, but **one door has been specially ramped to give flat access**. Flat inside to **seven (w) spaces** in boxes at the back of the Stalls. Box doors are 75cm, and there is a waitress service for refreshments. Good view. Limited price concessions. **A (w) loo has been provided with flat access**, and there are also ordinary loos at this level. Other parts of the theatre are up at least 30 steps, the Balcony about 80, but there is a **lift** which (s) may use, if you ask the house manager.

A ⬚ ⬚⬚ ⬚wc (A/B/C)

Comedy Panton St SW1 (930-2578). Entrance 2 steps. **Usually (w) can use the boxes** at Dress Circle level, −6 steps and 65cm door; slightly restricted view but they are frequently available. The one on the left has a staff loo on the same level, also with a 65cm door. For (w) who can transfer, the back of the Dress Circle is flat from the foyer, but then stepped.

■ E2N6 ⬚ (A/B/C)

Cottesloe *See entry on National Theatre.*

Covent Garden (Royal Opera House) Bow St WC2 (BO 240-1066, M 240-1200). The BO is just around the corner at 48 Floral St; entrance 1 step. Main theatre entrance also has **1 step. There is a (w) space** in Grand Tier box 66 (for the best view), access by the entrance in Floral St, then 27 steps but help is normally available. Alternative (w) space by seat 98 in Stalls Circle, 16 steps. It may be possible to accommodate more (w) by taking some Stalls Circle seats out. For (s) and (w) who can transfer, the best seats are rows F and T in the Stalls. Access via the main entrance and then −3+15 steps. Ordinary loos at Stalls Circle level or off the foyer. Box 66 has a private loo en suite.

■ E1N27/16 ⬚ (A/B/C)

Criterion Piccadilly Circus W1 (930-3216). Entrance **1 step**; then −16−8 with a further 6+2 to the Grand Circle, or −3−9 to the Stalls. However, there is **flat access** to the Circle through an exit in Jermyn St. **There are three (w) spaces** in the Circle, one in the centre aisle and two in side aisles. There is flat access to ordinary loos.

■ E1 A ⬚ (A/B/C)

Donmar Warehouse *See entry on Warehouse.*

Duchess Catherine St WC2 (836-8243). Entrance **1 step**. No (w) spaces. Inside there are −20 steps to Stalls, or 11 to Upper Circle. Row A of the Upper Circle (3 more steps) gives the minimum number of steps, and probably the best value seat. The Circle and Upper Circle are steeply stepped.

■ E1N14 (A/C)

Duke of York's St Martin's La WC2 (836-5122). **Entrance flat. Two (w) spaces** in Royal Circle with flat access. Adapted loo on same level. **Induction loop** covering the Stalls and the front of the Royal Circle. Commended and **recommended**!

E0 [♿] [♿ wc] [(?)] (A/B/C)

Fortune Russell St WC2 (BO 836-2238, M 836-6260). **Entrance flat.** No (w) spaces. Easiest part for transfer is the rear of the Dress Circle, row F: 7 steps from foyer, or 5 from exit in Crown Ct. The Stalls are −20 steps, the Upper Circle 21. Ordinary loos 1 step from rear of the Dress Circle.

E0 ■ N7/5 (A/C)

Garrick Charing Cross Rd WC2 (BO 836-4601, M 836-9396). Entrance **2 small steps**. The Dress Circle is at GF level which is obviously the best area for transfer, and there is flat access if you use the exit. **Two (w) can be accommodated** in the Royal Box, −12 steps from the Dress Circle. Loos on the Dress Circle level; the Ladies' has a 72cm cub door, and with negotiation gents in a wheelchair might be allowed to use this.

■ E2 [A] N12 [♿] (A/B/C)

Globe Shaftesbury Av W1 (437-1592). Entrance **1 step. Flat access** to the Dress Circle via an exit in Rupert St. No (w) spaces, but (w) can transfer in the Dress Circle at either end of row B. Stalls involve −12 steps.

■ E1 [A] [♿] (A/C)

Her Majesty's Haymarket SW1 (930-6606). **Entrance flat. One (w) space,** and opportunity for two (w) to transfer at the back of the Stalls. Normal route −21+17 steps, but alternative entrances from Charles II St, one with −4 steps, the other with none. Dress Circle up 23 steps.

E0 [A] ■ N4/0 [♿] (A/B/C)

Jeanetta Cochrane Theobalds Rd WC1 (242-7040). At junction with Southampton Row. **Entrance flat.** Auditorium sloped. **Four (w) spaces** at the front. Alternatively, (w) may transfer. Ordinary loos, with narrow cubicles, are near the front.

E0 [♿] (A/B/C)

London Coliseum *See entry on Coliseum.*

London Palladium *See entry on Palladium.*

Lyric Shaftesbury Av W1 (437-3686). Entrance **4 steps. Level access** to Dress Circle from alternative entrance in Shaftesbury Av. **Two (w) spaces** in boxes.

■ E4 [A] [♿] (A/B/C)

Lyttelton *See entry on National Theatre.*

May Fair Stratton St W2 (BO 629-3036, M 629-7777). Inside the May Fair Hotel. Entrance **1 step.** Inside there are −15 steps to the auditorium which is all one level (Stalls). There is a **lift** (D 83cm, W 83cm, L 144cm), but there are still 5 steps to the Stalls. **Four (w) spaces,** two at each end of the front row (and when used, the seats behind them are not sold). Ordinary loos, −5 steps: Gents' cub door 67cm, Ladies' 58cm.

⬛ E1 ⬛ ⬛ N5 ⬛ (A/B/C)

Mermaid Puddle Dock EC4 (236-9521). Small CP adjacent to theatre. NCP about 200m away in Queen Victoria St. As it's away from the West End, evening parking isn't too difficult. **Superb access**, perhaps because it is one of the relatively few venues where access has been taken seriously. **There are four (w) spaces,** and also seats where it is easy to transfer. **There is a (w) loo** on the GF, down the passageway to the left of the bar, which also gives access to the (w) spaces. The theatre complex includes a restaurant and facilities for conferences and exhibitions. Access to the 1st and 2nd floors is by **lift** from the entrance further down Puddle Dock. Full plans of the theatre are readily available if you write in. There is an **induction loop. Recommended.**

P E0 ⬛ 90% ⬛ ⬛ wc ⬛ X ⬛ (A/B/C)

National Theatre South Bank SE1 (BO 928-2252, M 633-0880). The National Theatre is a spacious and basically well designed complex containing three theatres, a number of bars and restaurants and comfortable lounge areas with bookstands, temporary exhibitions and live performances. There are, however, a number of irritating split levels. It's a good idea to arrive early and have a drink and listen to the jazz or classical musicians, or whoever else may be providing the foyer entertainment. This can also be a very pleasant place to visit even if you are not actually going to a play. There are **free (w) spaces** at all three theatres and seats for two friends or escorts can normally be booked alongside each space.

The **main entrance** serves the Lyttelton and Olivier theatres (but not the Cottesloe) and has **flat access** through wide but heavy swing doors. The BO has an outside entrance but this involves several steps, so you might be better off going round to the main entrance and then back along inside, where only 3 steps are involved. **The Cottesloe has a separate flat entrance** on the east side of the building. *Cottesloe* This is round the side of the complex with a separate entrance. **Ramped access to the two (w) spaces** at the first Gallery level, or −20 steps or so to the Pit, where some plays are presented promenade-style. There is a **(w) loo** off the foyer.

P E0 ⬛ ⬛ wc (A/B/C)

Lyttelton The Lyttelton information desk, which also serves as the main information desk, is opposite the main entrance. Directly behind it is the cloakroom where a spare wheelchair is available. **There are four (w) spaces** at the back of the stalls with reserved seats for the necessary companion; **access to these is flat** from the information desk. It is advisable to use the Rear Stalls entrance wherever your seat is, as the signposted way in to the Front Stalls involves a number of steps. The Circle is up a large number of stairs, but (w) and (s) may be taken up in a **service lift** if you ask at the desk. The main bar (*open pub hours*) and a coffee bar serving sandwiches, cakes and so forth, are on the same level as the desk. At first sight the Lyttelton Buffet (serving good medium-price salad-type meals) and the Restaurant (fixed-price menus) are inaccessible on the mezzanine, but again if you ask at the information desk, someone will take you in the service lift to either, with (we are told) no problem. **There is an excellent (w) loo** on the information desk level with a 95cm door, cub 165cm×180cm. There are also ordinary loos elsewhere.

P E0 [&] [††] [& wc] [& ✕] U (A/B/C)

Olivier The Olivier is on a level above the Lyttelton and parts of it, although not the auditorium itself, present access problems. The Stalls, where there are **six (w) spaces** at the back, and the Circle, which has no special spaces, are both served by **large lifts.** The Olivier information desk and the cloakroom, however, are on a mezzanine and involve either 11 steps from the Terrace or −13 steps from the Stalls level (both of these levels are served by the lift). This, however, is not desperate as the information desk opens only two hours before the performance; the Lyttelton desk, which is accessible, can always give you any necessary advice. The same problem also applies to the Olivier Buffet and there is no way to avoid −11 steps from Circle level or 9+13 from Stalls level. The Olivier's bars open only for performances. **The (w) loo** for the Olivier, of the same basic design as the Lyttelton's, is situated at Stalls level in the auditorium which means that in theory it is available only 30 minutes before the performance and during the interval, though access at other times could certainly be negotiated. There are ordinary loos elsewhere.

P [A] [&] [††] [& wc] (A/B/C)

New London Drury La WC2 (BO 405-0072, M 242-9802). **Entrance flat.** The theatre is unusual in that it is in the upper part of a new block. There is a NCP underneath the building. Small **lift** with 57cm door to 3rd floor (Stalls level) or a larger service lift with 68cm door to 2nd floor then 14+4 steps. The normal route up is by escalator or 16+16+16 then 20 to 3rd floor, and up to another 70 to the 6th floor (Dress Circle). For (w) it is easiest to transfer to the front of the Stalls (flat from the small lift). Staff very helpful, but (as always) ring or write first. The loos are up more steps.

P E0 [††] [⊞/††] [◼] N18 [&] (A/C)

Old Vic Waterloo Rd SE1 (928-7616). Re-opened during 1983 with facilities for disabled patrons including **(w) spaces** in the Stalls and an adapted loo.

E0 [&] [& wc] (A/B/C)

Olivier *See entry on National Theatre.*

Palace Shaftesbury Av W1 (437-6834). Entrance 2 steps. **Two (w) spaces** in a box at the side of the Stalls. **Flat access from exit** in Shaftesbury Av. The Stalls are the easiest for transfer, 3 steps from foyer by normal entrance. Loos are reached by 9 steps from Stalls.

[◼] E2 [A] [◼] N3 [&] (A/B/C)

Palladium (London Palladium) Argylle St W1 (437-7373). Entrance 5 steps to the BO. **There are three (w) spaces** in the Stalls, **accessed on the flat from a side exit** in Ramillies Pl.

🔲 E5 🅰 ♿ (A/B/C)

Phoenix Charing Cross Rd WC2 (836-8611). Entrance 2 steps. No (w) spaces. **Flat access to Dress Circle from exit** in Flitcroft St for transfer. By prior arrangement, loo in Royal Box in the Circle may be used, with flat access. Stalls are −5−8 steps, Upper Circle 38.

🔲 E2 🅰 ♿ (A/C)

Piccadilly Denman St W1 (437-4506). Entrance 1 step **Two (w) spaces** in box C. Access to Royal Circle area from a passageway in Sherwood St, and the Royal Circle is also recommended for transfer.

🔲 E1 🅰 ♿ (A/B/C)

The Pit *See entry on Barbican Centre in 'Arts complexes' chapter.*

Players Villiers St WC2 (839-1134). An unusual theatre, since it admits only members to its Victorian music hall shows, and you must become a member at least 48 hours before attending a performance. Flat to BO, then −3 steps to auditorium, with sloping aisle. **One (w) space**. Loos in the basement down a steep and narrow flight of steps. Restaurant facilities up 4 steps from the auditorium.

E0 🔲 N3 ♿ (A/B/C)

Prince Edward Old Compton St W1 (BO 437-6877, M 437-2024). Entrance 1 step, then steps up or down to all parts of the theatre. **Two (w) spaces** in x E with **flat access from an exit** in Greek St.

🔲 E1 🅰 ♿ (A/B/C)

Prince of Wales Coventry St W1 (930-8681). Entrance 2 steps, then −4 to the Stalls (or −2 via an exit). No (w) spaces. Up to six (w) who can transfer may occupy seats at the end of rows J, K, and L in the Stalls.

🔲 E2 N4/2 (A/C)

Queen's Shaftesbury Av WC1 (BO 734-1166, M 734-1348). **Entrance flat,** then −6−11−4 steps to Stalls or 2 to Dress Circle; more steps in the auditorium. The only entrance to the Upper Circle is from Wardour St, either 16+16 steps or via a small lift. The Upper Circle, however, is not always used. Only four seats available for (w) who can transfer, two at either end of the fourth row in the Circle, from which there is an exit door on street level. The seats are not reserved for (w) and therefore should be booked well in advance. Ordinary loos behind the Stalls; Ladies' at Circle level, but with small cubicles.

E0 🅰 🔲 N2 (A/C)

Regent's Park Open-Air Theatre Regent's Pk NW1 (486-2431). Parking available by arrangement. Although there are 10 steps at the main entrance to the theatre, there is an **alternative ramped route** via a side entrance from the CP. **Ten (w) spaces. Unaccompanied (w) are welcomed.** The refreshment facilities are accessible. The ordinary seating is very steeply tiered.

P ◼ E10 [A] [&] (A/B/C)

Royal Court Sloane Sq SW1 (730-1745). Entrance **4 steps, then flat** to back of Dress Circle. No (w) spaces. Only one (w) can transfer. Loos: foyer, −20 steps to Stalls, and 16 to Gallery. The *Theatre Upstairs* (a separate auditorium) is up 80+ steps.

Theatre ◼ E4 (A/C)

Theatre Upstairs ◼ 80+

Royal Opera House *See entry on Covent Garden.*

Sadler's Wells Rosebery Av EC1 (278-8916). Entrance has **1 tiny step,** but if you use the doors on the left you won't even notice it. **Flat to Stalls. Two (w) spaces** in the Stalls adjacent to D1 and D30. Transfer is advised in the Stalls because of access. Loos off foyer, Gents' with 63cm cub door. Bar/restaurant 8+9+8, then 8+8 to Dress Circle. There are 64 steps to the Upper Circle. **Induction loop.**

[A] [&] [(?)] (A/B/C)

St Martin's West St WC2 (836-1443). Entrance **3 steps, then 3 more** to the Dress Circle. **One (w) space** in box D, or transfer possible in the Dress Circle. A ramp for the inside curved stairs is available. Over 20 steps down to Stalls, 45 to the Upper Circle.

◼ E3N3 [&] (A/B/C)

Savoy Strand WC2 (BO 836-8888, M 836-8117). Entrance flat, but a flight of steps down to all parts of the theatre. However, there is an **alternative entrance via an exit** in Carting La involving only 8 steps. **One (w) space** in box A, and the easiest place for transfer is row F in the Dress Circle. Steps to loos.

[A] ◼ N8 [&] (A/B/C)

Shaftesbury Shaftesbury Av WC2 (836-4255/6596). Entrance has a **small threshold. Four (w) spaces** in boxes A/B at Royal Circle level, and transfer possible to some seats in the Royal Circle. The management said that they were very willing to look after a guide dog (as is the case at most theatres).

E0 [&] (A/B/C)

Shaw Theatre *See entry on Camden Festival in 'Sport' chapter.*

Strand Aldwych WC2 (836-2660/4143). Entrance **7 steps. One (w) space** in box A, −4−4−3 steps, loo en suite. For transfer, −4 to Dress Circle from foyer. Loos are on that level, but the doors are only 50cm wide.

◼ E7N4/11 [&] (A/B/C)

Theatre Royal Drury Lane Catherine St WC2 (BO 836-8108, M 836-3687). Entrance: 4+1 steps to BO, 2+1 to foyer, then flat to the Stalls. No (w) spaces, but up to six can transfer and there is a **level entrance**, from Russell St to the front of the Stalls, opened on request. Grand Circle involves +39−1 (stepped inside) and a further 36 to the Upper Circle (also stepped). The Gallery is above that level, and is approached separately from Russell St. Loos at Stalls level with ordinary cubicles.

▟ E5 🄰 ▟ N3 ♿ (A/C)

Theatre Royal Haymarket Haymarket SW1 (930-9832). Entrance 3 steps. No (w) spaces. **Flat access** to Stalls from an exit, so the Stalls is the best area for transfer. Loos are −11 steps from the Stalls. Dress Circle up 25 steps.

▟ E3 🄰 ♿ (A/C)

Vaudeville Strand WC2 (836-9988). **Entrance flat. One (w) space** in a box reached via 3 steps and a narrow door. There are 6 steps to Stalls, 27 to Dress Circle, and 45 to the Upper Circle.

E0 ▟ N3 ➕ /6 ♿ (A/B/C)

Victoria Palace Victoria St SW1 (834-1317). There are **4 steps** down to Stalls. **Two (w) spaces**, and the possibility of others transferring. Steps to loos.

▟ N4 ♿ (A/B/C)

Warehouse (Donmar) Earlham St WC2 (240-2766). Entrance **30 steps. Up to four (w) spaces** if seats are removed, for which there must be a prior written arrangement. All facilities are accessible once you've got up to the auditorium. Loos with narrow cubicles.

▟ E30 ♿ (A/B/C)

Westminster Palace St SW1 (BO 834-0283, M 834-7882). Entrance 13 steps. Foyer flat. There are −2 steps to Stalls or +34−18 to Circle, but there is a lift (D 58cm, W 71cm, L 122cm) to each level. **Normally six (w) spaces** in two boxes on each side of the Stalls, but this depends on the particular show. The boxes are occasionally used for lights or musicians. **Easy access from the side entrance** in Palace St, which opens level with the boxes and row O of the Stalls. Plenty of possibilities for transferring into a seat. Refreshments may be served to (w) in their seats on request. Small staff loo available near the boxes, on request. **Induction loop** for both Stalls and Circle, and one of the many theatres where guide dogs would be accommodated subject to the availability of the right seats.

▟ E13 🄰 ♿ 🅸🅸 ⍰ (A/B/C)

Wyndhams Charing Cross Rd WC2 (836-3028). Entrance 1 step. **Two (w) spaces** in a box behind the Stalls reached via an exit and −3 steps. Loo en suite. Also the possibility of transfer in the Stalls. **Hearing aids using the Sennheiser system** are available, as at the Albery Theatre.

▟ E1 🄰 ▟ N3 ♿ ⍰ (A/B/C)

Young Vic 66 The Cut SE1 (928-6363). **Entrance flat. (NB** The BO is separate from the main theatre.) There are **two (w) spaces** and, given notice, seats can be removed to accommodate more (w). Coffee bar −3 steps. Loos in the foyer, cub doors 63cm.

E0 ⟨♿⟩ (A/B/C)

Outer London

Albany Douglas Wy SE8 (691-3333). **Flat access, (w) spaces** and adapted loos.

E0 ⟨♿⟩ ⟨♿ wc⟩ (A/B/C)

Little Angel Marionette Theatre 14 Dagmar Pas N1 (226-1787). **Flat access and (w) spaces.** Adapted loo.

E0 ⟨♿⟩ ⟨♿ wc⟩ (A/B/C)

Lyric Hammersmith King St W6 (741-2311). Entertainment centre including two theatres, a restaurant, conference facilities and live lunchtime music. Surface CP near the Odeon, under the flyover. **Entrance flat** to the BO and **lifts** (110cm×140cm), which go to all five floors. On the 1st floor are the foyer, restaurant and the 150-seat *Studio* (1 step). On the 2nd floor are the main theatre Stalls with **three (w) spaces**. Both the Circle and the Upper Circle are stepped inside, although there is lift access. There are no (w) spaces in the *Studio* and if you want to transfer, note that the seats are bench-style with no side support. **Two (w) loos**, one on foyer level opposite the lifts (door unmarked) and the other at Stalls level near the (w) spaces, again opposite the lifts. **Induction loop** available in the Theatre. **Recommended.**

Theatre E0 ⟨♿⟩ ⟨♙⟩ ⟨♿ wc⟩ ⟨♿ X⟩ ⟨?⟩ (A/B/C)

Studio E0 ⟨♿⟩ ⟨♙⟩ ⟨♿ wc⟩ ⟨♿ X⟩ (A/C)

Polka Children's Theatre 240 The Broadway SW19 (BO 543-4888, M 542-4258). **Flat access, lifts, (w) spaces** and adapted loo. They have gone to considerable trouble to make things easy.

E0 ⟨♿⟩ ⟨♿ wc⟩ (A/B/C)

Riverside Studios Crisp Rd W6 (748-3354). A wide variety of activities and some fringe theatre. Lively place. **Flat access, plus (w) spaces and (w) loo.** Café accessible. Shop is up 2 steps but these can be ramped. Generally, very easy access.

E0 ⟨♿⟩ ⟨♿ wc⟩ ⟨♿ X⟩ (A/B/C)

St George's Elizabethan Theatre Tufnell Park Rd N7 (607-1128). This is a converted chapel where Shakespearean drama is the main offering. **Flat access** from rear CP, **(w) spaces** and adapted loos.

⟨A⟩ ⟨♿⟩ ⟨♿ wc⟩ (A/B/C)

Theatre Royal Stratford Salway Rd E15 (BO 534-0310, M 534-7374). **Ramped access via an exit.** Normally 3 steps to Stalls level. About **ten (w) spaces**. Ordinary loos.

⬛Ａ ♿ (A/B/C)

Tricycle 269 Kilburn High Rd NW6 (BO 328-8626, M 624-5300). A fringe theatre with good access. **Entrance ramped. Two (w) spaces and a (w) loo.** There are 6 steps into the theatre, but helpful management. The theatre, catering facilities, bar and exhibition space are all accessible, or can be made so with a little help. **Induction loop** available.

E0 ▟ N6 ♿ ♿ wc ♿ X ⟨?⟩ (A/B/C)

Further afield

Around London there are a considerable number of theatres with good (w) access. We list below some of those that have flat access, (w) spaces and adapted loos. They would all, therefore, be suitable for (s) as well.

Ashcroft—see entry on Fairfield Halls in 'Arts complexes' chapter.
Beck Grange Rd, Hayes, Mddx (561-7506).
Churchill High St, Bromley, Kent (460-6677).
Compass Glebe Av, Ickenham, Mddx (Ruislip (71) 73200).
Hexagon Centre Reading, Berks (Reading (0734) 56215).
Kenneth More Oakfield Rd, Ilford, Essex (553-4466).
Queen's Billet La, Hornchurch, Essex (Hornchurch (49) 43333).
Redgrave Brightwell, Farnham, Surrey (Farnham (0252) 715301).
Secombe Centre Cheam Rd, Sutton, Surrey (661-0416).
Sybil Thorndike Church St, Leatherhead, Surrey (Leatherhead (0372) 377677).
Yvonne Arnaud Millbrook, Guildford, Surrey (Guildford (0483) 64571).

E0 ♿ ♿ wc (A/B/C)

Arts complexes, cinemas & music venues

Arts complexes

There are a number of small arts centres in London as well as the two major ones detailed here. The advantage of a complex is that you'll find a number of facilities close together, often with a place to eat and parking space as well. Also, most of the buildings are relatively modern and access tends to be better than in traditional theatres, cinemas and galleries.

The Barbican Centre Silk St EC2 (BO 628-8795, M 638-4141, restaurant 588-3008, library 638-0569). This modern centre for theatre, concerts, cinema and arts exhibitions was opened in 1982 and has relatively good access. It is surrounded by a large pedestrian area on two levels, and there is a wide range of facilities. Unfortunately, (w) routes are not signposted in the Barbican area nor are there adequate maps. Similarly, particulary for (w) users, signposting inside the centre is not all that clear. There is a free leaflet for disabled people and it's worth getting hold of, together with their monthly magazine/programme, 'Welcome to the Barbican Theatre', which includes a cut-away diagram. Because of split levels, especially around levels 3, 4 and 5, it is important to understand certain basics about the nine-storey building. There is heavy carpeting in places (literally a drag for (w)); it is hot inside and there are many heavy doors. Wheelchairs tend to accumulate 'static'. Having said that, the centre provides unique facilities which are potentially valuable. It is compact, and there's a lot of different things to see and do without moving very far. There are reduced price ticket arrangements for (w).

Finding it & parking There are 30 steps at Moorgate Underground station to the Circle line and just over 50 at the Barbican station, which shuts at *22.00 on Sat* and is *closed Sun*. Both stations are some 400/500m away. By road, there are signs to lead you along London Wall and round Wood St and Moor La into Silk St, but they're small and easily missed. The main entrance is at the junction of Silk St and Whitecross St and whether or not you have come by car, **(w) or (s) are advised to go down towards the CP and level 3 where there are lifts** on the LHS. Note that the road running through the building is narrow and may be congested at the time of performances. Even stopping to let someone get out may be a problem, particularly from the front passenger seat on the left since the setting down spot is on the RHS. For (w) it may be better to get out of the car in the road outside where there should be less hassle. The best approach from there is still to go down towards level 3, unless you're going to the theatre when level 5 (upwards) is OK. There is CP space for 500 cars and there are special spaces for orange badge holders/(w), which can be reserved in advance through the BO. The charge is waived for disabled visitors if you pick up a card at the information desk. The card is handed in to the CP attendant on your way out. There are alternative CPs run by NCP in Aldersgate St (*open 24 hours*), Finsbury Sq and London Wall by the Museum of London (both *daytime only*). Around Silk St the kerbs are new but unramped, and from the level 3

The Barbican Centre

(Diagramatic Representation)

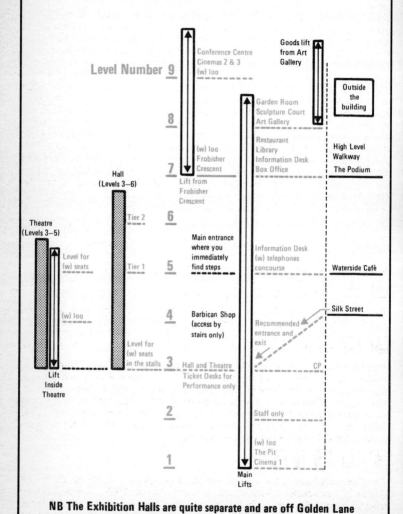

Level Number **9** — Conference Centre / Cinemas 2 & 3 / (w) loo

Goods lift from Art Gallery

Outside the building

8 — Garden Room / Sculpture Court / Art Gallery

7 — (w) loo / Frobisher Crescent — Restaurant / Library / Information Desk / Box Office — High Level Walkway / The Podium

Lift from Frobisher Crescent

Hall (Levels 3–6)

6 — Tier 2

Theatre (Levels 3–5)

5 — Tier 1 — Level for (w) seats — Main entrance where you immediately find steps — Information Desk / (w) telephones / concourse — Waterside Café

4 — (w) loo — Barbican Shop (access by stairs only) — Silk Street — Recommended entrance and exit

3 — Level for (w) seats in the stalls — Hall and Theatre Ticket Desks for Performance only — CP

Lift Inside Theatre

2 — Staff only

1 — (w) loo / The Pit / Cinema 1

Main Lifts

NB The Exhibition Halls are quite separate and are off Golden Lane

roadway there is a steeply ramped kerb and heavy doors leading to the lifts.

If you are coming from another part of the City, there are ways of getting up on the high level walkway (the Upper Podium) at level 7, but they're not signposted. **There's a very useful lift** near St Giles Cripplegate Church, at the left-hand end of Andrewes House (by Crowderswell pub on ground level) and there are, in fact, **four ramps** leading upwards, but without signposting they're quite difficult to find. The normal signs to the Barbican Centre involve routes with steps or escalators. There are ramps in Fore Street Av (near Moorgate), by BP Britannic House in Chiswell St and at the junction of London Wall and Wood St on the south east side.

Inside the building There are a considerable number of split levels and the **flat (w) routes** are not obvious. Since the building is quite big, it is important to know where you want to go and how to get there, as otherwise you can waste a lot of time and energy. The diagram accompanying this section indicates where the various facilities are. The split levels are mainly round the main concert hall and theatre. For the upper storeys, (w) and (s) are basically dependent on four **lifts**, which are grouped together. It is assumed that you will start either on level 3 (CP level described above) or on level 7 from the high-level walkway. If you go to the main entrance on level 5 you will immediately be faced with steps, except when the theatre is open when you can use the theatre lift. On the plus side, **all the telephones are at a suitable height for (w)**, eg those in the BO area on level 7 and in the foyer on level 5. There are **unisex (w) loos** on level 1 (go through the door marked MEN), level 4 (in the theatre area), level 7 and level 9 (door unmarked). The most important one is on level 7 and is extremely well concealed. From the lifts, go past the cloakroom and through the BO foyer, through the doors and turn left into the crescent. The loo is down the first passage on your right and is then on the LHS about 20m along, past another passage to the left, near the first aid centre. This is the only one that is always available.

Art gallery On level 8 right by the lifts. There may be an entrance charge. Access to level 9 can be obtained by using the **goods lift** at the far end (for which you will have to ask a staff member). Ordinary loos outside. Nearest (w) loo on level 7.

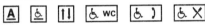

The Cut Above is a full-blown restaurant/carvery on level 7. View out over St Giles and the Lake. **Flat access and near the lifts with a (w) loo** on the same level.

Frobisher Crescent on level 9 is a section primarily for private functions and conferences and contains Cinemas 2 and 3 and Conference Rooms 1–5. You get there from level 7. There are **two lifts** going to level 9: a goods lift from about half-way round the crescent and a passenger/public lift (74cm×150cm) reached by passing through the BO foyer to the LSO administration centre—the lift is on the left opposite the reception desk. There is a **(w) loo** on level 9 between the reception desks (though it was locked when we surveyed).

The Hall is used mainly for concerts and has **16 (w) spaces** and a further facility for those who can transfer. These spaces are in row U of the Stalls. They are reached from level 3 and if you arrive by lift you must then cross the service road (**NB** steep ramp). **For the hard of hearing there are plug-in head-sets** for specific seats available on request from the information point on level 3; a small deposit is required. The nearest (w) loos are on level 4, accessible by the theatre lift on level 7.

P [A] [&] [¶¶] [& wc] [&)] [& X] [(?)] (A/B/C)

The library (a public library with a reference section) is on level 7. **Flat easy access.** A music library is planned underneath, on level 5. Access through the children's section and then use the goods lift (ask a staff member).

[A] [&] [¶¶] [& wc]

The Pit and the main cinema are in the basement on level 1. **The Pit has four (w) spaces** and additional seats assigned for those who can transfer. **In Cinema 1 there are boxes for two (w)** as well as seats for those who can transfer. **Plug-in headsets for the hard of hearing** are available from the level 1 BO for particular seats in the back row; a small deposit is required. There is a **unisex (w) loo** on level 1, but you have to go through the first door marked MEN: the (w) loo is on one side and the entrance to the Gents' is on the other!

P [A] [&] [¶¶] [& wc] [&)] [& X] [(?)] (A/B/C)

The Theatre has **four (w) spaces** in Circle 2 and additional seats assigned for those who can transfer into a seat. Circle 2 is on level 5 and can be reached via the internal theatre lift, or the main lifts, or from the upper Silk St entrance. Each (w) position has a lift which can lower the (w) if necessary to improve sight lines, but you are left with a stage view that is somewhat obstructed by a concrete beam and this is particularly difficult if the back of the stage is used and/or any of the action is high up. The internal lift in the theatre which goes to levels 3, 4 and 5 can only be used when the theatre is open for performances. The theatre has an **induction loop system**. The **(w) loo** is on level 4 inside the auditorium; if you want to use it during the interval you've got to be pretty slick, because you've got to go down a level.

P [A] [&] [¶¶] [& wc] [&)] [& X] [(?)] (A/B/C)

The Waterside Café is on level 5, with tables and chairs alongside the artificial lake. The café is buffet-style but serves quite a variety of food. **Flat access** but it gets congested and there are sometimes long queues.

[A] [&] [¶¶] [& wc] [& X]

The South Bank Arts Centre A modern complex on the south bank of the river, between Hungerford Br and Waterloo Br. There is an open-air sculpture exhibition in the forecourts of the buildings and in fine weather there are often free entertainments (music, street theatre etc) outside, both during the day and in the evening. The Centre includes the National Theatre (*see 'Theatres' chapter*), the National Film Theatre (*see 'Cinemas'*), the Hayward Gallery (*see 'Museums' chapter*) and the Queen Elizabeth Hall, Royal Festival Hall and Purcell Room (*see 'Music venues'*). The Centre can be approached from ground (road) level, from the overhead walkway from Hungerford Br (+40−20 steps) or from Waterloo station (−4−16+18−8 steps). The ground level approach is by far the simplest. There is a reasonably priced surface CP to the west near Hungerford Br or you can use the UGCP at the National Theatre. There are (w) spaces on the perimeter road, although whether orange badge holders may park there depends on how many (w) are booked in for a particular performance; this is at the discretion of the staff. There is also a new pier for riverboats outside the Royal Festival Hall, with ramped access. A ferry service from Westminster is planned.

Cinemas

Access to cinemas has become considerably more difficult over the past ten or fifteen years, particularly in central London, where very few cinemas admit B category patrons. This is partly because many cinemas have been split up into several screens, and partly because of the more rigid licensing procedure. Where cinemas have been divided, few modifications have been made to ease access, even for the ground-level screens. In addition, we have found that managements, perhaps conscious of the problems but unable to do much about them, frequently take a very defensive line. Several have said that they were caught between the company who owned the premises and who would have to pay for modifications, and the GLC who grant licences for places of public entertainment and who identify the wheelchair as a potential hazard.

However, there are a few places with good access, and with the others we have tried to highlight the principal access barriers so that you can decide whether you can negotiate them. The GLC leaflet, 'Just the Ticket', lists cinemas in suburban areas where there are licensed (w) spaces. We would particularly mention the Barbican cinema, the Classic and the Odeon Leicester Square and the ABCs in Catford and Putney. The arrangement at the Odeon Leicester Square, where seats are movable, could be more widely copied.

When you ring the telephone numbers given here, you may get a pre-recorded message about programme times. Note that the manager's number is usually given at the end of the recording, but if it's not you'll have to try Artsline or the headquarters of the cinema chain. One thing we were told is that if you particularly want to see a film that's on at an inaccessible screen, some managers may, at an off-peak time or towards the end of a run, be able to show it on a GF/accessible screen.

ABC Bayswater Bishops Bridge Rd, opposite junction with Queensway W2 (229-6620). Up 3 steps to BO. Screen 1 involves 23+12 steps and **(w) are not allowed**. Screens 2 and 3 are **flat from BO/foyer**. No (w) spaces but up to four (w) who can transfer can use Screens 2/3. There are 2/3 steps to the loos from Screens 2/3.

Screens 2 & 3 ◼ E3 ⬛ (A/C)

ABC Edgware Road By the junction with Harrow Rd W2 (402-4740). Flat to BO. Screen 1 has −8 steps; Screen 2, 12+7 steps; Screen 3, 12+7+8 steps; Screen 4, −8 steps but only −3 via an exit into Herbert St. No (w) spaces and (w) who can transfer are allowed only in Screen 4. Loos on the same level as Screen 4, but −5 steps inside. **Induction loop** in Screens 1 and 2.

Screens 1 & 2 ⬛ Screen 4 ◼ E8/3 ⬛ (A/C)

ABC Fulham Road At junction with Drayton Rd SW6 (370-2110). Flat to BO. Screen 1, 28+10 steps; Screen 2, 28 steps. **Two (w) spaces** in both Screen 3 and 4, where there is **flat access via an exit**. The (w) spaces are right at the back in a corner. There's an **induction loop** in Screen 1 and one is planned for Screen 2.

Screens 1 & 2 ⬛ Screens 3 & 4 ◼A ⬛ (A/B/C)

ABC Shaftesbury Avenue Just before the junction with High Holborn WC2 (836-8861). Basically **inaccessible to (w)** because of steps, so not surveyed in detail.

◼ (A)

Academy 1, 2 & 3 165 Oxford St W1 (437-2981). BO up **1 step**. Screen 1, **flat access**; Screen 2, −25 steps; Screen 3, 26 steps but there is a **lift** large enough for most (w). No licensed (w) spaces.

Screen 1 E0 (A/C) Screen 3 🔢 (A/C)

Barbican Cinema 1 *See entry on Barbican Centre in 'Arts complexes'.*

Cinecenta 1, 2, 3 & 4 Panton St, off Leicester Sq WC2 (930-0632). Flat access to BO. No licensed (w) spaces, but (w) who can transfer and are with (ab) friends will be admitted. Screens 1 and 2 are **accessible on the flat** through an exit door. Screens 3 and 4 are both up 25 steps.

Screens 1 & 2 🅰 ♿ Screens 3 & 4 ▰ N25 (A/C)

Cinecenta 1 & 2 Piccadilly W1 (437-3561). Flat to BO, then −39 steps to each section of the cinema.

E0 ▰ N39

Classic Haymarket Haymarket SW1 (839-1527). Our surveyors weren't allowed to look, nor given access details. The manager simply said, "No (w)".

Classic Leicester Square 35 Charing Cross Rd WC2 (930-6915). BO up **2 steps. All flat inside.** Up to six (w) can be accommodated at the front of the auditorium. There is flat access to the loos, where cub doors in both Ladies' and Gents' are 72cm.

▰ E2 ♿ (A/B/C)

Classic Praed Street Praed St W2 (723-5716). Entrance has **6 steps and then flat** to the Stalls, and to ordinary loos.

▰ E6 ♿ (A/C)

Classic Shaftesbury Avenue Shaftesbury Av SW1 (734-5414). BO up 1 step, then −18−25 to the Stalls. Only one level. If accompanied by strong friends, (w) who can transfer will be admitted.

▰ E1N43 (A/C)

Curzon Curzon St W1 (499-3737). BO down 5 steps, a further 11+11 steps to the auditorium, then stepped in each direction. If (w) come with (ab) friends and can transfer, they will be admitted. Loos are off the foyer, with narrow cub doors (64cm) and 90° turn.

▰ E5N22 (A/C)

Dominion Tottenham Court Rd, by St Giles Circus W1 (636-2295). Flat to BO, then −10 steps to Stalls, 38 to Royal Circle and 58 to Centre Circle. Again, (w) who can transfer and who come with (ab) friends will be admitted.

E0 ▰ N10 (A/C)

Empire Leicester Sq WC2 (437-1234). Flat access to BO. No (w) spaces, but (w) who can transfer can get into Screen 1, where the auditorium is up 7+7 steps but via an exit in Lisle St there are only 1+3. Screen 2 has −30 steps (and is in the old Ritz cinema). There are loos on the level from each cinema with 63cm cub doors.

Screen 1 E0 🖼 N14/4 ♿ (A/C) Screen 2 🖼 N30 (A)

Filmcentre 1, 2 & 3 Charing Cross Rd WC2 (437-4815). Flat access to BO. No (w) spaces, and −13 steps to Screens 1 and 2, but there are easier exits in each case for (w) who can transfer: Screen 1, 2 steps; Screen 2, 5 steps. There are an additional 15 steps to Screen 3.

Screen 1 🖼 N13/2 Screen 2 🖼 N13/5 Screen 3 🖼 N20 (A/C)

Gate Notting Hill Gate W11 (221-0220). **Flat access.** Small membership charge.

E0 (A/C)

Gate Bloomsbury 1 & 2 Brunswick Sq WC1 (837-8402). Foyer flat, but the cinema auditorium is below ground level. Normal access is via 42 steps (−10−10−12−5−5). If there's something on you particularly want to see, it is possible to gain access (after prior negotiation) through an exit into the UGCP. This involves going down the CP exit ramp, bearing to the right and then asking a staff member to open a roll-over door leading to the cinema.

E0 Ⓐ 🖼 N42 (A/C)

ICA *See 'Museums' chapter.*

Leicester Square Theatre Leicester Sq WC2 (930-5252). Flat to BO. No (w) spaces, and there are −30 steps to the Stalls or 11−3+10 to the Circle or Royal Circle. A maximum of two (w) who can transfer can be accommodated in the Stalls. **Induction loop** available, but it's advisable to 'phone first to check it's 'on'.

E0 🖼 N30 🔊 (A/C)

Lumière St Martin's La WC2 (836-0691). **Flat access** to BO. Basement auditorium −12−18−18 steps but there is a **lift** (D 80cm, W 150cm, L 140cm) giving flat access. No (w) spaces but (w) who can transfer and are with (ab) friends will be admitted.

E0 🖼 N48/ 🛗 (A/C)

National Film Theatre South Bank, under Waterloo Br SE1 (928-3232). The majority of the NFT programmes are open only to members of the British Film Institute; membership details may be obtained either from the NFT or from the BFI Membership Department, 81 Dean St W1. Members may bring three guests for reserved seats or one guest for unreserved seats, which are available half an hour before the performance.

There are two levels in the NFT and access to either is flat, although the area for 10m on either side of the restaurant entrance on the riverside is cobbled. Inside there are two cinemas: NFT 1, holding more than 450, and NFT 2, holding a little over 150. There is also a restaurant and bar.
NFT 1 is best reached from the Riverside Wlk entrance, from which there is flat access. There are **six (w) spaces** at the back of the auditorium (which should be booked in advance). There are also some empty spaces at the front of the hall which (w) could use. On the upper level with NFT 1 are the restaurant and bar, a bookshop and a self-operated cloakroom. The bar is open normal *pub hours* except

that it doesn't open until noon; the restaurant is open *daily 12.00–14.20 & 17.30–22.00*; the coffee bar, *daily 12.00–22.00*. Both are spacious with movable seating.
NFT 2 is best reached from the road entrance, level with the BO. No special (w) spaces, but wide flat access to the auditorium; the floor is sloping but the aisle seats are accessible both to (s) and to (w) who can transfer.

Loos There are ordinary Ladies' and Gents' loos on both levels, but the **(w) loo** is situated on the restaurant/NFT 1 (upper) level. **Flat access** on that level, or 7 steps from BO/NFT 2 level.

Facilities for the hard of hearing NFT 1 has an **induction loop** system for people with hearing aids with a T switch, and both cinemas have a number of seats with **special earphone facilities**. Earphones can be obtained from the theatre manager after paying a small deposit. **If you want either of these facilities, say so when booking.**

[A] [&] [& WC] [& X] [?] NFT 1 (A/B/C) NFT 2 (A/C)

Odeon Haymarket Haymarket SW1 (930-2738). There are **3 steps** to BO. No (w) spaces. To avoid 45 steps to auditorium, use the **lift** (D 66cm, W 83cm, L 98cm); the management will help if possible. **Special hearing aids** are available on request.

[▪] E3N45/ [¦¦] [&] [?] (A/C)

Odeon Kensington High Street Kensington High St W8 (602-6644). Opposite the Commonwealth Institute. **Flat to BO.** Screen 1, 45 steps to stepped auditorium. Screens 2, 3 and 4 involve 10 or 12 steps by the normal route from the BO but with prior negotiation exits can be opened so that there are only **1 or 2 steps** to get in and (w) who can transfer can be accommodated. Seats are normally bookable.

Screen 1 [▪] 45(A)

Screens 2, 3 & 4 [▪] E10/12 [A] [▪] N1/2 (A/C)

Odeon Leicester Square Leicester Sq W1 (930-6111). **Flat access** to the Stalls and the management have an excellent system of a removable seat at the back of the Stalls to provide a (w) space. It has been operating successfully for some 15 years but unfortunately we haven't found other cinemas who have copied the idea. There are ordinary loos on the flat.

E0 [&] (A/B/C)

Odeon Marble Arch Entrance just up Edgware Rd W2 (723-2011). Up **1 step** to BO. No (w) spaces. Massive cinema on 1st and 2nd floors. Normal access by escalators, which are reversed after the performance. Alternatively, about 50 steps to Stalls and 22 to Circle. A **lift is available** to bypass the steps, approached from the back of the cinema; ask the staff. **Hearing aids available.**

[▪] E1N50/ [¦¦] [&] (A/C)

Plaza 1, 2, 3 & 4 Lower Regent St W1 (930-0144 or 437-1234). The Plaza is under the same management as the Empire. Flat access to BO, but after that, there are steps to every screen: Screen 1, 33 steps; Screen 2, +4−39; Screen 3, −32; Screen 4, −28 steps. **The management say that (w) cannot be admitted.**

Screen 1 [▪] N33 Screen 2 [▪] N43 Screen 3 [▪] N32

Screen 4 [▪] N28 (A)

Prince Charles Leicester Pl WC2 (437-7003). BO 1 step, then −20+3 to Stalls but flat access to Circle (and **direct flat access** from Lisle St). Unfortunately the Circle is not always open, though a telephone call should secure (w) access. There are no (w) spaces, although presumably it would be easy to provide some in the Circle. Transfer OK. Loos a step or so from Stalls level.

[▟] E1N23/0 [♿] (A/C)

Scene 1, 2, 3 & 4 Swiss Centre, 10 Wardour St WC2 (437-2096). There are 3 steps to the BO. Lift to all auditoria. **The management say that no (w) can be admitted.**

[▟] E3 [⇕] (A)

Sherlock Holmes Centa 96 Baker St NW1 (935-2772). Basement cinema, both screens −26−3 steps. No (w) spaces and (w) who can transfer would need a couple of competent friends, because of the steps.

[▟] N29 (A/C)

Studio 1, 2, 3 & 4 225 Oxford St W1 (439-0710/3300). **Flat to BO.** No (w) spaces. **Screens 1 and 2 flat**; Screen 3, 27 steps and loos at this level; Screen 4, −26 steps.

Screens 1 & 2 [♿] Screen 3 [▟] N27 Screen 4 [▟] N26 (A/C)

Times Centa Marylebone Rd, by Baker St NW1 (935-9772). Flat to BO, then 5 steps to Screens 1 and 2. The management will try and be helpful over (w) accommodation. Loos via 6 steps and 4 doors, and very narrow.

E0 [▟] N5 [♿] (A/C)

Warner West End Leicester Sq WC2 (437-3874 or 439-0791). As with the Times Centa, the management will try and be helpful. There is flat access to BO, but steps to every screen. Screens 1 and 2, 26 via an exit; Screen 3, −23−5; Screen 4, −23+8; Screen 5, −23.

[▟] N23 (A/C)

Music venues

The Barbican and Fairfield Halls are covered elsewhere in this chapter. The remaining principal concert halls are described here, together with a few of the rock/popular music venues. Facilities at the main concert halls are good compared to other venues. Jazz, folk and rock all tend to be performed in rooms attached to pubs which are not easily accessible, although many places will give disabled fans a warm welcome. We mention a few of the more accessible places here, and plan to extend the section in the next edition; we would welcome people's comments and details of their experiences at other places. *Please see 'Tailpiece' chapter for the survey checklist and contact address.*

Concert halls

Queen Elizabeth Hall South Bank SE1 (928-3191). There are **two (w) spaces** reached via the artists' entrance at ground level, easily identified because it has a canopy over it. There's a **(w) loo** at this level also. The main foyer and bar, are inaccessible from this level but (w) can use the artists' bar. We advise (s) to ask for seats level with the main foyer, or with the (w) spaces approached via the artists' entrance. There are **special aids for the hard of hearing** in the back row of the auditorium and seats where a guide dog can be accommodated.

P [A] [&] [& wc] [(?)] [✻] (A/B)

Purcell Room This is for recitals and is deemed **inaccessible to (w)** by the authorities. There are 4 steps. Accessible to (s).

P [A] [▄] N4 (A/C)

Royal Albert Hall Kensington Gore SW7 (589-3203). This massive circular hall houses events ranging from the promenade concerts to the Festival of Remembrance. **Access is excellent**. There is a ramp by door 14 (near the artists' entrance), bypassing the 4 steps at most other entrances. There are 4 steps to the BO. There are **a number of (w) spaces** at each end of the Loggia boxes, although they are not ideally placed acoustically. It is possible for (w) to get into most boxes, and there are **two lifts**. Some boxes have split levels that may cause a slight problem. There are 5 steps from the GF to the Loggia boxes which have the widest doors (generally 68cm). Via the lift, there are no steps to the Grand and Second Tier boxes (doors 62cm approx). The lift goes to the Gallery which is open and flat and from which you can get a bird's-eye view. **The easiest seats for** (s) are in the boxes and the back rows of the Stalls. The Arena is relatively difficult to reach, involving about 50/60 steps, and the Balcony is steeply stepped.

There is a **(w) loo** on the GF, by door 8. The key will probably be held by the St John's Ambulance personnel. Their main office is between Stalls entrances K and J on the GF. **A wheelchair is available.** The (w) spaces are free, though your friend or escort pays. The BO will advise on the most accessible seats for (s).

[A] [&] [‖] [& wc] U (A/B/C)

Royal Festival Hall South Bank SE1 (BO 928-3191, M 928-3641, information 928-3002). The Festival Hall was one of the first venues to provide (w) spaces and access for disabled people right from the design stage. As the hall was opened in 1951 this was very imaginative. The entrances face the river and there is **flat/lift access to most parts**. There is a **(w) loo** on the GF, on the same level as the BO; turn to your right on entering and the loo is on your left before you reach the lift. There are **eight (w) spaces** at the back of the Terrace, with concessionary prices for both (w) and escorts giving exceptionally good value. We were told that **(w) are not allowed to transfer to a seat**, which is unusual. Access to the (w) spaces is from the **lift** at level 5. It should be possible to use one or more of the boxes which have movable seats and flat access. **For (s)**, the seats involving the minimum number of steps and with extra leg-room are at the front of the Stalls or Terrace. There is also an **induction loop system**. The foyer/exhibition/refreshments area on the upper level is sometimes open during the day and there are tables outside in the summer. Other facilities include a bar, −4 steps; exhibition area, −8 steps; cafeteria on the GF with some movable chairs and tables. Flat access elsewhere.

A recent development is the provision of two special seats in each hall where **blind or partially sighted patrons can sit with their guide dogs**. The management felt that a 'dog-sitting' service which separates the dog from its owner could unintentionally injure the very special relationship between them.

P [A] [&] [‖] [& wc] [& X] [(?)] [✻] (A/B)

Wigmore Hall 36 Wigmore St, near junction with Wimpole St W1 (935-2141, M 486-1907). There is **flat access** to the foyer and Stalls. Inside there are **two (w) spaces** and transfer is possible. There is an **induction loop**. Access to loos is by −19 steps.

E0 ♿ 🔈 (A/B/C)

Other venues

Dingwall's Camden Lock, Chalk Farm Rd NW1 (267-4967). Live bands. There is a **flat entrance** and the bar, stage area and video are all accessible. The restaurant area is up 3/4 steps. There are no seats in the stage area; ordinary loos.

E0 🍽 N4 ♿ (A/B/C)

National Jazz Centre 9 Floral St WC2 (240-2430). A facility providing an auditorium, library and rehearsal and practice rooms. There is **flat access to a large lift**, which goes to the auditorium on the 1st and 2nd floors. There is no fixed seating on the 1st floor and therefore (w) can easily be accommodated. There's a **unisex (w) loo** in the basement, also reached by a lift, and a bar/restaurant on the GF with flat access. The provision of an induction loop is being considered.

E0 ♿ 🍽 ♿wc ♿✗ (A/B/C)

The Venue 160 Victoria St SW1 (828-9441/2/3). The BO has 5 steps. There is **no problem over (w) access**, as the staff are willing (and accustomed) to help. There are steps (−12+3+2) to the bar and concert hall, plus the odd step or two inside. Access to the loos is 19 steps to the Gents', −3 to the Ladies', but remember that there are **(w) loos** across the road in Victoria station.

🍽 E5N17 ♿ (A/B/C)

Further afield
Arts complex

Fairfield Halls Park La, Croydon, Surrey (688-9291, M 681-0821). There are three major facilities, listed below. **Both access and provisions for (w) are good** and the management are helpful. There is only a nominal charge for a (w) visitor together with a friend, although (w) seats are in considerable demand. There are plans to install an induction loop in the Ashcroft Theatre. There's a CP, but it's a little walk from the Halls. For special provision, contact the senior house manager.

Access is flat/ramped to the main BO and foyer. There is a (w) loo on the GF, but it is not signposted and is quite difficult to find: go to the rear LHS of the foyer, turn left past the ordinary loos and follow the passage through the double doors and past the first aid room; then turn right and the (w) loo is on the left with a sign on the door saying LADIES, although it is intended as a unisex loo. The cafeteria bar and restaurant has **flat access**. Guide dogs are admitted throughout but patrons are asked to notify the BO when booking.

Arnheim Gallery **Flat access** into the suite from the foyer. No fixed seats. Officially **four (w) spaces**.

PE 0 ♿ ♿wc ♿✗

Ashcroft Theatre **Three (w) spaces** in a box on the 2nd level. **Flat access via large lift.** Stalls entrance for (s) is 6 steps from the main foyer, then −1 step per row. There are plans for a (w) loo in the Gents'.

P E0 [⚬] [↑↓] [⚬ WC] [⚬ ✕]

Fairfield Hall (concert hall). **Eight (w) spaces** at the 3rd level (Upper Stalls). **Access by large lift.** Ordinary loos at this level. Most seats have easy access but if you want to transfer the front row of the Lower Stalls (2nd level) is particularly easy.

P E0 [⚬] [↑↓] [⚬ WC] [⚬ ✕]

Cinemas

ABC Catford (Screen 1) Catford SE6 (697-6579). Adapted loo and (w) spaces.
ABC Putney (Screen 2) Putney SW15 (788-2263). Adapted loo and (w) spaces.

[A] [⚬] [⚬ WC]

Music venues

Chat's Palace 42 Brooksby's Wlk, Homerton E9 (986-6714). Opposite the Stag pub. For theatre, jazz and rock. Chat's Palace has a flat entrance and the main hall and bar are **fully accessible**. There is a **(w) loo. Recommended.**

E0 [⚬] [⚬ WC] [(?)]

Hammersmith Odeon 42 Queen Caroline St W6 (748-4081). Mainly for pop concerts. There are 3 steps into the foyer, but there is a side entrance with just **1 step** straight into the Stalls. **Once inside, access to the Stalls and foyer is flat**, but there are 13+4+13 steps up to the Circle foyer, with no lift, and another 10 up to the Circle seats with a further 2 for every row. Officials are on hand to help lift wheelchairs and to give assistance generally. There are only **two official (w) spaces**, but (w) are allowed to transfer, especially to the Circle front seats. It is worth trying to get these seats, because at a popular concert with over 3500 people, many standing, it will be difficult to see satisfactorily from anywhere else.

There is no (w) loo, but there is a Ladies' and Gents' on each level. On the GF there are −3 steps into the loo area and four cubicles (door 62cm). There is a bar in the Circle foyer and a snack bar for hot dogs etc in the Stalls foyer, but remember that at a big concert these will be extremely congested.

The management is willing to help, and they regularly look after the guide dogs of blind people, but it is best to ring up as early as possible for access to the big concerts, as most are sold out months ahead.

P [▪] E3/1 [⚬] (A/B/C)

Wembley Arena Empire Wy, Wembley, Mddx (902-1234). Venue for large pop concerts, among other things. Large CP. There are **(w) spaces** on both north and south sides and more than 20 (w) can be accommodated. Adapted loo near the wheelchair enclosure on the north side.

P E0 [⚬] [⚬ WC] (A/B/C)

Museums & galleries

On the whole, much more thought and effort has been put into providing access facilities at museums than at most other public places. There is sometimes a lack of attention to detail; particularly widespread are inadequate signposting and lack of information about specific facilities. Museum managements have also made more provision than others for the partially sighted and hard of hearing, and it is always worth asking about what is available. Some (w) entrances to museums and galleries are kept locked, usually for security reasons. It sometimes takes time to get special routes unlocked, but be patient; art and historical collections are valuable and security is therefore important. If you 'phone in advance, remember that the Education Service at the big museums is frequently the section with the best knowledge of access. Also, if you can avoid it don't turn up just before closing time; the staff tend to get jittery thinking you'll stop them from getting home on time, and you may have a rushed visit.

Cultural Enterprise Ltd 59 Sheldon St WC2 publish a super little book called 'London's Museums', which includes information for disabled people, It's one of the few guides we've come across that attempt to give access information and even though some of it is incomplete, the intention is excellent and we hope that other publishers will follow this example.

The Museums Association 34 Bloomsbury Wy WC1 (404-4767) keep access data and print lists of museums throughout the country with basic access details.

Inner London

Apsley House *See entry on Wellington Museum.*

Barbican Art Gallery *See entry on Barbican Centre in 'Arts complexes' chapter.*

Bear Gardens Museum & Arts Centre 1 Bear Gdns, Bankside SE1 (928-6342). Elizabethan theatre history. There are museum tours for the partially sighted and hard of hearing by prior arrangement. There is a large and awkward threshold into the first room, then a ramp with a step at the top into the second room. Friendly people there will normally help. **All accessible** except the reconstructed theatre, which is up narrow stairs. There is flat access to the loos with ordinary cubicles.

 E1N1

British Museum Great Russell St WC2 (636-1555, access enquiries ext 427 or 508). One of the largest and most important museums in the world. The natural history department (*see entry on Natural History Museum*) is in Kensington and the ethnography department (*see entry on Museum of Mankind*) is in Burlington Gdns. Special arrangements can be made for (w) or (s) to park in the forecourt if there is a real need. Advance notice would be helpful (ring ext 387). While it is easier for coaches to offload by the north entrance in Montague Pl, it is a longish route through the museum to the main information desk and for (w) it is certainly easier to start at the main entrance.

At the main entrance (Great Russell St) there are 12 steps but well hidden to the left there is a **(w) lift** to bypass these. There's a button to press to summon help. A plan of the museum and an information sheet for disabled visitors are available from the information desk at the main entrance; all good stuff. Most (though not all) of the GF is **accessible without steps** (rooms 1–32) as is most of the upper floor (rooms 35–66) which is reached by the **lift** to the right of the bookshop, past the information desk. Rooms on the GF involving steps with no available bypass are 6, 8, 11, 13, 14 and 33. There are 6+6 steps to the coffee shop but these can be bypassed by using a **staff lift** if you ask one of the warders nearby. Again, this is not signposted. The seating arrangement in the coffee shop is particularly good for (w). The basement is reached by −27 steps from rooms 16 or 18, but if you are particularly keen to get to the Assyrian basement or the lecture theatre, ask at the information desk and you will be able to use a staff lift to get there. (**NB** It takes a little while, as the route is somewhat tortuous.) There are 18 steps between rooms 32 and 33, and −3 more to room 34. The main reading room of the British Library has **flat access** from the main foyer. Admission is by reader's card only, issued to people with a special research interest. There are **two (w) loos** in the museum, both shown on the plan and both on the GF. One is off room 25 and the other is past the bookstall on the left.

If you arrive at the north entrance and look at the plan you will be confused (at least, we were). The information desk there is not always manned. From this entrance there are 2+8+2+10+3 steps up to the GF, while the libraries are off the staircase from a split level part-way up. There is a **lift** to bypass the stairs, which goes to the libraries, the GF (but not giving flat access to the main part of the museum, only to room 34) and to the upper floor from which, if you ask, you can get flat access to room 66 via a private part of the museum. Otherwise there are +3−3 steps to negotiate and then flat access to the main front lift by room 40 and therefore to most of the rest of the museum via the GF.

The museum is very large and you would be sensible to try and see only part of it in any one visit. **Wheelchairs are available** for use if needed. Educational visits can be organised and some exhibits can be made available for handling by visually handicapped visitors. There are sometimes special exhibitions for the partially sighted (contact the Education Service). Generally the museum staff are very willing to help and to talk about the exhibits, so if you want to know anything, do ask. It is clear that access around the museum is generally very good, once you've worked it out, and someone has gone to considerable trouble to achieve this, although the signposting of facilities does need improvement.

P D ◪ E12/ Ⓐ ♿ 90% ⑪ ♿ wc ♿ ✕ ◉ U

Commonwealth Institute Kensington High St W8 (603-4535, recorded information 602-3257). A tent-like building housing colourful displays from 47 Commonwealth countries. There is a monthly calendar of events, 'What's On', and also an excellent leaflet, 'Facilities for Disabled Visitors'. There is a small CP in front of the building; 'phone in advance for a place. The way in for (w) via the CP and the west entrance is well signposted. The main entrance involves steps. **Access is possible to most of the building** and the staff are helpful. The three floors of permanent exhibitions, art gallery, library and activities room can all be reached from a **lift** entered from the CP. Have a word at reception at the west entrance.

The Theatre/Cinema is accessible via a rear entrance and there are **six (w) spaces**. There's a **(w) loo** on the 1st floor in the Middle Gallery.
Flags restaurant involves 3 steps from the west entrance.

P � E ▣A▣ ▣&▣ 90% ▣&wc▣

Courtauld Institute Galleries Woburn Sq WC1 (580-1015). A reasonably small art gallery and not quite so overwhelming as some. Entrance has **3 steps**, then inside there's a large **lift** to get anywhere. Ordinary loos with level access but narrow cubicles.

▣ E3 ▣&▣ 90% ▣↑↑▣

Crafts Council Gallery 12 Waterloo Pl W1 (930-4811). **Access here is excellent**. There is ramped access and lifts to anywhere and everywhere and a **(w) loo**. Coffee bar for drinks and light snacks with lift access. Posters and exhibition information readily available. **Highly recommended.**

E0 ▣&▣ ▣↑↑▣ ▣&wc▣ ▣&X▣

Design Centre 28 Haymarket SW1 (839-8000). Various exhibitions of the best of British design. **GF flat/ramped**. There's a two-section (s) stair-lift to the basement level, but it's only suitable for (w) who can transfer to a smallish seat and have a companion to carry the chair down. **A service lift** to the 1st floor is available on request.

E0 ▣&▣ 60% ▣↑↑▣

Dickens' House *See 'Historic buildings' chapter.*

Dr Johnson's House *See 'Historic buildings' chapter.*

Foundling Hospital of Art Treasures & Coram's Fields Brunswick Sq WC1 (278-2424). Captain Coram roped in Handel and Hogarth among others as supporters of his hospital for orphaned and deserted children. The building contains many mementos, and the Fields next door (now a park) are open to adults only when accompanied by a child. Access is via **6 steps**, then a small **lift** to the 1st floor. Ordinary loos on the flat.

▣ E6 ▣&▣ ▣↑↑▣

Geological Museum Exhibition Rd SW7 (589-3444). Illustrates the general principles of geological sciences with special features on Great Britain. Entrance 1+10 steps. **Alternative entrance** down the service road between the Geological and Science Museums, but this is neither signed nor advertised; ask at reception, up 1 step at the main entrance. Once inside, the **access is generally good**. There are three floors and most of the museum is flat, although there are some exhibition areas on new mezzanine levels with access via stairs only. The museum is about 100m long and the **lift** (D 90cm) is at the far end. There is a **(w) loo** available via the lift on the 1st floor of the office section. Ordinary loos on the GF, −8−5 steps.

▣ E11 ▣A▣ ▣&▣ 80% ▣&wc▣

Guildhall Clock Museum Guildhall, King St EC2 (606-3030). An extraordinary and fascinating collection of clocks and watches. **Flat access** via the Guildhall main entrance if you ask one of the attendants to unlock the door through the library. Otherwise there are 3 steps.

 E3

Hayward Gallery South Bank SE1 (928-5708). **Access to the gallery is flat** through wide double doors, reached via the upper walkway and 8 steps from the Festival Hall, or on the flat if you use the lift in the National Theatre to the 1st floor. Inside, the layout changes with each exhibition but there are basically two main floors and a mezzanine. The management say that they always provide ramps where possible. **There is an excellent lift** which can take you up from the UGCP to the gallery (you have to summon an attendant from the gallery office by entryphone) and which also goes to the upper floor of the gallery, thus eliminating 50 steps. it is a very big lift with room for at least four (w). There are no special (w) loos. The ordinary Ladies' and Gents' are situated on a split level involving a minimum of 20 difficult steps and so are basically inaccessible. However, if you ask an attendant they will give you access to the staff toilets which, although we were unable to survey, we were assured had been used by parties of (w) before with no problems. If necessary, use the loo in the National Theatre, crossing by the walkway under Waterloo Br and using the lift in the theatre. In general the people here were very helpful and have often catered for (w), both singly and in groups, in the past. They would appreciate prior warning of large groups, but say they feel the gallery presents no real problem for the handicapped visitor.

P  90%

ICA (Institute of Contemporary Arts) Gallery Nash House, The Mall SW1 (930-3647). Changing exhibitions to explore new ideas and themes. Just **1 step** at entrance. Events take place in various parts of the building, but the staff are helpful wherever possible. The video library and 'cinemathèque' both have **flat access**. The main gallery is −6 steps from the entrance. The upper gallery can be reached via a **lift** the other side of the restaurant. There are **(w) spaces** and the possibility of transferring.

 E1

The Imperial Collection Westminster Central Hall, Storey's Gate SW1 (222-0770). Brilliant collection of replicas of the crown jewels from many royal families. Well presented. Disabled visitors are welcomed, although groups are asked to telephone in advance. It is a particularly important collection because of the inaccessibility of the Crown Jewels in the Tower of London. The entrance is at the back of the hall in Matthew Parker St, with 2+14+5 steps with handrails. However, there is a **lift** (D 73cm, L 96cm, W 81cm) which bypasses these. As is all too common, there is no indication outside that this facility is available. You need to ask someone to go and let the ticket office know that the lift is needed, or to ring first. The inside is flat and most of the displays are readily seen. Loos off the middle landing, −5 steps from the exhibition.

 E21

Imperial War Museum Lambeth Rd SE1 (735-8922). A fascinating collection of historical military equipment. Generally good access, but some problems for a larger-than-average wheelchair. The facilities are not obvious, nor are they signposted and for almost everything (w) must ask—ie for getting in, using the lift and using the loo. The museum is about 50m from the road along a tarmac path. There are 10+3 steps at the main entrance but there's a **side entrance on the RHS with 1 step**. This is not signposted and you will need to get someone to ask a warder to open it for you. Inside there are two floors and most things can be seen. There are a few bumpy surfaces. There is a small lift (W 90cm, L 105cm) but it is necessary to ask the staff if you want to use it. On the upper floor near the lift there is a **(w) loo** with 80cm cub door. It is normally kept locked. Ordinary loos to the left from the main entrance and on the lower floor by the shop. There is another (w) loo in the Geraldine Mary Harmsworth Park, which surrounds the museum.

Jewish Museum Woburn House, Upper Woburn Pl WC1 (387-3081). Fascinating and well presented exhibition on the Jewish religion and famous Jewish people. **Flat access and a lift**, but some narrowish gaps between exhibits. Ordinary loos with flat access.

E0   🔲   ⬛

Leighton House Art Gallery 12 Holland Park Rd W14 (602-3316). Centre for Victorian studies and special exhibitions. Entrance 7 steps although there is an alternative at the back with only **3 steps**. There are three major rooms on the GF, which is about half the house, with **flat access**; −2 steps to one gallery. There are stairs to the 1st floor and no lift. Nearest (w) loos in the Commonwealth Institute.

📶 E7/3 🔲 50%

London Dungeon 34 Tooley St SE1 (403-0606). A series of dark, eerie vaults under the London Bridge railway arches with some gruesome waxworks representing aspects of British medieval history. A rival to the Chamber of Horrors at Madame Tussaud's. **Flat but slightly rough access** throughout. There's a **(w) loo** in the Ladies' (which can be cleared for gents if necessary).

E0 🔲   ▭   ♿ wc

London Planetarium Marylebone Rd NW1 (486-1121). Next to Madame Tussaud's. Although recently extensively modified, sadly (w) access was not provided. The main auditorium is on the 1st-floor level, and there's a ramp part-way and then about 15 steps.

📶 15

London Toy & Model Museum 23 Craven Hill W2 (262-7905/9450). A small family-run museum full of Victorian and Edwardian teddy bears, toys and model railways. Nearest NCP in Queensway. Entrance **1 step**, then most of GF accessible. Step and steep hump-back bridge to get into the level garden, where the tea room is. There are −17 steps to the basement, where there are further exhibits and the ordinary loos (cub door 63cm).

📶 E1N1/17 🔲 70% ♿ X

London Transport Museum *See entry on Covent Garden in 'Historic buildings' chapter.*

London War Museum Crucifix La SE1 (403-5881). The museum is dedicated to the fighting men of World War II and the Blitz figures prominently. It is sited between the arches underneath a railway. For parking, orange badges work in Southwark or there's a NCP at the east end of Tooley St. There's **1 step** at the entrance, **after that access is flat** almost everywhere; 1 step to NAAFI. Loos with 66cm cub doors; in the Ladies' there is room for sideways transfer, although there are no rails.

 E1

Madame Tussaud's Waxworks Marylebone Rd NW1 (935-6861). Near Baker St Underground station. One of London's most popular tourist spots, so it gets crowded at peak times. At the entrance there are 20 steps to the pay kiosk but (w) and (s) can on request use a **lift** to bypass the stairs. Inside, our survey team took about three hours to go around everything although it is obviously possible to bypass some exhibits. There is **flat access** to the Grand Hall (1st floor), to part of the 2nd floor and to the Chamber of Horrors (basement), although there is a rough cobbled surface there and a narrow bottleneck behind one of the exhibits. On the 2nd floor much can be seen, but there are 4 steps (10 more to the Sleeping Beauty exhibition). All steps have handrails. The Grand Hall has plenty of seats if you want to take a rest. It's advisable to bypass the Battle of Trafalgar exhibition on the GF as this involves $+15-6-5-4-3+3$ steps. Ordinary loos on the GF and 2nd floor, **(w) loo** on the GF. **The management tend to discourage (w) at busy times**.

A 50% [!!] & wc

Museum of London London Wall EC2 (600-3699). The museum is not only interesting and well laid out but has **excellent access and two (w) loos**. It is situated on the corner of London Wall and Aldersgate St. The main entrance is on the high-level walkway, with (w) access either via the lift on the RHS of Aldersgate St, opposite the NCP garage (go to the Podium level), or up the ramp at the junction of London Wall and Wood St or the ramp at the junction of Aldersgate St and Fann St. Ignore the notice for (w) by the steps at the roundabout, which is misleading. If you telephone in advance, permission is usually given for you to use the underground museum CP and you can then get to the Podium level via the museum's own lift in the CP (red door). Ring the bell once and the lift will come.

Inside, there is **flat, ramped or lift access everywhere**. There are **two lifts**, a staff-operated one just past reception—which you would use to get to the (w) loo, coffee shop, lecture theatre/cinema (with **(w) space**) or to the education department—and the other (D 80cm, L 110cm) 20m further on to the left of the main bookshop/sales area; it is not signposted. You could easily walk or wheel some 400/500m in going round the whole museum, but there are seats. The other **(w) loo** is near the Lord Mayor's Coach on the lower level. There are plenty of staff around who can direct or advise you, if you want, and we found them very helpful.

There is an **induction loop** in the lecture theatre and another in the Great Fire Experience (audio-visual display). There are six museum **wheelchairs available** for use, also **Braille sheets** listing objects in the galleries that can be touched, and the provision of a taped guide for blind and partially sighted visitors is planned. Also, (w) can see a section of the old City wall from a special window in the Roman gallery.

E0 & [!!] & wc & X [?] ⦿ U

Museum of Mankind Burlington Gdns SW1 (437-2224). Parking can be provided in cases of real need, if you 'phone and negotiate first. Entrance is via 8 steps. These can be bypassed, but there is no sign to say so and you must ask a staff member. Unaccompanied (w) would have either to cajole a passer-by, or to shout! There is a **level/ramped route** available from the outside of the building through a door which is normally locked. **The GF is flat.** Room 7 is accessible using a portable ramp; room 13 has several steps. The 1st floor is mainly flat: there are 3 steps but the same portable ramp can be used. The cinema is easily accessible. Ordinary loos on the GF, cub doors 72cm.

P 🔲 E8 Ⓐ 🦽 90%

National Army Museum Royal Hospital Rd SW3 (730-0717). Parking possible in the grounds if prior arrangements have been made. The entrance is up **3 small steps**. Steepish ramp (outside) or 10 steps (inside) down to the Weapons Gallery. Large **lift** to other floors, but several displays are on mezzanine between the main floors—for example, if you take the lift to the 2nd floor, there are then −7−7 steps to the Uniform and Art Gallery; −7−7 to 1st floor and a further −7−7 steps to the History of the Army 1485–1914, then −7−7 to the GF. There is a new gallery covering the years 1914–1982 at 1st-floor level which is flat from the lift. The **(w) loo** is near the main entrance just past the souvenir shop.

P 🔲 E3N10 🦽 50% 🚻 🦽 wc

National Gallery Trafalgar Sq WC2 (839-3321). Fine representative collection of various painting schools. Guided tours highlight selected pictures and there is an information sheet, 'A Quick Visit to the National Gallery'. Main entrance 35 steps. **Alternative flat access entrance** at the back in Orange St but it is inadequately signed. **Then flat/lift access throughout. Wheelchairs are available** for use, and there are **(w) loos** by the Orange St entrance and near the restaurant. There is a café reached via the Lower Galleries and, if you ask, a warder will take you through.

🔲 E35 Ⓐ 🦽 🚻 🦽 wc U

National Portrait Gallery 2 St Martins Pl WC2 (930-1552). Historical collection of contemporary portraits of many famous British people. You have to negotiate +2−8 steps at the entrance before you get to the lift. Much of the gallery is then accessible. Both ordinary and **(w) loos** are down about a dozen stairs. The staff will assist wherever possible, but it is helpful if people give prior notice, especially if a number of (w) are involved.

🔲 E10 🦽 80% 🚻

National Postal Museum King Edward St EC1 (432-3851 or 606-3769). Superb displays of stamps. There are **5 steps** at the entrance to the main post office building through to the enquiry and sales desk. The main exhibition room is on the 2nd floor up 12+11+11+12 steps which means that the museum is effectively inaccessible. There is, however, a **lift** inside the main building which could provide access. The current form is, that if you're very keen and/or want to take a group, then contact the chief security officer and ask for permission to use the lift.

🔲 E5N46/ 🚻

Natural History Museum Cromwell Rd SW7 (589-6323). Massive museum full of models, and the remains of all kinds of animals, fish and plants. Go and see the dinosaur skeletons and the massive model of a blue whale. Slope and 10 steps at main entrance but these can be avoided by the use of a ramp to an **alternative entrance** via the East Gardens, after contacting the front gate warder. A further alternative, with level access, is available via the service road between the Science Museum and the Geological Museum from Exhibition Rd; ask at the warder's post by the gate or at the museum control room at the rear entrance to the building. Prior arrangements should be made about parking, if necessary.

Inside, it is about 150m from the main entrance to the most distant galleries. There are split levels of 4 steps in each of the two main 1st-floor galleries and there is a tiny **lift** to the left of the main entrance serving the 1st and 2nd floors (D 70cm, W 90cm, L 90cm). An alternative but more distant lift is larger. The new British Natural History Exhibition is up a further 20 steps from the 2nd-floor level. In the Hall of Human Biology at ground level there are a few minor ramps and some of the special flooring is slightly bumpy. There is a **(w) loo** off the Main Hall, clearly signposted; a key for the door can be borrowed at the counter by the main entrance, or ask one of the warders to unlock it for you. The restaurant is up steps, but there is a snack area with flat access. There are plans to provide a new lift at the eastern end, improving access and giving a roof-top view of London.

There is a connecting corridor to the Science Museum but this involves 20 steps on the Science Museum side. It is not a good route for (w).

� E10 ▣ ♿ 70% ⧉ ♿ wc

Photographers Gallery 5 & 8 Great Newport St WC2 (240-5511). Interesting little gallery with varying exhibitions and a comprehensive bookshop. At No 8 there is **1 step** and (w) would have to get the other door unbolted. **Flat and easy inside**. At No 5 there are 4 steps but there's a **ramped alternative**, available if you ask. **Flat inside**. There's a useful refreshment place in No 5 in the gallery itself. Easily accessible. Ordinary loos with very narrow doors.

No 5 ▪ E4 ▣ ♿ ♿✗   No 8 ▪ E1 ♿

Public Record Office Museum *See 'Historic buildings' chapter.*

Queen's Gallery Buckingham Palace Rd SW1 (930-4832). A changing exhibition of works from various parts of the royal collection. About 100m to walk from the road. There are **7 steps** to the lower section where many of the major exhibits can be seen, then 17 quite steep steps to the upper section.

▪ E7N17 ♿ 40%

Royal Academy Burlington House, Piccadilly W1 (734-9052). There is a regular Summer Exhibition during May and other special exhibitions during the year. Small CP outside which (w) may be able to use with prior notice. There is a **ramp** to bypass the 8 steps at the entrance. Double doors, of which one needs to be unlocked for (w). The arrangements for (w) visitors are generally good, but use of the **lift** means bypassing the main route and going through a security zone (locked doors and all that). There are **wheelchairs available** for use, and (s) who have difficulty with stairs or crowds would be well advised to use one. Taped commentaries on exhibitions are available. The business gallery is on the 3rd floor with lift access and then 3 steps. The loos are on the 1st floor in the vestibule; cub doors are 75cm and open inwards. One cubicle has handrails. Restaurant/cafeteria −4 steps from the GF.

P E0 ♿ 80% ⧉ U

Science Museum Exhibition Rd SW7 (589-3456). This is one of the country's most popular museums. There is a large collection of engineering models, and various special sections. Parking can be arranged by prior appointment, particularly for parties of disabled people. **Only 1 step** at the entrance, then a **ramp** down to main GF. **Lift access** to all other floors, except the basement. The museum shop is just to the right of the entrance. A great deal can be seen but it is unfortunate that the very popular children's gallery is in the basement (-26 steps) and the space exhibition on the GF includes some important sections that are up $9+7$ steps. Other than that, access is fairly good. Each floor is some 250m long. There is a tea bar up 6 steps at the west end of the aeroplane gallery on the 3rd floor. The interconnecting passage to the Natural History Museum involves 20 steps and is not the easiest route for (w). **Unisex (w) loo** on the GF; take the ramp, through the steam engine section and past the space exhibition. There are also loos with 80cm cub doors on the 2nd floor.

P D ▨ E1 ♿ 70% ⏫ ♿ wc

Serpentine Gallery Kensington Gdns W8 (402-2107). Changing exhibitions of contemporary art. Entrance involves **1 step, then flat** throughout. Loos on the flat, but tiny cubicles and difficult access for (w).

▨ E1 ♿

Sir John Soane's Museum Lincoln's Inn Fields WC2 (405-2107). Fascinating house that's a sort of time-capsule. Unfortunately by its nature not very accessible, with **8 steps** at entrance. **GF flat** with one or two narrow doors but including some interesting exhibits. Basement $-3-14$ spiral steps, 1st floor 27. Only about 25% of the collection is visible on the GF, but well worth a visit to step into the magpie mind of this great collector and architect.

▨ E8N27/17 ♿ 25% ✚

Tate Gallery Millbank SW1 (821-1313). One of the major collections, including many modern works and a selection of British paintings, notably a fine exhibition of Turners. There is also a continuous programme of special exhibitions. There's a flight of steps at the front but a **ramped (w) entrance** in Atterbury St. The ramp leads to the basement, from whence there is **lift/flat access** virtually everywhere. **Wheelchairs are available** for use. The coffee shop and restaurant are accessible and there's a **(w) loo**. In principle, the number of (w) admitted is limited to six at any one time. The lecture room/cinema has an **induction loop**.

A ♿ ⏫ ♿ wc ♿ ✗ (?) U

Tradescent Trust St Mary's Church, Lambeth Rd SE1 (373-4030). Just at the south end of Lambeth Br. The church is a museum of garden history, and Captain Bligh is buried in the churchyard. There is **1 lintel step** in and after that access is generally good, with **ramps** in the garden and the church. Teas are sometimes available.

▨ E1 ♿

Victoria & Albert Museum Cromwell Rd SW7 (589-6371). The collection ranges from furniture of all ages to paintings, Renaissance jewellery, costume etc.

Whatever your interests, there's almost bound to be something that appeals. For parking, ring the chief warder on ext 270. The entrance to the small CP is via the Secretariat gate. Alternatively, you can try one of the other major museums nearby in Exhibition Rd, where there are also limited facilities.

There are 5+2 steps at the main entrance in Cromwell Rd but there are easier **level ways in** via the Henry Cole Wing in Exhibition Rd or via the Secretariat gate (near Brompton Oratory), where one of the warders will open a fire door for you. There are **wheelchairs with large back wheels available** for the use of (s). As the museum is so large, using a wheelchair is well worth considering.

A leaflet called 'Victoria and Albert Museum: Information and Plans' is available from the bookshop and there is a separate plan of the Henry Cole Wing. You are strongly advised to get hold of both, as our description is based on them. **Flat access** to many parts of the building is possible from the Henry Cole entrance, provided you can work out the routes.

In the Henry Cole Wing (which is a separate entity) access is possible to about 80% of the exhibits via the **lifts** (D 80cm, W 105cm, L 152cm). Only level 2 (with split levels), level 3 (−3 steps) and the Boilerhouse Project (−12 steps) are awkward. The best **(w) loos** are in this wing; the other smaller one is off room 16.

In the main building, about 20% is readily accessible. The green-coloured areas on the plan are easiest and can be reached by the Secretariat gate or by a ramp from the Henry Cole Wing. This area also contains the flat self-service restaurant, which is civilised enough to provide proper pots of tea. To get to the yellow area on the 1st floor, ask a warden to take you in the **service lift** (D 75cm, W 100cm, L 136cm) behind room 21a, which brings you up to room 74a. From there, once you're down the 4 steps into room 73, 80% of the area is flat.

The easiest way to see the rest of the museum is to ask at the Secretariat gate for a warder to take you through the photographic sales area to room 8, from which there is a **lift** (D 78cm, W 155cm, L 144cm) to the top of the building and the intervening floors. At the top of the building (red area on the plan), you can cross to room 139 and take another lift down to reach the rooms on the other side. It is hoped that planned improvements will soon make access easier.
The lecture theatre is up 20 steps.

P D ▣ E7 Ⓐ ⬚ 30% 🍴 ⬚ wc ⬚ ✕ ⬚ U

Wallace Collection Hertford House, Manchester Sq W1 (935-0687). A private art collection bequeathed to the nation by Lady Wallace in 1897. Entrance has 3 steps, but a portable **ramp** is available if needed. **Basically flat inside with lift access** to the 1st floor. Museum size about 75m×50m. Ordinary loos on the GF (−6 steps) with cub door 80cm, but it opens inwards. No facilities for refreshments. Nearest CP is in Gloucester Pl.

▣ E3 Ⓐ ⬚ 🍴

Wellington Museum (Apsley House) 149 Piccadilly W1 (499-5676). The Duke of Wellington's House, known as 'No 1 London', it is situated on the north side of Hyde Park Corner overlooking the Wellington Arch. There are **7 steps** to the GF, **then −9 to get to the lift**, which gives access to the 1st floor. Ordinary loos in the basement with lift access. No refreshment facilities. There is a **wheelchair available** for use.

▣ E7N9 ⬚ 20% 🍴 U

Battle of Britain Museum & Bomber Command Museum Grahame Park Wy NW9 (205-2266). There are three major aircraft and war history museums in the same area (*see also entry on RAF Museum*). They all have good facilities including parking, access, restaurants, displays and (w) loos. Ample parking space available. **Flat access** everywhere. **Lift** to upper floor (D 84cm, L 150cm, W 96cm) opposite the main larger entrance. **Two (w) loos** behind the BO. Battle of Britain Museum approximately 100m×50m. Bomber Command Museum approximately 200m×60m. **Recommended.**

P E0 [🚹] [⑪] [🚾 wc]

Bethnal Green Museum Cambridge Heath Rd E2 (980-2415). All kinds of things of interest to children; holiday activities include painting competitions, storytelling and Punch and Judy shows. Access 2+1+1 steps at the main entrance, then 9 steps to 1st floor. However, there's a **goods lift** at the back which will take you to the 1st floor, top floor or basement. The only place it doesn't go to is the foyer level where there is a **(w) loo** in the Gents', but the staff are helpful wherever possible.

▟ E4N9 [A] [⑪] [🚹] 75% [🚾 wc]

Dulwich College Picture Gallery College Rd SE21 (693-5254). This building, designed by Sir John Soane, provides one of the finest settings for an art collection anywhere in this country. There are 2 steep steps at the entrance and heavy swing doors. **Alternative ramped access** at the back which can be opened on request. The gallery is quite large; it is **all on the flat** and there are a number of seats around. There are ordinary loos, also with flat access. The park opposite is a good place for a picnic, but motorists should look out for the 'sleeping policemen' in the road.

P ▟ E2 [A] [🚹]

Geffrye Museum Kingsland Rd E2 (739-8368). Built as almshouses in 1715, and later turned into an exhibition of furniture and furnishings from as early as 1600. Access by 3 steps at the entrance, though an alternative with only **1 step** can be opened. **Flat throughout** but carpeted, which can be tiring for (w). **Unisex (w) loo** in the refurbished north wing and (w) loo in the Gents'. Small refreshment room with tiny threshold.

▟ E3/1 [🚹] [🚾 wc]

Horniman Museum London Rd SE13 (699-2339). A museum of ethnography, concerned with mankind's arts, crafts and religion. Problematic 6+10+8 steps at the main entrance but there is a **sloped bypass** to either the GF or the mezzanine as the museum is built on a hillside. We advise (w) to either ring first or get someone to ask at the reception desk for the alternative route to be opened. The top floor, where the famous Apostle Clock is, can only be reached up 10+7+6 steps. There are loos near reception, with a (w) cubicle in the Gents', and there are plans to provide one in the Ladies' as well. The lecture theatre has an **induction loop**.

▟ E24 [A] ▟ N23 [🚹] 70% [🚾 wc] [⑦]

Kenwood House The Iveagh Bequest, Kenwood, Hampstead La NW3 (348-1286). The entrance is **flat**. There are some exhibition rooms and the Orangery for concerts and poetry reading on the GF. A lecture room and special exhibition rooms are upstairs, with no lift. There are (w) spaces in the Orangery. The cafeteria and adapted loos are reached by a small step from GF.

E0 ⌊&⌋ 60%

National Maritime Museum *See 'Historic buildings' chapter.*

RAF Museum Grahame Park Wy NW9 (205-2266). Ample parking. **Flat or ramped access** almost everywhere. **Lift** to upper floor can be made available on request and there's a (w) loo. The museum is about 220m×60m. **Recommended.** (*See also entry on Battle of Britain Museum.*)

P E0 ⌊&⌋ ⌊↑↓⌋ ⌊& wc⌋

Whitechapel Art Gallery Whitechapel High St E1 (377-0107). Due to re-open in early 1985 with good access. There's a MSCP about 150m away with entrance in Buckle St. It is planned to provide flat/ramped/lift access everywhere with a unisex (w) loo on the 2nd floor.

E0 ⌊&⌋ ⌊↑↓⌋ ⌊& wc⌋

William Morris Gallery & Brangwyn Gift Lloyd Pk, Forest Rd E17 (527-5544). A venue for various art exhibtions including paintings, carving and design. **Entrance 4 steps. GF flat,** then 25 steps to 1st floor. Public loo outside with 63cm cub doors.

▪ E4N25 ⌊&⌋ 50%

Further afield

Epping Forest Museum Queen Elizabeth Hunting Lodge, Rangers Rd, Chingford, Essex (529-6681). A Tudor, timber-framed building. Nearest BR station is 800m away at Chingford. Parking outside. **Slight threshold** at the entrance. One exhibition room on each floor. **GF accessible** with wildlife exhibition, then 16 steps to 1st floor and 20 to 2nd floor. Loos 100m away with ordinary cub door 64cm. There's a Berni Inn nearby—The Royal Forest restaurant: access 2 steps then level, and level to loos (64cm doors).

P ▪ E1N36 ⌊&⌋ 40%

Kodak Museum Headstone Dr, Harrow, Mddx (863-0534). A history of the camera, including early movie machines, peep shows and spy cameras. It is the largest collection of photographic exhibits and apparatus in Great Britain. Easy **ramped access and (w) loo** available if you ask. Parking outside.

P E0 ⌊&⌋ ⌊& wc⌋

Orleans House Gallery Riverside, Twickenham, Surrey (892-0221). A small gallery near Marble Hill House (*see 'Historic buildings' chapter*) housing changing exhibitions, usually of local interest. CP 50m. There's **1 step** at the entry and to one exhibition room, the second room is reached from the outside via a **ramp** into the Octagon and the third is on the 1st floor up steps. There is a (w) loo.

P ▪ E1N1 ⌊&⌋ 50% ⌊& wc⌋

Shops, pubs & restaurants

Shopping

One of London's main attractions is its big department stores and its long streets full of shops. The most popular area is around Regent St and Oxford St (they go with Bond St, if you're familiar with the Monopoly board!). The main problem is that the area is big. Also, at Christmas time and during the sales the whole area gets very crowded and parking isn't easy. However, if that's where you want to go, we can give you a few hints. Well known shops outside this area include Harrods in Knightsbridge, Peter Jones in Sloane Sq, the Army & Navy stores in Victoria St, Heal's in the Tottenham Court Rd and the shops in Kensington High St. Surveys of all of these are detailed here. Since the opening of the adapted (w) rooms in the Tara Hotel, the Kensington shops have assumed a greater importance than before. In addition to those covered below there's a British Home Stores with flat access, and a large Boots. There are many other, smaller stores in Kensington High St and Kensington Church St.

Many of the big stores rely heavily on escalators for getting people between floors. Although most also have lifts often you have to walk or wheel further to get from floor to floor if you go by lift; Selfridges is a classic example. Also, most of the department stores are heated and, particularly if you're dressed up for winter weather outside, they can be unbearably hot. In general, London's shops are reasonably accessible, and you will get a friendly reception. We have surveyed only a tiny number and our selection is inevitably somewhat arbitrary. We hope that you won't feel in any way limited by the listings here.

Most big shops have a store guide near the main entrance or the lifts. These guides don't normally take account of split levels or of the fact that some stores are in two buildings (eg the Army & Navy stores and Liberty's). Also, departments are sometimes moved around without the listing being amended, so do ask for directions. People are usually willing to help.

If shopping is important to you, but you don't want the hassle of coming to central London, why not consider using one of the new compact shopping centres in the suburbs? Many have branches of the big department stores, and can offer nearly as wide a choice as those in the centre. Prices may be lower as well. You'll have much less trouble parking and not nearly so far to walk or wheel. The ones we've covered here are Brent Cross, Ealing, Croydon and Stratford. Our criteria were the presence of a good range of shops, good access, a nearby CP (normally a MSCP) and provision of a (w) loo. There will be other places you can go—the list is by no means exhaustive—but if you don't know where to begin, one of these should be easier than most.

Remember too the street and open-air markets which have, in principle, good access although they can be very congested and may not be suitable for some (s). (*See entries on Markets in 'Sport' chapter.*)

Shop locations are shown on the map illustrating this chapter, which we've included because the principal shops are spread over a very wide area. In the text, the shops are listed in alphabetical order.

Principal Shops Map

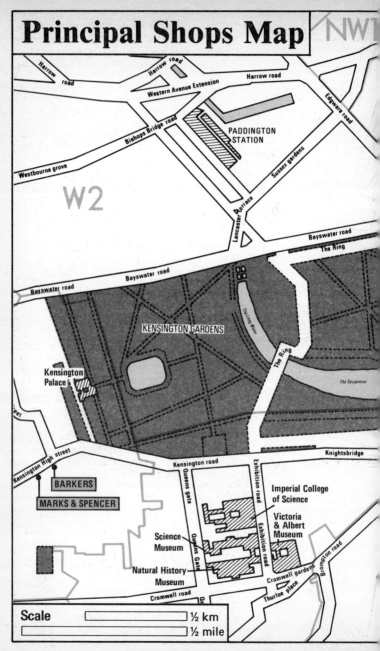

NW1

Harrow road

Harrow road

Harrow road

Western Avenue Extension

Edgware road

Bishops Bridge road

PADDINGTON STATION

Sussex gardens

Westbourne grove

W2

Lancaster Terrace

Bayswater road

The Ring

Bayswater road

Bayswater road

Bayswater road

KENSINGTON GARDENS

The Long Water

The Ring

The Serpentine

Kensington Palace

Kensington High street

eet

Knightsbridge

Kensington road

Queens gate

Exhibition road

Imperial College of Science

BARKERS

MARKS & SPENCER

Victoria & Albert Museum

Science Museum

Exhibition road

Natural History Museum

Queens Gate

Cromwell gardens

Brompton road

Cromwell road

Thurloe place

Scale

½ km

½ mile

118

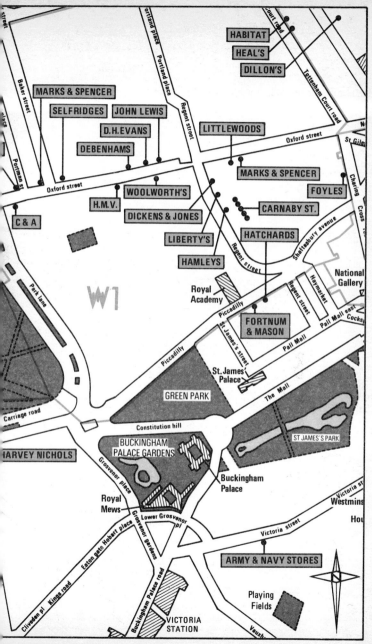

HABITAT

HEAL'S

DILLON'S

MARKS & SPENCER

SELFRIDGES　JOHN LEWIS

D.H.EVANS

DEBENHAMS

LITTLEWOODS

Oxford street

MARKS & SPENCER

FOYLES

WOOLWORTH'S

H.M.V.

DICKENS & JONES

CARNABY ST.

C & A

LIBERTY'S

HATCHARDS

HAMLEYS

W1

Royal
Academy

National
Gallery

FORTNUM
& MASON

Piccadilly

St James's street

St.James'
Palace

Piccadilly

GREEN PARK

The Mall

Carriage road

Constitution hill

ST JAMES'S PARK

HARVEY NICHOLS

BUCKINGHAM
PALACE GARDENS

Buckingham
Palace

Royal
Mews

Lower Grosvenor pl

Victoria st

Westmins

Hou

Victoria street

ARMY & NAVY STORES

Playing
Fields

VICTORIA
STATION

Vaush

Baker street

Portland place

Regent street

Portland place

Portman st

Oxford street

Regent street

Tottenham Court road

St Giles

Charing Cross

Shaftesbury avenue

Haymarket

Regent street

Pall Mall east

Cocks

Pall Mall

Park lane

Grosvenor place

Grosvenor gardens

Eaton gate Hobart place

Grosvenor gardens

Cliveden pl Kings road

Buckingham Palace road

Central London

Army & Navy stores 105 Victoria St SW1 (834-1234). Big department store on four floors with its main frontage on Victoria St but a second building behind this one, across Howick Pl. The main store is **fully accessible** with flat entrances and lifts to all floors. There is a **(w) loo** on the 2nd floor quite near the lifts, but it is not well signposted; ask the staff if necessary. The restaurant on the 2nd floor is accessible with plenty of space round self-service counters.

E0 [♿] [↑↓] [♿ wc] [♿ ✗]

The second building is not quite as easy, as there are **2/3 steps** at each entrance or about 12 via a connecting passage from the main store, above road level. There is a **lift**, but be prepared for split levels inside with up to 10 steps. There are plans for redevelopment of the shop and consequently these details may change. Note that the store guide does not make it clear which building the various departments are in.

[▪] E3/2N10 [♿] [↑↓]

Barkers 63 Kensington High St W8 (937-5432). Very large and spacious department store on four floors with **flat access everywhere, huge lifts** at the back of the shop and both male and female **(w) loos** in the basement near the Gents'. (The loos are not listed in the store guide.) The Rendezvous restaurant in the basement is readily (w) accessible; there are 2 steps to the Terrace restaurant on the 2nd floor.

E0 [▪] N2 [♿] [↑↓] [♿ wc] [♿ ✗]

C & A 505 Oxford St W1 (629-7272). Large store on three floors with good selection of clothing. **Lifts** at the back. **Flat access** everywhere. No loos or refreshment facilities.

E0 [♿] [↑↓]

Carnaby Street W1. This is the pedestrianised area behind Regent St. Although it has lost its 'swinging sixties' image, it's still quite interesting to see. Most of the shops have a step to get in and are slightly cramped and cluttered, but they vary. Generally not excessively crowded.

Debenhams 334 Oxford St W1 (580-3000). Large department store on four floors. **Flat access** via the Vere St/Oxford St entrance. **Lift** (not in main store area but adjacent to the stairs) gives access to most of the store except the GF. Split level on GF with 5 steps, which can be bypassed by going up in the lift by the entrance, crossing over to one of the lifts at the back of the shop, and coming down to the upper GF. Ordinary loos.

[▪] E3 [A] [♿] [↑↓]

Dickins & Jones 224 Regent St W1 (734-7070). Large department store on five floors with **flat access** everywhere. There's a group of **large lifts** in the centre of the store giving access to all floors. Some departments are slightly congested with only just enough room for (w) to pass between displays. Accessible restaurant on the 4th floor (movable chairs and tables). Loos also on the 4th floor: Gents' has 1 step but largish cubicle with 70cm door opening outwards; adapted cubicle in the Ladies'.

E0 ⬦ ⬦ X

Dillon's Torrington Pl/Malet St WC1 (636-1577). University bookshop on four floors, specialising in academic books. Typical bookshop layout—a bit narrow throughout with many shelves over 2m off the ground. **Flat access to most parts and there is a lift.** Records and tapes department is on a mezzanine, up 15 steps.

E0 ⬦ 80% ⬦ ⬦

D H Evans 318 Oxford St W1 (629-8800). Large department store on seven floors. **Flat entrance, large lifts giving flat access everywhere** including to the 6th-floor restaurant. Ordinary loos on 5th floor (cub door 60cm). No (w) loos.

E0 ⬦ ⬦ ⬦ X

Fortnum & Mason 181 Piccadilly W1 (734-8040). One of London's traditional shops with a style all its own. Parking in the immediate area is difficult. **Flat entrance** from Piccadilly involves two sets of swing doors; 4 steps at Duke St entrance; 1 step into The Fountain restaurant from the corner of Duke St and Jermyn St. Inside, there are **lifts** to most parts of the building, including the St James's restaurant on the 4th floor. Mezzanine floor 10 steps from GF (no lift access) and best access to Fountain restaurant is from the street entrance (*see above*) as inside there are −2−10−1 steps. Ordinary (small) loos.

E0/4 ⬦ 80% ⬦

Foyle's 119 Charing Cross Rd WC2 (437-5660). Massive bookshop on five floors in two buildings, but very cramped and crowded. Although (w) can get to some parts, you would need help in finding books on high shelves. There are plans for extending the main shop and moving the sections from across the road. In the main shop there is an (ancient) **lift** (D 68cm, L 116cm, W 91cm). **Access is flat**—there's just not much room!

E0 ⬦ ⬦ ⬦

Habitat 156 Tottenham Court Rd W1 (388-1721). A smallish shop on two floors well known for its modern furnishings and household goods. There is **flat access** with just enough room for manoeuvre on both the GF (for large furnishings) and the basement, but if they have stock blocking the way to the service lift, access to the basement is by staircase. No loos.

E0 ⬦ ⬦

Hamleys 188 Regent St W1 (734-3161). The world's largest toy shop on six floors. It's certainly big. **Lift/flat access everywhere**, but 4th-floor café is a bit cramped. Some displays are also a little cramped, but generally it's OK. Gets very crowded before Christmas. There's a **(w) loo** on the 4th floor but passage to it has been blocked when surveyed on two different occasions.

E0 ⬦ ⬦ ⬦ wc

Harrods Brompton Rd/Knightsbridge SW1 (730-1234). Harrods department store is a unique institution with its own special atmosphere and a world-wide reputation. It is truly massive, on five floors, and it is not particularly well signposted. There are some good floor plans showing where all the **lifts** are, at the entrance on the corner of Brompton Rd and Hans Cres. They have a **wheelchair available** for use and some (s) would be wise to use it because of the size of the place. The GF, 1st and 2nd floors have **flat/ramped access** almost everywhere. On the 3rd and 4th floors there are **split levels** which are not shown on the floor plans. On the 3rd floor it is a question of 2 or 3 steps here and there, but on the 4th there are up to about 8, eg to reach the restaurant.

As there are five sets of lifts in different parts of the store it is possible, by using the right lift, to bypass the steps but it all gets quite complicated. Harrods have issued a small leaflet for disabled shoppers which is of limited value. The staff will always help, but it is understandable that they may not realise the hassle caused by the split levels that they've never even noticed. There are adapted loos in the 3rd-floor Gents' (but quite difficult to find, and locked when we surveyed them) and in the Ladies' on the 4th and 1st floors. There are plans to provide a unisex (w) loo on the 1st floor. There's also an LTB information desk on the 4th floor.

D E0 ⌈&⌉ 80% ⌈↑↓⌉ ⌈& ✗⌉ U

Harvey Nichols Knightsbridge SW1 (235-5000). High-class store specialising in ladies' outfitting, but with some general departments. Four floors, with **lifts and flat access** almost everywhere.

E0 ⌈&⌉ 90% ⌈↑↓⌉

Hatchards 187 Piccadilly W1 (439-9921). A smallish but well-stocked bookshop on four floors with **flat access and a lift** (not working when the shop was surveyed) which goes to the 2nd floor. Ordinary loos with very narrow (49cm) cub doors but flat access.

E0 ⌈&⌉ 60% ⌈↑↓⌉

Heal's 196 Tottenham Court Rd W1 (636-1666). One of London's premier shops for furniture and fabrics. **Flat entrance** from Tottenham Court Rd. **Large lift** in the centre of the store to all four floors and two smaller lifts (D 68cm) away to the right from the main entrance. Most floors accessible although there are a few displays up 2 or 3 steps. Loos on the 4th floor (3 steps, narrow doors) and on the lower GF (flat access, Gents' cub door 63cm but door opens outwards).

E0 ⌈&⌉ 90% ⌈↑↓⌉

HMV 363 Oxford St W1 (629-1240). One of the biggest shops in London for recorded music. **Lift access** to all floors (L 170cm, W 170cm) and the lower floor is reached by service lift on request. A few of the counters/displays have narrowish gaps. No Loos.

E0 ⌈&⌉ 90% ⌈↑↓⌉ ⌈⊞⌉

John Lewis 278 Oxford St W1 (629-7711). Large department store. **Flat access almost everywhere.** Two sets of **lifts** to all five floors and a **(w) loo** on the 2nd floor behind the lifts (go through the door marked 'Exit A, stairs to Cavendish Sq' and the loo is immediately on the left). There are public telephones both there and on a number of other staircase landings which are both accessible and a reasonable height for (w), a self-service restaurant on the 3rd floor and a coffee lounge on the 4th.

E0 ⌊&⌋ ⌊↑↓⌋ ⌊& wc⌋ ⌊& ⌉⌋ ⌊& X⌋

Liberty's 210 Regent St W1 (734-1234). The store has more character than most and is certainly one to see, even if you can't afford to buy anything! It consists of two separate buildings linked by a bridge (involving steps) at the 1st- and 4th-floor levels. Access within each building is reasonably good, although some departments are a bit congested. In the main building in Great Marlborough St there is **flat access** at the main entrance and the security guard will always open the revolving doors for (w). There are **lifts** at each end of that building. There are also lifts in the other building and flat access from Regent St. The restaurant (flat access from lifts) is in the main building on the 4th floor, but access to the loos is poor and the cubicles are narrow (51cm). There is a larger staff loo which (w) might be able to use on request.

⌊A⌋ ⌊&⌋ ⌊↑↓⌋

Littlewoods 207 Oxford St W1, near Oxford Circus (437-1718). **Flat access** and only two floors. **Goods lift** to lower GF. Loos on lower GF but with narrow cubicles and the WC pedestal is on a step. Cafeteria on the GF but with fixed seating.

E0 ⌊&⌋ ⌊↑↓⌋

Littlewoods 508 Oxford St W1, near Marble Arch (629-7840). **Flat access. Goods lift** to lower GF available on request on two floors. Reasonably priced cafeteria and tea bar on lower GF but narrowish passage past the counter and fixed tables and chairs. Loos on lower GF with narrow cubicles.

E0 ⌊&⌋ ⌊↑↓⌋

Marks & Spencer 99 Kensington High St W8 (937-1654). **Flat access**, two floors and a **lift**, but no loos. For a (w) loo, Barkers is just next door.

E0 ⌊&⌋ ⌊↑↓⌋

Marks & Spencer 173 Oxford St W1 (437-3761). Pantheon Store, east of Oxford Circus. Large with **flat access and lifts** to the upper floor, though not well signed. Customer lift on the left, in the middle of the store; service lift at the far end. **Unisex (w) loo.** Signs advise the hard of hearing and partially sighted to ask for help.

E0 ⌊&⌋ ⌊↑↓⌋ ⌊& wc⌋

Marks & Spencer 458 Oxford St W1 (935-7954). Near Marble Arch. Large with **flat access and lifts** to both floors. Ask at Ladies' Footwear (back of 1st floor) for the **unisex (w) loo.**

E0 ⌊&⌋ ⌊↑↓⌋ ⌊& wc⌋

Peter Jones Sloane Sq SW1 (730-3434). Large department store on five floors with **flat access** almost everywhere. Split level (4 steps) on the lower GF and also on the

4th floor. Two groups of **lifts**, one group going to each level and virtually all of the store is accessible on the flat from one set or the other. There's a **(w) loo** on the 3rd floor alongside the lifts nearest to Sloane Sq, opposite the accounts desk. Generally good access as the two floors with a split level can be reached by using the lift back to the GF and then going back up in one of the other group. Coffee shop on the 5th floor with flat access. The restaurant is on the 4th, −5 steps from the lift.

E0 ⌨ 90% ⥮ ♿ wc

Selfridges 400 Oxford St W1 (629-1234). One of London's biggest department stores, situated between Marble Arch and Bond St. It is enormous, each floor measuring some 200m×200m. There is a MSCP attached to the store, run by NCP. Access to the store is flat from CP. There are some **flat entrances** from the street, including the main central one from Oxford St; several entrances have steps, however, especially those from Orchard St. If you come in from the side you'll find steps either at the door or inside the shop. Starting from the main entrance, over 90% of the store has **flat access via the lifts**, which are near the centre of the shop. Like many other big stores, Selfridges tends to be hot inside and you may have long distances to go to get from one department to another, unless they are near the lifts. There's a **(w) loo** on the 3rd floor.

P D ▣ E0/6 Ⓐ ⌨ 95% ⥮ ♿ wc

Woolworths 311 Oxford St W1 (629-8611). On two floors with **flat/lift access** everywhere. There is a service lift at the back of the shop. No loos.

E0 ⌨ ⥮

Outer London

Brent Cross Shopping Centre Templehof Av NW4. Situated just off the A406 North Circular road by the Brent flyover, the centre is reasonably well signposted locally. It is a compact two-level indoor centre with excellent parking facilities and **good access** to branches of several of London's big department stores. If you can't face the hassle and parking problems round Oxford St this provides an excellent substitute, although *on Sat* and at Christmas time etc, it gets very crowded. There are seven **(w) parking spaces** available on your right as you go past John Lewis (follow the sign to service area V). If you park in the main MSCP there is a gently sloping covered way to the shops.

There is **flat access** to most areas and shops. Surprisingly, there is only one public **lift** (D 105cm, L 130cm). There is another lift in Marks and Spencer which can be used if you ask the staff. **Unisex (w) loo** near the lift, on the GF.

Croydon Shopping Centre Croydon, Surrey. This is a very large but generally accessible shopping centre to the south of London. The new Whitgift Centre lies between North End Rd and Wellesley Rd, and is on two levels with two spiral ramps. There's a **lift** in the Dingwall Av MSCP. There are also at least three lots of **(w) loos**. There are over 1000 shops either in the Whitgift Centre or in the immediate vicinity, including most of the big name chain-stores. Rail access to East Croydon station is good as there are **ramps** to all platforms. There are three MSCPs: one on the corner of Dingwall Av and Wellesley Rd, giving access to both levels, near the back entrance to Adlers; one on the corner of Poplar Wlk and

Wellesley Rd, giving access to the lower level; and one in Frith St about 150m away.

The Centre is uncovered, but there are canopies running along the shop-fronts of each level, so that in the event of bad weather you needn't be out in the rain for long, even though the ramps aren't covered. Most of the shops have flat access; we haven't attempted to give details, partly because a total survey would have taken a very long time and partly because there's not much to say!

'*Access in Croydon*', published in 1979 and available from RADAR, is useful and we hope it will be updated regularly.

The Croydon Voluntary Association for the Blind Bedford Hall, 72 Wellesley Rd, Croydon, can provide tactile maps of the town centre.

Loos The (w) loos are to be found by the lower level of the Dingwall Av MSCP, near the lower level of W H Smiths (**NB** there are two W H Smith branches in the Centre); in the entrance to the Wellesley Rd MSCP—head towards Marks & Spencer until you get to Boro's Boutique and then turn right into the passage towards the CP and the loos are on the LHS; in the Frith St CP to the left of the car entrance. Other (w) loos listed in 'Access in Croydon' are on the upper level of the Whitgift Centre; in College Rd opposite the Dingwall Rd/George St junction; and in Kesley Rd, adjoining the MSCP.

Ealing shops Ealing Bdwy W5. A large new development substantially completed in 1984 which provides a compact and accessible centre with a wide variety of shops. There are MSCPs nearby, lifts and (w) loos—one on the east side of the development near Oxford Rd and another in the Spring Bridge Rd MSCP. There are two large department stores, Bentalls and Sanders, and the Safeway super-market has a (w) checkout. Rail access is poor, unfortunately—there are about 40 steps from both the BR and Underground stations.

Stratford shops Stratford E15. A compact, mainly covered shopping centre, recently redeveloped, to the east of London. Using Stratford Underground station involves lots of steps. There's a MSCP on top of the new centre with **lift access** near the station exit from the Centre. There's another MSCP on top of the adjacent bus station. The **(w) loo** is in the Centre near the exit to the station subway and near Sainsbury's. There's one unisex cubicle and the key is available from the attendant. We noted also that the Mainstop supermarket has a (w) checkout.

Pubs & restaurants

Access to places for eating and drinking is surprisingly bad, especially when the difficulties of reaching the loos are taken into account. The loos are commonly up or down steps, or along awkward, narrow passageways. The cubicles are also frequently small. It is not too difficult to find a pub bar or a restaurant which has flat access or only one step but no thought has been given to the disabled customer who, like anyone else, needs to go to the loo. Some of the obvious places to suggest are the catering facilities at the Barbican Centre and on the South Bank, where there are (w) loos in the buildings, and the restaurants at several large stores which have a (w) loo such as Selfridges, Harrods and Peter Jones (*see 'Shopping'*). Some of the major museums have both (w) loos and adequate refreshment places (*see 'Museums' chapter*). After that, there are some major hotels with reasonably priced carveries and moderately accessible loos or you might try and find a restaurant near a public (w) loo. The Hilton Roof Bar is worth a visit both for the prestige and the exceptional view, and the hotel has a (w) loo on the 1st floor. The fixed menu is quite expensive, though.

We are indebted for the information here to a Manpower Services Commission (MSC) team carrying out a study in central London. They found very few remotely accessible places but without the MSC help the section would have been even shorter. We will be working towards extending it considerably in the next edition. In this section, the loos are inaccessible unless details are given and we apologise to (s) if the lack of detail means that the information is inadequate for their use. The MSC survey from which the data was drawn was based simply on accessibility for (w). Having said all that, we hope that the listing will be of some use even to (s) since the places listed will probably be the easiest for them too.

The Restaurant Switchboard (444-0044) available from *10.00 to 24.00 daily* is a very useful enquiry service. Whilst it is basically a general enquiry point, they are trying to build up a bank of access data alongside details about the service, cuisine and price range of the restaurants. For general information, Nicholson's 'London Restaurant Guide' is also very useful.

W1

Gallery Rendezvous 53 Beak St (437-4446). Peking Chinese. 1 step. **£££**
Glory Kebab House 57–59 Goodge St (636-9093). Greek. 1 step. **£££**
Golden Egg 64 Tottenham Court Rd (636-3587). English. 2 steps inside. **££**
The Grecian Taverna 27a Percy St (636-8913). Greek. Level. Loos: 1 step then cub door 71cm. **£££**
Hostaria Romana 70 Dean St (734-2869). Italian. Level. **£££**
Villa Carlotta 33 Charlotte St (636-6011). Italian. Level. Restaurant **£££**, cafeteria **££**

WC1

L'Almacas 15 Leigh St (388-1461). Wine bar. 1 step. **£/££**
Bordigiana 5 Bernard St (837-8744). Italian. 2 steps. **££/£££**
Cagney's 13 Cosmo Pl (278-8498). International. 1 step. **£££**
Carpenter's Arms 105 King's Cross Rd (278-5708). Pub food. 1 step at the Frederick St entrance. **£**
Chung's Chinese 15–17 Brunswick Centre (278-4945). Chinese. 1 step. **£££**
Ham & Egg 19–21 Brunswick Centre (278-4559). English. Level. **££**
Ivanhoe Hotel bar Bloomsbury St (636-5601). Pub food at lunchtime only. 1 step. Loos: level, cub door 71cm. **£**
Lord John Russell 91–93 Marchmont St (387-1513). Pub snacks. 1 step. Loos: Gents' level, cub door 71cm; Ladies' inaccessible to (w). **£**
Marlborough Arms 36 Torrington Pl (636-0120). Pub food. 1 step. Loos: Ladies' accessible (if you are slightly mobile). **£**
Marquis of Cornwallis 31 Marchmont St (837-6072). Pub food. Level. **£**
Northumberland Arms 141 King's Cross Rd (837-6146). Pub food. 1 step. **£**
Oodles 42 New Oxford St (580-9521). Mainly vegetarian. Level. **££**
Pizza Express 30 Coptic St (636-3232). Pizzas. 1 step. Loos: level, cub door 71cm. **£**
Prince Albert 2–4 Acton St (837-0120). Pub food. 1 step. **£**
Spaghetti House 20 Sicilian Av (405-5215). Italian. Level. Loos: level, cub door 71cm. **£££**
Tagore Tandoori 8 Brunswick Centre (837-9397). Indian. 1 step. **£££**
White Lion 16 Northington St (405-9705). Pub food. Level. **£**

WC2

Evergreens 36 Drury La (836-2019). American. 1 step. **£££**
Flounders 19 Tavistock St (836-3925). Seafood. 1 step. **£££**
Jerusalem 150 Shaftesbury Av (836-7145). Middle-Eastern. 1 step. **£££**
Mr Rockwell's American Diner 1/3 The Piazza (836-5873). Mexican/American. 1
step. **££**
Neal Street Restaurant 26 Neal St (836-8368). International. 1 step. **££££**
Porters 17 Henrietta St (836-6466). English. Level. **£££**
Ristorante Aurora 1/3 Catherine St (836-7585). Italian. 2 steps. **££**
Splitz 4 Great Queen St (405-6598). American. 1 step. **£££**
Thomas de Quincey 36 Tavistock St (240-3972). French. Level. Loos: only the
Ladies' is accessible, but gents can use it. **££££**

NW1

Asuka Berkeley Arcade, 209a Baker St (486-5026). Japanese. Level. Lunch **£££**,
dinner **££££**
Pizzaland 187 Baker St (935-9100). Pizzas. 1 step. Loos: Ladies' level, cub door
71cm; Gents' inaccessible to (w). **£/££**
Primrose 64 Parkway (485-0678). English/Continental. Level. **££**
Sagarmatha 339 Euston Rd (387-6531). Nepalese, Indian, selected Asian. Level.
£££
Tonino's 12 Glentworth St (935-4220). Italian. 1 step. **£££**

SW1

L'Arco 79 Buckingham Palace Rd (834-1151). Italian. Level. **£££**
Bag o' Nails 6 Buckingham Palace Rd (834-6946). Pub food. Level. Loos: Gents'
level, cub door 71cm; Ladies' inaccessible to (w). **£**
Mandarin House 26 Buckingham Palace Rd (834-0192). Chinese. 1 step. **£££**
Pickles 6 Old Queen St (222-8749). Sandwich bar. Level. **£**
Pizza Hut 125 Victoria St (828-1757). Pizzas. 1 step. Loos: level, cub door 71cm. **££**
Pizza on the Park 11 Knightsbridge (235-5550). Pizzas. 1 step. **££**
Shakes 91 Buckingham Palace Rd (828-4913). English. 1 step. **£**

Sport, open-air & special events

Sport

Access to the main venues for sport is of great importance. The emphasis here is on spectating, but participation is also a vital interest for many and the **British Sports Association for the Disabled** (BSAD), Hayward House, Harvey Rd, Aylesbury, Bucks (Aylesbury (0296) 27889) is the central co-ordinating body. Note that many new sports centres have provided facilities for disabled people, particularly changing facilities, (w) loos and access to the swimming pools. In the survey we have covered venues for interests as varied as athletics, football—both soccer and rugby—racing, rowing and tennis.

Association football (Soccer)

In spite of the current troubles, and much talk of violence and confrontation, watching football remains a very popular and generally perfectly safe activity. Access for disabled spectators to the various grounds has improved enormously over the last few years and it is now more widely recognised that disabled people should have the right of entry just like anyone else. However, attitudes and facilities do vary, and **some clubs operate a pre-match reservation system for the (w) spaces**. At most grounds there are terraces for standing, and seats, some of which are pre-booked and some of which may be available only on the day of the match. A few particularly important games are designated 'all-ticket' matches by the clubs involved. Standing on the terraces and sitting in the stands makes a nonsense of the language, but that's what you do.

If you have a problem with mobility, it is usually best to contact the club and check on what the form is. The chances are that they will be helpful if they can, either booking you into the most accessible seats or reserving a (w) space. The normal route into the ground for (ab) is via very narrow turnstiles, so (w) or (s) may need a gate opened specially for them; it is important to be clear about which gate when negotiating with the club. Also, remember that there isn't normally much leg-room in the seats, and in a few cases they are just benches without backs.

If you meet opposition but are particularly determined to see the match, the thing to do is to turn up with enough helpful friends to enable you to get over any barriers and up the steps to a seat. Get there reasonably early and the officials will almost always be friendly and helpful.

Arsenal Arsenal Stadium, Avenall Rd N5 (226-0304). The club who have been in the First Division longer than anyone else. Finsbury Pk BR station is about 750m away. There are no reserved parking places, and the stadium is in the middle of a residential area. If you want or need to park nearby, get there very early (perhaps even as much as two hours before kick off). There are **(w) spaces with flat access** in the corner of the terrace in front of the East Stand and it's best to telephone to reserve a place. There are **steps to all the seats**. The easiest to get to are in row G in blocks G and H in the East Stand lower tier, where there are only 8 steps. The entrance for these seats and for (w) spaces is almost opposite Elphinstone St. There is less than 50m to go inside the ground and there are loos nearby (Gents' cub door 63cm). The refreshment bar is −15 steps from this area. Access to other parts of the East Stand and to the West Stand involves considerably more steps.

Brentford Braemar Rd, Brentford, Mddx (560-2121). A small club with a famous history. Brentford Central BR station is about 500m away. Parking is in the surrounding streets. There is **touchline space** in the corner **for a few (w)**, reached by going through the main entrance in Braemar Rd and using the players' tunnel to give **flat access. The 'easiest' seats for (s)** are in blocks A and B but both **involve steps**: 14+7 to row F and a further 12 to row A. The only seats are behind and above a terraced section. There's a tea bar by the main gate and another next to the entrance to block F. Loos are under the Braemar Rd stand by the entrance to block C (Gents' 1 step, cub door 66cm).

Charlton Athletic The Valley SE7 (858-3711/853-0444). Charlton station is 300m away. It may be possible to use the club CP if really necessary, if you contact the club in advance and arrive early—go through the main entrance in Floyd Rd. The **enclosure for (w) has 15 spaces with flat access** and affords a good view as it is above the pitch level. Go through the main entrance (as above), turn left on to a fairly steep concrete ramp 10m long. **The best seats for both (s) and (w) who can transfer are in the North Stand, with flat access to some of them**. Get there early. Refreshments and (normal) loos behind the enclosure with flat access.

P [A] [image] N [&] (A/B/C)

Chelsea Stamford Bridge Ground, Fulham Rd SW6 (381-0111). A vast ground with a greyhound track as well as a football pitch. The nearest station is Fulham Broadway. Parking in the streets around. There are **(w) spaces with flat access** from the main entrance in shelters by the East Stand. The **easiest seats for (s)** are in the lower tier of the East Stand, **13 steps** to Gate 1 and **then steps down**, depending on how far down your row is. The easiest is the back row (row W) but there is a slightly restricted view from there. Rows T downwards give an uninterrupted view. The (w) spaces can be reserved a month in advance by post, or a fortnight in advance by 'phone. A refreshment kiosk and toilets (Gents' cub door 60cm) are situated by gate 1.

The club are hoping to provide headsets and a commentary for blind supporters, when funds are available.

[A] [image] N [&] (A/B/C)

Crystal Palace Selhurst Park Ground, Park St SE25 (653-2223). Parking is in the streets around. There is a club CP some 300m from the Park St entrance which may be used by prior arrangement if there is a real need. The nearest stations are Norwood Junction and Selhurst. Palace have been for years one of the best clubs in London for (w) access and you can generally expect a friendly reception. Groups should obviously contact the club first and there is a system of **(w) passes**, so it's worth checking on the position for popular games and getting your ticket in advance. There is a **marked entrance for (w)** in Park St and **flat access** to a section of the Arthur Waite Stand giving a good view. For reserve games, ask at the box office, as the Arthur Waite Stand is shut and you will be let in behind the advertising boards. All flat access. There are also **easily accessible seats** in the Arthur Waite Stand **for (s)** but make sure you make your needs known when booking.

A ▄ N ⑤ (A/B/C)

Fulham Craven Cottage, Stevenage Rd SW6 (736-6561). Parking is in the residential area around, which tends to get very congested. The nearest station is Putney Bridge. **Excellent access for (w)**. Entrance at the gate opposite Finlay St and **(w) spaces** on the running track in front of the Eric Miller Stand (about 100m to wheel). **For (s)** and for **(w)** who prefer to transfer there are 15+7 steps minimum in the Stevenage Rd Stand or **7 steps minimum** in the Eric Miller Stand (entrance at the Hammersmith end). A gate next to the turnstiles can be opened. Usual (limited) provision of loos. More facilities for disabled people are included in long-term plans.

A ▄ N ⑤ (A/B/C)

Orient Leyton Stadium, Brisbane Rd E10 (539-2223). About 1km from Leyton (Midland Rd) BR station and 400m from Leyton Central line tube station. Parking involves the usual congestion in the streets around, and some streets are closed off on match days. There is an **excellent covered (w) enclosure** with room for about 20 people. **Flat access** through an entrance in Brisbane Rd, opposite Balmoral Rd. Ring in advance to be sure of a place, but for most matches you can probably turn up on the day. The club has **up to six wheelchairs to lend** to (s) who want to use them, and they even provide a cup of tea and free programmes in the enclosure. Refreshments and loos (with normal cubicles) are nearby, under the Main Stand. The **best seats for (s)** and (w) who prefer to transfer are in the lower tier of the Main Stand, but **must be booked in advance**.

A ▄ N ⑤ U (A/B/C)

Millwall The Den, New Cross SE14 (639-3143). About 800m from New Cross Gate station. Street parking. **Small (w) enclosure** at pitch level **with flat access** through the main entrance in Cold Blow La. **The easiest seats for (s)** are in blocks A–F in the Grandstand, **bookable in advance**. There's a ramp to the stand from the main entrance. Normal toilets with flat access.

A ▄ N ⑤ (A/B/C)

Queens Park Rangers (QPR) Rangers Stadium, South Africa Rd W12 (743-0262). A small club with a completely modernised stadium with the controversial all-weather omniturf surface. QPR have been, over the years, one of the best London clubs for welcoming disabled spectators and we started going there in the mid-60s. Parking is the usual hassle in the streets around but the police are fairly helpful to (w) and will enable them to park in Ellerslie Rd. The nearest station is White City. There are **(w) spaces** in the corner of the ground **accessible on the flat** from the Ellerslie Rd entrance. Refreshments and ordinary loos with flat access. **The seats** are generally not very accessible as they **are all up steps**. The easiest for (s) would be those in the Ellerslie Rd Stand, where there are a minimum of about 15 steps.

A ▄ N ⑤ (A/B/C)

Tottenham Hotspur (Spurs) 748 High Rd N1 (801-3411). One of the prestigious clubs, located some 500m from White Hart Lane BR station (−30 steps). Parking in the streets around and in some commercial CPs along the High Rd which are opened on match days. There is a **small, new (w) enclosure** for 12 chairs at pitch level behind the goal. **Book in advance** for important or popular matches, and they like you to arrive well before kick-off. **Flat access** to the enclosure via the Officials and Directors entrance off the High Rd. Refreshments and **(w) loo** with flat access. **For (s)** and for transfer there are a few easily accessible seats in the lower tier of the West Stand. In the East Stand there is a lift situated between turnstiles 40 and 41 half-way down Worcester Av; **easiest access is to seats near the lift**.

[A] [▟] N [♿] [‖] [♿ wc] (A/B/C)

Watford Vicarage Rd, Watford, Herts (Watford (0923) 20393). The nearest stations are Watford Junction (1.5km) and Watford High St (800m). Parking in the streets around. There is a **covered (w) enclosure** for 24 chairs, and the club advises you to ring and **reserve** a space in advance. Access is flat/sloped via the entrance off the Directors CP; about 140m from Vicarage Rd and a moderate slope. Refreshments and normal loos near enclosure. **Easiest access seats** are in blocks A and B in the lower tier of the West Stand, which **are bookable**.

[A] [▟] N [♿] (A/B/C)

Wembley Stadium Wembley, Mddx (BO 902-1234, M 902-8833). The stadium stages the Cup Final, most international matches and various other events. It was built in 1924. In spite of the crowds and the excitement, provided you can organise yourself a ticket it is perfectly possible to go. We've been there many times and, although there are access hassles to everywhere except the (w) spaces, generally we've always found people accommodating and helpful on the day. **For big events there are enormous crowds** and the roads and transport system get choked up both before and after the event, so **allow at least an extra hour or two** for traffic delays and remember that it may take you a long time to get away afterwards as well. There is priority parking near the stadium offices for a limited number of Orange Badge holders with prior permission. Contact the chief security officer. The nearest stations are Wembley Park and Wembley Hill.

The **easiest entrance** for both (w) and (s) is via the stadium offices, which are between turnstiles G and H. There is 1 step, but this gives access to the level covered walkway which goes right round the ground. There are **12 (w) spaces** on the Flame Platform over the players entrance. The platform slopes the wrong way so the view from the second row is poor; however, improvements are planned. For the Cup Final, six spaces go to each team. For the England/Scotland game they are allocated via clubs and for other events they are administered from the Wembley BO. For all the big events it's important to apply and to arrive early. **For (s)** and also for (w) to transfer, note that the lower levels of seats are simply narrow benches without backs and although the top seats (row 34) have a wall behind them for support, it's a highly variable distance back. There are also 11+4 steps to reach it. The upper levels of seats have backs (and are more expensive) and all have steps up to them. There's a lift in the North Stand from the restaurant area but a **minimum of about 10 steps** to the seats (row 17—other rows involve more steps either up or down). There are quite a number of ordinary loos and there's a **(w) loo** in the first aid centre behind the Flame Platform. Alternatively, you might use the one in the Wembley Conference Centre before or after the game.

P [▟] E1N [♿] [‖] [▟] [♿ wc] (A/B/C)

West Ham Boleyn Ground, Green St E13 (472-2740). One of London's prestigious clubs with a very strong local following, but **poor access**. It is now the only club in London without proper (w) facilities. We were told that (w) are not allowed on the touchline under any circumstances, though we know one or two who've made it in the past! As at other clubs, the stands were designed long before access was thought of; however, it wouldn't be too difficult to do something to improve things for disabled spectators. As it is, you have to come in with everyone else and try to get to the unreserved seats. There are about 40 steps up to the back of each stand and then further steps to seats. There are also narrow gaps at the top (approx 50cm). When our survey team visited a little while ago we used a lift in the main club building to the side of the West Stand, which bypassed some of the steps. A visit is currently only possible with considerable (ab) help. Nearest Underground station is Upton Park. It is to be hoped that the club will look into the possibility of providing an enclosure for (w) towards the front of one of the terraces, which could be accessed from the touchline without too much hassle.

Wimbledon Durnsford Rd SW19 (946-6311). The nearest station is Haydons Rd. There are other stations in the vicinity, but it's probably best to study a street map to see if they're too far away. They are all surface lines around Wimbledon (BR Southern Region and District line), so there are only steps at the stations and no escalators. There is a small CP in the grounds where space may be reserved by asking in advance, otherwise park in the streets around. **A few (w) can be accommodated on the touchline** in the north-east corner in front of the North Stand. **Flat access** off Durnsford Rd. Go behind the stand and through the gate which is between the stand and the terrace. The club ask (w) to **'phone before the match** to check that there is space. **The best seats for (s)** or for (w) who prefer to transfer are in row A of the centre block of the North Stand. Refreshment facilities are up 13/14 steps. Loos are under the North Stand (Gents' 1 step, 72cm cub doors). **Wheelchairs are available** for use if needed.

P [A] N [img] [&] U (A/B/C)

Athletics

Crystal Palace National Sports Centre Ledrington Rd SE19 (778-0131). The area is fairly hilly which causes inevitable problems. Major athletics meetings are held in the stadium. There are extensive CPs, but 4 steps up from the main CP to the concourse. From Crystal Palace BR station there are about 60 steps to negotiate. In the stadium, the back row of the West Stand is accessible via a **ramp** and there is then **−1 step** to the seats (for (w) transfer). **If you need to stay in your chair, ring in advance,** and you can be driven to a spot near the final bend.

The indoor sports centre is on two levels, both **accessible by ramp**, but from different entrances. Both the competition pool and the spectator area are reached via 12 steps. The small pool in the annexe has flat access apart from the footbaths. There's a café with flat access in the main sports centre. There are two lots of **(w) loos**: in the changing rooms for the pool, **−4 steps**; and behind the Jubilee Stand (to the east) with flat access. There are also specially converted showers on the lower level of the main sports centre.

P H [img] E1/4 [A] [&] [& wc] [& X] (A/B/C)

Cricket

Lords St John's Wood NW8 (289-1611, prospects of play 286-8011). Nearest tube station is St John's Wood. The HQ of Marylebone and Middlesex Cricket Clubs, Lords is run on very traditional lines. Most privileges are for members and club membership is somewhat exclusive. Things are difficult, particularly for (w) on big match days, as virtually no special arrangements are made. They don't seem to have taken on board the fact that **in a test-match crowd there would be on average at least 15 to 20 (w)**.

Getting in to county matches isn't a problem. There's a CP off Wellington Rd and (w) can sit in front of the Taverners Bar. For big matches, CPs are for members only, and the area in front of the Taverners Bar isn't recommended as the 'noisy element' tends to take over and there can be aggro and broken glass and all the rest. The only other places to stay in your chair are in the gap between Q block and the Pavilion—**room for about six (w)** but strictly it's an area for members and guests—or in the area opposite the Pavilion just on either side of the sight screen. For (w) who can transfer and **for (s)** there are 12 steps at entrance M to the Mound Stand, where seats are reservable, or **4 steps** to the lower tier of the Grandstand where seats are unreserved but again it's an area that gets crowded and rowdy. There is a museum with 1 tiny step and part of the exhibition is on the GF; 19 steps to the 1st floor.

There are no (w) loos and in general, because of the tiered (stepped) stands everywhere **access is not good**. Adaptations to facilitate (w) access are essential and wouldn't cost that much. If you do go, take some friends with you and your own refreshments, arrive early and if you book seats, make sure they know you're (w) or (s). Good luck!

The Oval Kennington, SE11 (582-6660, match information 735-4911). Disabled spectators are welcomed. Limited CP space for those in real need if negotiated in advance. Nearest tube station is The Oval. Most public entrances involve turnstiles. To avoid these, go to the Hobbs gate or Vauxhall gate and ask. Once inside there is a flat roadway that circles the ground, and by prior arrangement a vehicle can be driven in to drop off (w) or (s) if necessary. **The best place for (w)** to watch is in the Nets Stand by the West Wing (about 100m from the Hobbs gate). It's advisable to **ring first** to ensure seats are cleared away if necessary. The Ladbroke tent for both betting and beer is nearby. **Flat access** to the bottom level of the Vauxhall Middle Stand is possible but most of the public stands are up above a dozen steps and are tiered. No (w) loos, but there are several loos around with minor access problems. Refreshments are available from hatches at the back of the Surrey Tavern, up 1 step. The Banqueting Suite is over the Surrey Tavern, up about 30 steps.

Greyhound racing

Walthamstow Greyhound Stadium Chingford Rd E4 (527-2252). There is a two-tier CP in front of the stadium. Walthamstow Central, Highams Pk, Wood St and Queen's Rd stations are all within 1.5km of the stadium: Highams Pk is the nearest. **Access is straightforward to most parts of the stadium.** A road goes right round between the stands and the track (which is raised about 1.5m above ground level).

Some (w) can be accommodated in the internal CP at the end of the North Stand, and others can transfer to seats, some of which are accessible. Through the North Stand is a corridor with a cloak/coats counter, sandwich kiosk, Tote windows and loos (cub doors 74cm) all flat access. The smaller South Stand has probably the best seats for (w) who want to transfer. It is accessible from the road between the track and the stands.

P ▣ N Ⓐ ⟨&⟩ (A/B/C)

White City Stadium Wood La W12 (743-5544, restaurant 743-5057). This is one of London's major stadiums and is used for a variety of events such as the International Horse Show as well as being a regular venue for greyhound racing. Remember that for some events there may be large crowds causing traffic congestion etc. The nearest tube station is White City, where access involves steps to the platforms. The management are generally friendly, and if you want any further information or need particular assistance they will help if they can. Special arrangements may be made for (w) in three-wheelers who have difficulty getting out to park on the paddock, but it is essential to **negotiate this beforehand**. There is limited parking space inside the grounds. Enter from the East Side main gate in Wood La; there's a NCP across the road in Wood La and organised parking two and three abreast in White City Rd (**NB**: There's no car access to White City Rd from Westway when the stadium or the nearby Queen's Park Rangers FC stadium is in use).

The main entrance is the East Side main gate, and there are **exit doors** which **can be opened for** (w) there to bypass the turnstiles. On the east and west of the stadium there are open terraces where people stand or sit to watch. On the north and south ends there are terraces with access only by stairs. From the main (east) entrance, **access is flat** through the CP to the road running right the way round under the stands, and it is also flat to the paddock area round the track. Access to the upper levels (East Side) is by stairs (3+10+10) or escalator to the 1st floor, then 9+14+14+6 or escalator to the 2nd floor. The bars are on the upper level—eg Lonsdale Bar, East Side 2nd floor—with tiered seating at the front of the bar so you can watch the racing. The American Bar (West Side 1st floor) has flat access from lifts and there are **viewing platforms outside with flat access**. The West Side would seem to be the best for (w). The restaurant is on the 2nd floor, West Side via −3 steps. The restaurant is also tiered to enable diners to watch what's going on.
Loos Those from the American Bar and Lonsdale Bar both have flat access but normal cubicles. There's a **(w) loo** on the access road under the stands, situated near the vehicle entrance at the junction of White City Rd and South Africa Rd.

P Ⓐ ▣ N ⟨&⟩ ⟨II⟩ ⟨& wc⟩ (A/B/C)

Wimbledon Stadium Plough La SW19 (946-5361). There is greyhound racing here all the year round, motorcycle speedway *Mar–Oct* and a variety of car races with stock cars, hot rods and bangers almost every week. There is a large CP. **The best view** is from the 2nd floor of the Grandstand, which is enclosed. Access **via 1 small step, a lift and a ramp**. It's all very easy. Although the restaurant in the Grandstand is tiered, with steps everywhere, full restaurant service can be provided for (w) at greyhound racing, on the flat 2nd floor. At speedway and car racing, (w) access to the restaurant is via 5 steps from the 1st floor. It is planned to provide a unisex (w) loo on the GF of the Grandstand.

If you want to use the cheaper enclosure, the entrance from the CP is entirely flat and there are no steps until you reach the terraces. **The best view** and access is from the backstraight where there are **4 steps**. Bars, buffets etc can be reached, as can ordinary loos. There are plenty of seats to transfer into. It seemed a very easy and friendly place to go.

P  E1N 🚻 ⏸ 🚻wc 🚻✗ (A/B/C)

Horseracing

London is well situated for racecourses, the three closest being Sandown, Kempton and Epsom. Slightly further out are Ascot, Windsor and Lingfield, but all are within about 40km of central London. The only one we have surveyed in detail is Sandown Park, but a fair amount of the information is the same for the other courses in the sense that the facilities are broadly similar. All are accessible from London by train, although there's usually quite a distance (approx 1km) from the stations to the main facilities, except at Kempton where the station is alongside the Grandstand. Most have reserved parking spaces for disabled drivers and passengers near a special entrance, but it is worth telephoning first. On arrival, let officials at the gate know about your needs. Be insistent. Generally, the CPs have rough surfaces. Racecourses are large, usually crowded places and the main facilities for viewing, betting and eating and drinking are concentrated in the Grandstand, which has various sections with different entry charges. Where you go depends on the company you want to keep and, naturally, to an extent you get what you pay for.

There are usually three kinds (and prices) of entry. The first and cheapest, usually about £1.50–£3.00, is often called the 'parking' area: this gives a reasonable view of the racing, but often there are no drink or snack facilities, toilets or betting offices—you can, however, take your own food and drink. The best place to go is probably what is often called 'The Tattersalls': this gives access to nearly all the bars/restaurants/loos/betting facilities and can provide an excellent view of what goes on. The prices usually range from £4.00–£6.00 but for that you get a full afternoon's entertainment. The most exclusive entry is to the Members Enclosure, but prices start from about £7.00–£7.50 and can often be very much more, especially on big race days, such as Royal Ascot and Derby Week at Epsom. Facilities are usually very good, but also very expensive. Champagne and seafood is the order of the day and if mixing with millionaires is what you want, then the Members Enclosure is the place to go.

Sandown Park Racecourse Esher, Surrey (Esher (78) 63072). Sandown is fairly accessible from London either by road or by train. The nearest station is Esher with trains from Waterloo. There is an entrance quite near to the station, but a longish walk to the main facilities. The course is on the Portsmouth Rd (A307) in the middle of Esher, just off the A3 Kingston/Esher bypass. The CPs off the Portsmouth Rd are free, but the terrain is rather rough. There is a special **disabled parking area** reached through the Owners/Trainers/Press entrance, and a **disabled persons' entrance** by the special CP; a short walk or wheel brings you to the Grandstand and main facilities, including the paddock and the Paddock Bar. Entrance to the GF of the Grandstand is flat and inside there is a bar, snack bar and the Tote betting offices. On the right as you go in is a large lift, otherwise there are a lot of steep steps—both giving access to the 1st and 2nd floors, where snacks and drinks are available. To gain access to the course, go through the Grandstand where you will find a slope and only 1 step to reach the tic-tac men and you can go right down the rails by the side of the course. There are **(w) loos** (one Gents' and

135

one Ladies') on the GF of the Grandstand and these are the only really accessible toilets.

Betting at the course can be very confusing. If you don't know a great deal about it but enjoy a little 'flutter', use the tote. It doesn't always give such a good return, but is much safer. The tic-tac men, (ie those on the course) are very sharp and often the minimum bet is £3 or £4. For those who know their racing (and are confident!!), they're worth investigating; for those who don't, it is still worth a look and gives a fascinating insight into the complex world of racing and betting. However, remember that if pickpockets are around, they'll probably be in that area.

P ⒜ ♿ 80% 🍴 ♿WC (A/B/C)

Enquiries about the other racecourses can be made as follows:
Ascot Racecourse Ascot, Berks (Ascot (0990) 22211).
Epsom Racecourse Racecourse Paddock, Epsom, Surrey (Epsom (78) 26311).
Kempton Park Racecourse Sunbury-on-Thames, Mddx (Sunbury (76) 82292).
Lingfield Park Racecourse Lingfield, Surrey (Lingfield (0342) 832009).
Windsor Racecourse Windsor, Berks (Windsor (95) 64726).

Rowing

Henley Royal Regatta This is the most important event in the rowing calendar and usually takes place in *early Jul*. The town gets extremely crowded, as do pubs, restaurants and hotels in the area, and parking is difficult. If you want to hire a boat so that you can moor alongside the course, you will have to book it months in advance and arrive very early in order to get a mooring. Similarly for parking, the trick is to arrive really early and make a day of it. Bring a picnic to avoid hassles with getting food. **Parking concessions to orange badge holders may be suspended** locally because of the volume of traffic. The towpath which, of course, gets crowded is tarmac on the south side of the river for about 500m. Thereafter it gets narrower and rougher. The Regatta Headquarters is just by the bridge on the south side and there are two enclosures set aside for watching the racing. Both are grass and get muddy when it's wet. There is a General Enclosure with seating, mainly in deck-chairs.The Stewards Enclosure (basically for members and friends) has a **small area set aside for (w)**. For membership details write to the Secretary, Regatta Headquarters, Henley-on-Thames, Oxon. **There is a (w) loo in the Stewards Enclosure and if you need to use it, ask at the entrance.** There are usually St John's Ambulance helpers around in this area if needed.

Rugby Union

Twickenham Rugby Ground Rugby Rd, Twickenham, Mddx. The home of both international and key Rugby Union matches. Tickets are allocated solely through rugby clubs and the telephone is ex-directory. Parking is possible near the south-west corner off Witham Rd if you make prior application. It's important to get there early, perhaps as much as two hours before kick-off for big matches, because the traffic gets very thick and many roads in the area are closed off. There are about **30 (w) spaces** in the south-west corner of the ground which give only a moderate view, as the area is below the level of the pitch so your eye-line is only a foot or so above the grass. However, demand usually exceeds supply for internationals and there's plenty of 'atmosphere'. Because of the ticket allocation system, it is difficult to book particular seats. There are stands almost all round the ground with stepped access. At the south end there are benches without backs at ground level. There are **(w) loos** near the (w) spaces, one unisex and one in the Ladies'. A rugby museum is planned to open shortly and there's a restaurant (1 step) but it's very expensive.

P [A] ◢ N [&] [& wc] (A/B/C)

Swimming

Facilities are generally improving, especially changing rooms, (w) loos and access to the pools. In central London one of the best is the Queen Mother Centre in Vauxhall Bridge Rd. If you're feeling hardy, the open-air pool in the Serpentine is reasonably accessible, though the facilities are fairly basic. In west London there's the Fulham Pool, Normand Pk, Hammersmith W6 (381-4498) which has (w) loos, a special changing area and four pools.

Tennis

Wimbledon The All England Lawn Tennis & Croquet Club, Church Rd SW19 (946-2244). The most famous tournament in the world takes place towards the *end of Jun* and attracts enormous crowds. There are parking areas nearby (about 500m away) and it is advisable to arrive early. **For (s) there are significant access barriers** in that there are steps to most seats and some of the corridors between the main courts are narrow. There are a **small number of (w) spaces** on the Centre Court and about ten on Court 6, which is a semi-show court. Written application clearly marked 'Wheelchair Application' should be made as far ahead as *Jan*, as all the spaces are balloted. There's a **(w) loo** in the South West Hall.

P [A] ◢ N [&] [& wc] (A/B)

Open-air attractions

Open-air events and venues have the attraction of being generally accessible and surprisingly varied. There's music, politics, art and shopping, in addition to the parks and historical statues. Doing things in the open can enable the visitor to get a real feel for London—and in fact to see and experience many things that the visitor intent on the standard tourist circuit will miss.

Bandstands

Details of performances are available from the LTB or the GLC. Some of them are of very high quality, and a stop to listen to an open-air concert can provide a welcome contrast and rest during a day spent sightseeing or shopping. Bandstands are to be found in many places in central London, including the following:
Cathedral Place Near St Paul's Cathedral, within the shopping precinct on the north side.

Hyde Park Just north of The Dell restaurant.
St James's Park Near the Guards' Memorial on Horse Guards Rd.
Tower Place EC3. Opposite the Tower of London.
Victoria Embankment Gardens Near Embankment Underground station.

Further out, stands are to be found in a number of parks, including Battersea Park SW1, Victoria Park E9 and Parliament Hill NW3.

Free speech

Speaker's Corner Hyde Pk W1, near Marble Arch. It operates mainly on *Sun* and anyone may get up and talk about (almost) anything. Mainly religion and politics. **Easily accessible.** UGCP in the same corner of Hyde Pk (400/500m to walk).

Tower Hill EC3. Politics at lunchtime. **Easily accessible.**

Markets

Street markets tend to be crowded, but the stalls are all basically accessible and they are lively and interesting places. There's a useful book called 'Markets of London' by Foreshaw and Bergstrom, and there's a section on markets in Nicholson's 'London Guide'. If you're selective you can often pick up a bargain, but there are a few points to remember. It's advisable to arrive early to avoid the worst of the crush, and bear in mind that crowds are a pickpocket's delight. Your purse or wallet are easily 'nicked', and the fact that you're disabled or in a wheelchair is no protection. Watch out too for 'set-up' sales where the valuable goods go to a few accomplices in the crowd and what is sold to the public is very poor quality, and for the slick three-card-trick type of gambling. It's an easy way to part with money. There are numerous small markets scattered around the city, but the main ones are:

Berwick Street & Rupert Street W1. Mainly food; centrally situated in the heart of Soho. *Mon–Fri.*

Club Row & Cheshire Street E2. General market with a strong East End flavour. Pets, old furniture. *Sun morning.*

Petticoat Lane Middlesex St E1 and surrounding streets. Usually crowded and parking nearby can be a problem. Something of a tourist trap, but very varied stalls and quite an atmosphere. Main market *Sun*, some stalls *Mon–Fri* too.

Portobello Road Notting Hill W11. This also spills over into the surrounding streets. Antiques and bric-à-brac *Sat*, fruit and vegetables *Mon–Sat*.

Other markets include: Brixton, Atlantic Rd SW9; Camden Lock NW1; Chapel Market, White Conduit St N1; Columbia Rd E2; The Cut SE1; East St SE17; High St Walthamstow E17; Kingsland Waste E8; Leather La EC1; Ridley Rd E8; Shepherd's Bush W12; Vallance Rd E1; Whitecross St EC2.

Parks

London has several large and delightful parks. Even near the centre you can get right away from the traffic and noise and bustle. The main parks were all parts of royal estates and their history is outlined in 'Discovering London's Parks and Squares' by John Wittich, published by Shire Publications. The main parks are described in some detail together with an account of the architecture and history of some of London's more interesting squares in Bloomsbury, Westminster and other centres. There is also a GLC Information Service on Parks for disabled persons on 633-1707, and a GLC leaflet listing events in parks.

Battersea Park SW11. An extensive park south of the river with various facilities. You can drive round the perimeter road and there are good parking facilities, which are free. There's a **unisex (w) loo** over towards Queenstown Rd and normal loos elsewhere. There's a children's zoo, paddling pool, adventure playground and a boating lake with facilities for fishing (in season). Not a bad spot to leave the car if you want to take a taxi or—if you're feeling energetic—to walk or wheel the 3km to the Kensington museums or to the Buckingham Palace area and don't want any hassle over parking. Good riverside views.

Holland Park W8 & W14. Access from Kensington High St or the CP in Abbotsbury Rd. Pleasant area with tarmac paths. Refreshment facilities near the house. Easiest access to area for snacks is from the back, and the **restaurant has flat access** from the side (73cm door). There is an open-air theatre nearby, 16 steps at the main entrance but flat access from the LHS. Loos are near the restaurant: Gents' 5 steps; outer door 74cm and 90° turn; cub door 70cm, relatively spacious. Ladies' similar.

Hyde Park & Kensington Gardens W2 & W8. This vast stretch covers over 240 hectares. It is fairly flat and there are tarmac paths throughout. There is limited parking on the road running between the two parks (West Carriage Dr), with small CPs either side of the Serpentine Br. There is also a large UGCP with entrances off Park La and North Carriage Dr; note that there's a longish walk to get out, though. There are some seats in the park and many more deck-chairs, for which there is a small hire charge. In summer, it's nice just to sit on the grass—you can almost forget that you're in the middle of an enormous city. There are **(w) loos** behind the shrubbery between the Serpentine Gallery and the Albert Memorial; both Ladies' and Gents' about 400m north of The Dell self-service restaurant; and in the Ladies' on the south side of Kensington Gdns opposite Hyde Park gate. Some of the parks' principal features are:
Boating on the Serpentine from the north side of the lake. Rowing boats and canoes available for hire. **Flat access**.
Fishing is allowed at the eastern end of the Serpentine.
The Lido is an open-air swimming area on the south side of the Serpentine. There are big marquees for changing and ordinary loos. Water only 1.3m deep. Children's pool and sandpit up 6 steps but otherwise **easy access**.
Open-air art market on the park railings, right down the Bayswater Rd as far as Queensway, on *Sun*.
The Orangery in front of Kensington Palace, with its attractive sunken gardens, is reached by −3 shallow steps.
Refreshments are available at two main places. The Dell is a self-service restaurant at the east end of the Serpentine and has **flat, easy access** and tables and chairs, both inside and out. It sometimes closes in winter. The main restaurant area is just south of the Serpentine Br and includes a restaurant, bar and snack bar. CP adjacent. There's **flat access** to the restaurant, +4−1 to the Plant House Bar and an awkward turnstile into the snack bar. Getting a (w) inside the snack bar looked a bit of a hassle—you can't even go in through the exit. There are tables and chairs outside, though. There are also kiosks near Marble Arch and by the Black Lion gate, Queensway.

The Round Pond for model boats, ducks and swimming dogs is over towards Kensington on high ground approached by a broad tarmac path.

Speaker's Corner is near Marble Arch with easy access. Here you can listen to people talking about anything and everything, particularly on *Sun afternoon*.

Physic Garden Swan Wlk, off Chelsea Embankment SW3. An ancient garden where apothecaries grew their herbs for medical treatments in days gone by. Access involves −1−3 steps and then gravelled paths which are heavy work for (w). Ordinary loos only. *Open infrequently*.

Regent's Park NW1 is a large and attractive area to the north of London. It is flat, and most of the paths are tarmac. There's a largish lake with boating and in the north-east corner is London Zoo (*see 'Historic buildings' chapter*). To the north is Primrose Hill and, in the Inner Circle, there's a small open-air theatre which is (w) accessible—an attractive spot during warm summer evenings. The only (w) loos we found were just outside the Inner Circle near where Broad Wlk crosses Chester Rd. Parking is possible at certain times on the perimeter roads and the Inner Circle. Orange badge holders shouldn't have much trouble, as it's generally a quiet area.

St James's Park & Green Park SW1 are both attractive, well shaded and very centrally placed. There are (w) loos on the north side of St James's Park opposite Marlborough Rd. From the bridge over the lake there's a unique view of the Whitehall offices.

Places to pause awhile

Small open stretches are scattered around all over London. A few are railed in and this is because they are, effectively, the private gardens of the houses surrounding the square and upkeep is paid for by the residents. Places worth a mention include the gardens at the Natural History Museum which are never crowded and have lots of seats, and another open space behind the Brompton Oratory. There's Postmans Pk on the edge of the City (which tends to get crowded) and also Lincoln's Inn Fields just north of the Law Courts. Also note the Westminster Abbey garden, open only on *Thur*.

If the weather's fine, the parks mentioned are obvious places, together with the Thames Embankment. If it's wet, things are not so easy. There are relatively few places one can sensibly suggest. Pubs don't have accessible loos (and are not always open) and main line railway stations are usually crowded and not very pleasant or clean. The two most obvious areas are the Barbican Centre and the South Bank complex around the Royal Festival Hall and National Theatre. There are attractive foyers, catering facilities and, sometimes, live entertainment. There are (w) loos nearby. In addition, some of the major museums provide shelter, something interesting to see, seats, catering facilities and (w) loos.

Street art displays

There are several large displays of painting, sculpture and handiwork to be seen in London, mainly on *Sun*. It's fun to wander along to look even if you don't intend to buy. They are to be found in the Bayswater Rd along the railings of Hyde Pk, stretching sometimes almost the entire length from Marble Arch to Queensway; in Piccadilly along the Green Pk railings from Hyde Park Corner; and in *summer only* in Heath St, Hampstead starting at Whitestone Rd. **All are easily accessible.**

Special events

There's a more comprehensive list in Nicholson's 'London Guide', but we mention most of the principal ones here. You can also get information from the LTB. We have included some annual events (listed in chronological order) and also permanent exhibition halls and venues for major shows and sporting events. Many of the events are open-air, and therefore accessible, and we have given access details for indoor attractions. For details of the Football Cup Final, Derby Week, Royal Ascot and Wimbledon, *see entries on Wembley Stadium, Horseracing and Tennis in 'Sport'*.

Annual events

The Chinese New Year is celebrated in the streets of Soho with paper dragons, processions and a mini-carnival. *Jan or Feb*.

Pancake races are held at Lincoln's Inn Fields on Shrove Tuesday, six weeks before Easter. *Feb or Mar*.

The Camden Festival takes place at a number of different venues with various possibilities of access, but if you want to go to something in particular, contact the Festival office in Camden Town Hall, 100 Euston Rd NW1 (278-4444 ext 2452) and they will try to help. Details are given below of three of the major venues used. *Late Mar*.
The Logan Hall Bedford Wy has −3 steps to a lift which will take you down to the auditorium. One row is at lift level, but (w) must transfer to a seat.
The Round House Chalk Farm Rd is reached by a large flight of steps, but if you go up the road to the CP there's only −2 steps to the entrance. There are (w) spaces, and the front row and the loos are all on the same level.
The Shaw Theatre Euston Rd has a side entrance which can be opened to give **flat access to (w) spaces**. The normal access is by about 20 steps to the top of the auditorium. There is a (w) **loo** in the office block above in the administrative section of the library.

The Oxford & Cambridge Boat Race is rowed from Putney to Mortlake. To get a view, get there early (Hammersmith Br is often a good spot) but remember that you'll only get a brief view of the crews and the pursuing launches and there'll be a lot of people around. *Late Mar or Apr*.

On Easter Sunday there's a parade of old cars in Battersea Pk and a carnival procession. Generally very colourful. The London Harness Horse Parade is on the following day with brewers' vans, drays and other horse-drawn vehicles on show. The parade goes twice round the Inner Circle in Regent's Pk at about midday. *Mar or Apr*.

The Chelsea Flower Show is organised by the Royal Horticultural Society and is held in the grounds of the Chelsea Hospital. Parking in the area is difficult, and entrance is not cheap. It may be possible for (w) to negotiate parking with the organisers (834-4333). A good time to go, to avoid the crowds, is first thing in the morning; or you could become a member of the Society and go to the preview day. It's a glorious show and **access is generally good**. Main entrance on the Embankment, with flat access. Paths are either tarmac or grass but there are some kerbs and gentle slopes. There are two well signposted portable **(w) loos**, not quite big enough for sideways transfer but very adequate. If you can cope with the crowds and want to see a fantastic flower show, this is the place to go. There are picnic areas, plenty of shade, and bands playing. Note that guide dogs are not allowed to go round, but the organisers can normally provide an escort if needed. Contact them in advance. *Late May*.

Trooping the Colour is the best known of several events held during the summer in Horse Guards Pde. Temporary stands built on scaffolding are erected around the square. Access is up **steps** and there are bench-type seats and few handrails. *Sat nearest 11 Jun*.

The other events include *Beating Retreat* by different regiments and a *Son et Lumière* production, 'The Heart of the Nation', organised by the Soldiers', Sailors' & Airmen's Families Association (SSAFA). The central contact for tickets is the Ticket Centre, 16 Bridge St SW1, opposite Big Ben (839-6815/6732). Disabled spectators for the military events should contact the HQ London District, Horse Guards, Whitehall SW1 (930-4466). For Trooping the Colour ask for the brigade major; (w) are normally admitted only to the rehearsal for this event. For Beating Retreat contact the public information office (PIO) (ext 2396 or 2357). The PIO can arrange for **(w) spaces** and for chairs to be put out at GF level for friends or for (s) if needed. For the Son et Lumière performance, the BO is at 27 Queen Anne's Gate SW1 (222-9228). They say that (w) can be accommodated but that chairs are not available for (s) or for (w) friends and escorts. We suggest that this may change if disabled people start to go to the performances and the difficulties are evident.

The Festival of the City of London consists mainly of concerts and exhibitions in various churches and halls, some of which aren't otherwise open to the public. The main BO is normally situated in St Paul's Churchyard EC4 at the top of Ludgate Hill (236-0451). Although most of the concerts and events take place in old buildings where there are steps (at one or two venues there are quite a lot of steps), the organisers say that they can help any (w) to get in, provided they know about it. The organiser we spoke to was very clued up and knew how many steps there were at most of the halls and where there was a lift to bypass them. If he didn't know precisely, he would find out. As they use different places each year, there is little point in giving too much detail here, but the kind of information you may want to know about some of the places used in 1982 is as follows: St Mary-le-Bow, 5 steps; Mansion House, up 2 steps (special entrance), lift; Guildhall Old Library, 10 steps; Baltic Exchange, 6 steps; Bishopsgate Hall, 2 steps; 10 Trinity Square, lift. We would rate this as being one of the easier arts events to get in to, because of the very helpful attitude taken by the organisers. *Jul*.

On August Bank Holiday there's a fair on Hampstead Heath NW3 (near North End Wy) and there are likely to be other fairs at other places on spring and summer bank holidays. See the local press and 'Time Out' or 'City Limits'.

The Promenade Concert season takes place at the Albert Hall during *Aug & Sept*. The famous 'last night of the Proms' is on the *Sat nearest 15 Sept*. *(See entry on Royal Albert Hall in 'Arts complexes' chapter.)*

Thamesday is a one-day event held on and around the river between Westminster and Hungerford Br. A viewing platform for disabled people and **(w) loos** are provided. *Sept*.

On Guy Fawkes' Night there are both private and public fireworks displays. All, generally, accessible. *5 Nov.*

The London to Brighton Veteran Car Rally starts at Hyde Park Corner. It commemorates the Anniversary of Emancipation and is an opportunity to see period costumes as well as cars. *First Sun in Nov.*

The Lord Mayor's Show is a large carnival-style procession through the City. The LTB can advise about the precise route. *Second Sat in Nov.*

Christmas decorations There are usually spectacular ones in Oxford St and Regent St, and traditionally a large Norwegian pine tree in Trafalgar Sq *during Dec.*

These are only a fraction of the events that take place every year. In general, provision for disabled spectators is now made at most events, and certainly things have improved. Sometimes you have to make enquiries and arrangements well in advance. Currently, (w) are perhaps better provided for than (s) in the sense that there are special arrangements made and enclosures at viewing points provided. A practical suggestion is for disabled people who can walk a bit but who find crowds and steps and distances a problem to use a wheelchair just occasionally, in order to go to the Proms, Beating Retreat or even to Wimbledon. It's not cheating and it might open up possibilities of getting around that you just hadn't thought of.

Year-round venues

Exhibitions and special events are held at various places in London throughout the year; we've listed the five main ones. Access provisions have improved considerably during the past few years, but for some exhibitions the problem is simply the number of people who want to go and therefore the parking problem outside and the difficulty of seeing, inside. Obviously, an off-peak visit (such as on a weekday morning) has its attractions, but not all disabled people and their friends can avoid the crowded peak periods and organisers need to take note of this. The responsibility for the use of the building lies with the exhibition or event organiser and not primarily with the building manager or owner. The user hires the hall lock, stock and barrel and decides how it shall be organised and used—and that includes the use of lifts, catering facilities and so on. The number of (w) admitted is at the discretion of the hall management and the event organiser.

Earl's Court and Olympia Ltd, Exhibition Centre, Warwick Rd SW5 (395-1200) produce a useful leaflet including plans of the halls for the disabled visitor. If you are thinking of visiting it is well worth getting hold of one; alternatively you can ask for one from the Traffic Office at Earl's Court or the appropriate main entrance at Olympia on arrival. The plans show the locations of the (w) loos and lifts as well as helping you find your way around.

The Barbican Exhibition Halls in Golden La EC1 (588-8211) have **flat/lift access everywhere and (w) loos**.

E0   🚻   ♿   ♿ wc

The Central Hall Westminster SW1 (222-7472) is sometimes used for exhibitions but has very poor access. *See 'Churches' chapter.*

Earls Court Warwick Rd SW5 (385-1200). Very limited CP for disabled drivers by hall manager's office. Cars with disabled passengers should use the public CP behind the building. There are 6+6 steps at the main Warwick Rd entrance and turnstiles. **An alternative entrance** will be opened by a staff member some 50m to the left of the main entrance and gate giving flat access. **Most of the hall is accessible** on the flat or by lift, though there are a few facilities (mainly unimportant) between floors and reached by stairs. The lifts are large. There's one to the left of the foyer and there are two lots on the perimeter wall on your right as you come in from the foyer. There are **(w) loos** on both the GF and 1st floor but they are not well signposted. There are plenty of accessible buffets, but the main restaurant areas are all up or down quite a number of steps and are without lift access. To get to level 2 you need lift 1 or 2 by the Warwick Rd entrance or lift 12 from the GF.

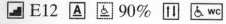 E12 [A] [&] 90% [¶1] [& wc]

Olympia Hammersmith Rd W14 (hall manager 603-3344). There is limited CP space, some of it on the other side of the railway line. By arrangement, ramp ambulances and special coaches may use the Blythe Rd yard for unloading. There are three main exhibition halls and sometimes different exhibitions in each. There are steps at both the main entrances, but **entrances without steps can be opened** by the staff for **(w)** visitors, if you ask. Having bypassed the steps at the entrance **virtually everything is flat**. There are **lifts and (w) loos** on the GF in the West Hall. In the Grand Hall there's a (w) loo in the Gents' only and currently none in the National Hall, though provision of a (w) loo there is under consideration. Buffets etc are generally accessible. For major shows there is a **(w) box** in a corner at 1st-floor level; it's also easy to transfer into certain balcony seats.

 E [A] [&] 90% [¶1] [& wc]

Wembley Conference Centre Wembley, Mddx (902-8833, BO 902-1234). Alongside Wembley Stadium. **Ramped access, basically very accessible, (w) loo on the GF.** (Note that if there's an event like NAIDEX, involving a lot of disabled people, you may have to queue for quite a while!) There are **eight (w) spaces** in the Grand Hall, made available by removing some seats in block 16. Access everywhere is by **large lifts**. You can get to the Greenwich Room on the lower GF only by a key-operated lift—ask one of the staff. There is parking outside the main entrance for (w) drivers. If you want full details, write in for the brochure mentioned above.

E0 [&] [¶1] [& wc]

The good loo guide

This section draws together the information on (w) loos, by which we mean specially converted or provided ones where it is possible to make a sideways transfer. Unfortunately, the biggest problem with (w) loos is not whether they're there or not, but whether they're open and where you have to go to get the key. It can be a frustrating business. In addition, some listings fail to distinguish between an ordinary cubicle with grab rails and a cubicle large enough for (w). Generally speaking, there are (w) loos at the main railway stations, at a number of major museums, a few expensive hotels, some major stores and in modern public complexes like the Barbican and South Bank. Access to the (w) loos in public toilets is frequently dependent on whether the attendant is there. We found, in fact, that something approaching a third of the loos listed here were locked at the time of the survey. In some cases we drew this to the attention of the management and found that they sometimes hadn't realised what a let-down this can be. It is therefore unfortunately impossible to give reliable information about opening times and availability here, since both may vary even from day to day. Where loos are locked, we hope that RADAR's National Key Scheme (*see below*) will be adopted so that keyholders can always get in. The other common problem is that because (w) loos are used less often than others, the cleaners or attendants use them as store cupboards and all too often you can only get at the toilet past a variety of buckets, brooms and cans of disinfectant!

As with other sections of the guide, most of the loos have been visited and measured by one of our survey teams or surveyors. Just a few have been included because we've been told about them by reliable sources. We've tried very hard to ensure that the information is correct, knowing how important it is, but with the best will in the world it's not possible to be absolutely accurate. The loos in central London are shown on the map, and a key follows. Adapted cubicles which are not proper (w) loos are indicated like this $\boxed{2}$. There's an additional list of those just outside the map area, and beyond this you will find (w) loos detailed in the text. All are either purpose-built or have had substantial modifications made. A few are in private buildings, or a private section of a building, but staff rarely turn away a (w) in need, provided they aren't disturbed too often.

Map key
W1

1   *Hilton Hotel* 22 Park La. Unisex. 3 steps at the entrance. On the 1st floor with lift access.

$\boxed{2}$ *May Fair Hotel* Stratton St. 1 step at entrance. Loos only in specially adapted bedrooms and therefore not available for general use. (We were originally told that there would be a unisex (w) loo.)

3   *Hamleys* Regent St. Unisex. On the 4th floor with lift access.

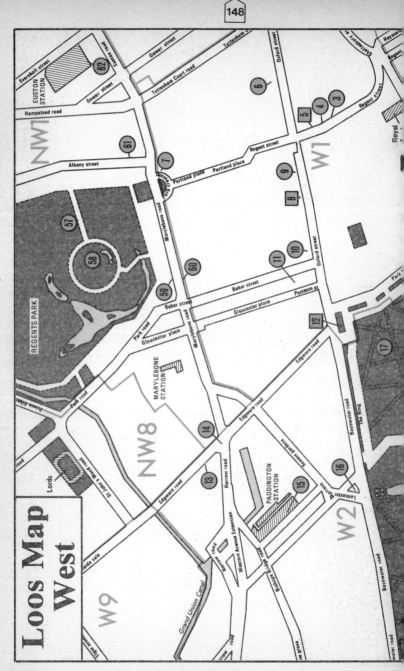

Loos Map
West

REGENTS PARK

MARYLEBONE STATION

PADDINGTON STATION

Lords

EUSTON STATION

NW1

NW8

NW9

W9

W1

W2

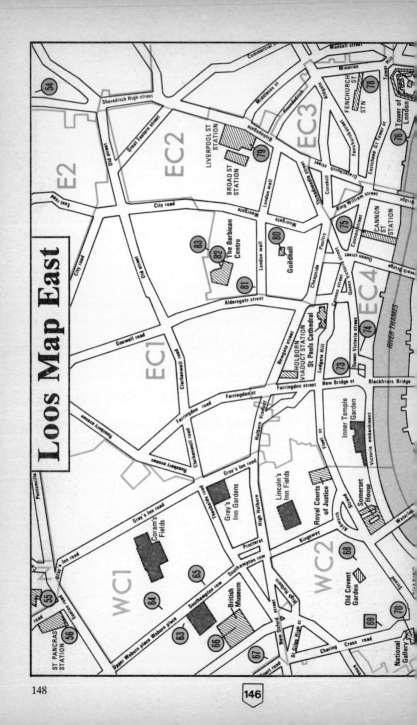

Loos Map East

4   *Liberty's* Regent St. Gents' staff loo in basement, with lift access. Ask a staff member. No rails, but sideways transfer possible.

⑤   *Dickins & Jones* Regent St. Ladies' only, on the 4th floor through the powder room. Has hand rails, but is too narrow for sideways transfer.

6   *New Berners Hotel* 10 Berners St. Unisex. On the lower GF with lift access.

7   *Spastics Society* 12 Park Cres. Unisex. In the basement via a lift. Ask at the desk.

⑧   *Debenhams* Oxford St. Ladies' has a special cubicle. Ordinary Gents' loo on the 3rd floor. Lift access.

9   *John Lewis* Oxford St. Unisex on the 2nd floor behind lifts. Go through the door marked 'Exit A', towards the stairs to Cavendish Sq; the loo is immediately on the left. Also note that *Marks & Spencer* between Oxford Circus and Tottenham Court Rd has a unisex (w) loo available.

10   *Selfridges* Oxford St. Unisex on the 3rd floor, with lift access. Also note that *Marks & Spencer* at Marble Arch has a unisex (w) loo available on request.

11   *Portman Intercontinental Hotel* 22 Portman Sq. Unisex on the 1st floor with lift access.

⑫   *Subway under Marble Arch* One in Gents', one in Ladies'. Ramped access. Doors open inwards and (w) need to remove foot plates to manoeuvre. Also note that a (w) loo is planned in the *Cumberland Hotel*.

W2

13   *London Metropole Hotel* Edgware Rd. Unisex on the GF. Ask at the desk.

14   *Subway under the junction of Edgware Rd and Westway* One in Gents', one in Ladies'.

15   *Paddington station* Eastbourne Ter. Unisex in the first aid room on platform 1.

16   *Royal Lancaster Hotel* Bayswater Rd. Unisex on the 1st floor, with lift access.

17   *Hyde Park* Approximately 400m north of the restaurant at the eastern end of the Serpentine. One in Gents', one in Ladies'. Attendant has the key.

18   *Hyde Park* Just south of Serpentine Gallery. Unisex.

W8

⑲   *Kensington Gardens* Opposite T-junction of Palace Gate and Kensington Rd in Flower Wlk. Ladies' only. Door opens inwards.

20   *Barkers* Kensington High St. One in Gents', one in Ladies', in basement by the gas showroom.

21   *Kensington Town Hall* Kensington High St. One in Gents', one in Ladies'. Entry by exit ramp to CP where Phillimore Wlk crosses Hornton St.

SW7

22   *London Penta Hotel* 97 Cromwell Rd. Unisex. On the mezzanine floor, with access via lift no 4.

㉓   *Baden-Powell Guest House* Queen's Gate. Specially adapted.

24   *Royal Albert Hall* Kensington Gore. Ramped access at door 14. Two unisex on the GF.

25 *Science Museum* Exhibition Rd. Unisex on the GF via ramp down to the stationary steam engine level, through exploration section, then ask. 1 step at entrance.
26 *Geological Museum* Exhibition Rd. *See 'Museums' chapter.*
27 *Natural History Museum* Cromwell Rd. *See 'Museums' chapter.*
28 *Victoria and Albert Museum* Cromwell Gdns. Entry is via the service road to the east of the museum. Enquire at the car checkpoint for directions to adapted unisex loo in room 16. Only front transfer possible. In the new Cole Wing, entrance in Exhibition Rd, there is flat/ramped access to (w) loos. *See 'Museums' chapter.*

SW3

29 *National Army Museum* Royal Hospital Rd. 3 shallow steps at entrance. Special loo on the GF near the bookshop.

SW1

30 *Peter Jones* Sloane Sq. Unisex on the 3rd floor with lift access. Near toys, opposite accounts desk alongside the lifts nearest to Sloane Sq.
31 *Harrods* Brompton Rd. Well adapted. Gents' on the 3rd floor, 64.5cm door—a couple of rails, but sideways transfer is not possible. Similar Ladies' on the 1st floor, plus one on the 4th floor with a 68cm door. Lift access. Provision of a unisex (w) loo on the 1st floor is planned.
32 *Victoria coach station* By bay 23. Key at station office. Unisex. Kerb.
33 *Victoria station* Buckingham Palace Rd. Unisex, by Ladies' loo. Unlocked by the attendant.
34 *Army & Navy stores* Victoria St. Unisex on the 2nd floor, with lift access.
35 *Queen Mother Centre* Vauxhall Bridge Rd. Flat access.
36 *Grosvenor Road Gardens* Opposite St Georges's Sq. One in Gents', one in Ladies'. Sanitary towel incinerator makes sideways transfer difficult in latter.
37 *Tate Gallery* Millbank. Flat entry via Atterbury St. One in Gents', one in Ladies', and one unisex. Gents' too narrow for sideways transfer.
38 *St James's Park* The Mall. One in Gents', one in Ladies'. Should be unlocked, even when the attendant is not around.
39 *Crafts Council Gallery* 12 Waterloo Pl. Flat access.
40 *Westminster Pier* Victoria Embankment. One in Gents', one in Ladies'. Entrance very near the bridge, from the low-level walkway accessed from the Embankment to the east.

SE1

41 *County Hall* Belvedere Rd. Unisex. Ask at the desk.
42 *Imperial War Museum* Lambeth Rd. Unisex on upper level near the (w) lift. *See 'Museums' chapter.*
43 *Lower Marsh* Lancelot St. Unisex.
44 *Waterloo station* Unisex (w) loo off the Ladies' waiting room has RADAR key scheme lock. Key can be got from the area manager's office (at the other end of the station).
45 *Royal Festival Hall* Belvedere Rd. Unisex on the GF. Turn right after going through the glass doors. Difficult entrance doors.

46 *Hayward Gallery* Belvedere Rd. Access by lift to level 1 of National Theatre, then walking under Waterloo Br to the gallery. Toilets in staff area.

47 *Queen Elizabeth Hall* Belvedere Rd. Unisex. Take artists entry to south of National Film Theatre. Ask attendant.

48 *National Film Theatre* Belvedere Rd. Unisex. Flat access on restaurant level. Narrowest door 68.5cm, so slightly awkward access, and a handrail blocks sideways transfer.

49 *National Theatre* Waterloo Br. Unisex, off the corridor leading to the Ladies' on the GF.

50 *London Bridge station* Tooley St. Unisex. Key available from attendant in Ladies'.

51 *London Dungeon* Tooley St. Ladies' only.

52 *Tower Bridge Museum* Unisex. Big kerb.

E1

53 *Tower Hotel* St Katherine's Wy. Unisex. 2 steps at entrance or use the separate ramped baggage entrance. Loo on the 1st floor.

E2

54 *Geffrye Museum* Kingsland Rd. 3 steps (or alternatively 1) at entrance. (w) loo in Gents'.

N1

55 *Kings Cross station* York Wy. Unisex. For attendant, press the bell at the top of the steps down to the Ladies'.

NW1

56 *St Pancras station* Euston Rd. In the first aid centre beyond the ticket barrier on platform 7. Ask at the station supervisor's office next to platform 1.

57 *Regent's Park* Chester Rd. One in Ladies', one in Gents'.

58 *Regent's Park* Inner Circle. Gents' only.

59 *Madame Tussaud's* Marylebone Rd. Unisex loo on the GF. *See 'Museums' chapter.*

60 *Opposite Madame Tussaud's* Marylebone Rd. Unisex. Attendant has key.

61 *The White House* Albany St. 3+3 steps at entrance. Specially adapted unisex loo on the GF.

62 *Euston station* Euston Sq. On the east side of the station concourse past the platform entrances. Unisex. If locked, ask a staff member for the key.

WC1

63 *The Royal National Hotel* Bedford Wy. Specially adapted Gents' and Ladies' on the GF with 77cm cubicle doors. Access by lift from CP, or 1 step at entrance.

64 *Bloomsbury Crest Hotel* Coram St. Specially adapted loo in the Ladies' on the GF.

65 *Bonnington Hotel* 92 Southampton Row. Specially adapted unisex loo on the 1st floor with lift access.

66 *British Museum* Great Russell St. Two unisex loos on the GF: one off room 25, the other on the left, past the bookstall. Entry by a staff-activated lift to the left of main steps.

67 *YMCA* 112 Great Russell St. In the basement. Ask at the desk for access.

WC2

68 *London Transport Museum* 39 Wellington St. One in Gents', one in Ladies'. Free admittance for (w). Flat. Also note nearby alternative in *National Jazz Centre*.

69 *Duke of York's Theatre* St Martin's La. Flat access to theatre; (w) loo on Royal Circle level but sideways transfer not possible.

70 *National Gallery* Trafalgar Sq. Flat access in Orange St. One in Gents', one in Ladies' near this entrance.

71 *Charing Cross station* Strand. Opposite ticket sales booth—press the button and the ticket seller opens the door using an entryphone.

72 *Victoria Embankment* By Embankment tube. One in Gents' (used as a storage area, but attendant will clear it), one in Ladies'.

EC4

73 *Blackfriars station* Queen Victoria St. Next to platform 1, with lift access.

74 *Mermaid Theatre* Puddle Dock. Unisex on the GF, along passageway to the left of the bar. Easy access.

75 *Cannon Street station* Cannon St. Access by lift.

EC3

76 *Tower Hill Precinct* Tower Hill. Unisex. Near escalator, on GF. Press bell for attendant to come and unlock it.

77 *Tower of London* Tower Hill. Unisex. Near the Bowyer Tower close to the main entrance.

78 *Subway between Tower Hill tube and the Tower of London* under Tower Hill Rd. Unisex. Attendant has key.

EC2

79 *Liverpool Street station* Unisex, in first aid room. Access by ramp to Underground at the west side of the station. Key kept in the booking or enquiry office.

80 *Guildhall* Guildhall Yd. Unisex, in the offices above Watch Museum. Not strictly for the public, but can be used if you ask.

81 *Museum of London* London Wall. Two (w) loos: one on the coffee shop level (access via the keyed lift), and the other near the Lord Mayor's Coach on the GF.

82   *The Barbican* Silk St. There are unisex (w) loos on Levels 1, 4, 7 and 9. *See 'Arts complexes' chapter.*

EC1

83   *Whitbread Brewery* Chiswell St. Unisex (w) loo in the building across the courtyard, which used to house the Overlord Embroidery.

Other (w) loos within the map area include: the Ivanhoe Hotel; RADAR, 25 Mortimer St W1; the Spinal Injuries Association, 5 Crowndale Rd SW1; and the Piccadilly Trocadero Development (due to be opened shortly).

Loos outside the map area

North London

London Zoo, Regent's Pk NW1. Two loos.
Holiday Inn, King Henry's Rd NW3.
King's Fund Centre, 126 Albert St NW1.

South London

Battersea Park, Battersea SW11.

South-west London

West Centre Hotel, 47 Lillie Rd SW6.

West London

London Tara Hotel, Wright's La W8.
Commonwealth Institute, Kensington High St W8.
Disabled Living Foundation, 346 Kensington High St W14.
Cunard International Hotel, Shortlands W6.
Westbourne Grove W2.
Portobello Road W11.
Ladbroke Grove W11.

RADAR's National Key Scheme (NKS)

The National Key Scheme for toilets for disabled people has grown considerably in recent years. The key currently costs £2.00 from RADAR and we would like to recommend the scheme to local authorities and other organisations. We would also stress that (w) loos should always be left open wherever possible, although we understand that some places are subject to vandalism and damage and it may be necessary to lock them. If that is so, there should be a standard lock so that keyholders can gain access.

Further afield

Chessington Zoo Leatherhead Rd, Chessington, Surrey (Epsom (78) 27227). Small, compact out-of-town zoo with a funfair, miniature train and circus (circus free and accessible). Good CP. **Flat access everywhere**, although slightly hilly. Paths are mainly tarmac'd. Shop, 1 step. Maps and plans available. There's a **(w) loo** near the café in the centre of the site. **Recommended.**

P H 🚻 🚻 wc

Chislehurst Caves Chislehurst, Kent (467-3264). These are an extraordinary complex, cut through chalk. Remains include part of an Ichthyosaurus fossil, an area associated with the Druids and the remains left when the caves became an air-raid shelter during World War II. CP with narrowish entry 50m away; BR station about 200m away. Note that even the short tour will take you something approaching 1km, and there are no seats. Ticket booth has 2 steps. Inside, the caves are cool (always 45°F) but **access is flat**, although the surface is quite **rough and bumpy**. Even the hardiest (w) would need a good pusher and it's even advisable to take a torch. The long tour isn't really practicable for either (w) or (s), as you have to crawl part of the way. A **(w) loo** is signposted near Chislehurst Library (on the RHS as you take the A208 from the caves towards London). There is also a small, cramped tea room at the caves. It makes a fascinating visit and disabled visitors are welcomed.

P ⊟ D 🚻

Guildford Cathedral Guildford, Surrey (Guildford (0483) 37446). Parking outside but up to 100m to walk. The main entrance has been **ramped** but is not always open; the side entrance has 2/3 steps. Thereafter **flat access** to most areas, including café and loos on the left. There is a **(w) loo** in both Ladies' and Gents'.

P 🔳 E3 A 🚻 80% 🚻 wc

Hampton Court East Molesey, Surrey (977-8441). A large historic riverside palace, with extensive gardens. CP outside and there are also special (w) places opposite the police entrance, about 75m from the entrance to the palace. Hampton Court station (Southern Region) is about 400m from the entrance across the bridge and there are frequent trains to Waterloo. Flat access to platforms but 2 steps from the road into the station. Alternatively, you could come by riverboat from Richmond or Kingston, but there are 12 steps to one pier and the other one is reached by a steep, bumpy track. Once there, **access is generally flat**. Slightly bumpy surfaces here and there.
Café is up 1 step.
Care of Buildings exhibition involves 1 step to the GF, but about half the exhibits are on the 1st floor.
King's Private Apartments are accessible via 1+1 steps.
The Kitchens are on the GF with virtually flat access.

Loos There is a **(w) loo** near the ticket sales area and loos with adapted cubicles (not quite (w) loos) by Laburnum Wlk to the north-east of Wilderness Gdns.

The Maze is flat but rough and the paths are narrow.

The Palace The route through the courtyard is flat but rough in places. The ticket office is about 75m from the entrance. As at other Department of the Environment sites, the (w) pays for entrance but his or her friend/escort doesn't.

Real Tennis Court involves −1 step and a tight 90° turn.

State Apartments Normal access is via 34 steps and then exit via −24 steps from the Great Hall, but a lift was under construction at the time of the survey towards the north-eastern end of the palace and should be operating by now. There is a small alternative lift from Fountain Ct. **You will have to ask if you want to use either lift.** Once upstairs, the majority of the rooms are flat and there are only minor hassles, but it's a big place—about 400/500m all the way round.

Tiltyard restaurant 1 step.

The Vine has flat access.

All in all, this is a possible place for a day's visit complete with picnic. Signposting is generally good but it's advisable to get a plan as well. **Recommended.**

P ⊟ D ☒ 80% ⬍ ☒ wc

Hatfield House Hatfield, Herts (Hatfield (30) 62823). Very adequate parking. Hatfield BR station is about 2km away. The entrance involves 15 steps, then there are 25 steps to the 1st floor but there is a **lift** (D 80cm) from the bottom of the Grand Staircase to bypass these. The grounds and garden are nearly all on the same level. There's a café up 1 step and a small shop −1 step, both situated in Palace Yd. There are **(w) loos** in the courtyard. The normal guided tour lasts about an hour.

P ▣ E15 ☒ ⬍ ☒ wc

The Old Palace (Hatfield (30) 62055) is nearby. Elizabethan banquets are held here. In our researches we found this to be the only truly accessible venue near London for this type of thing. Dress is fairly formal and the banquets are not cheap—nor are they suitable for young children. They are hosted by 'Good Queen Bess' accompanied by her court and, of course, her jester. There is **flat access** via a door in the tower and all seats are movable. It is important to **mention your disability when booking** to ensure that the flat access route is unlocked and the (w) loos are left open. Be sure to arrive in good time, too, to avoid the rush. Special diets can be catered for. The **(w) loos** in the courtyard are about 150m away.

P ▣A ☒ ☒ wc

Knole House Near Sevenoaks, Kent (Sevenoaks (0732) 450608). A really large 15thC house. Entrance is off Sevenoaks High St and is well signposted. The main exhibits are on the 1st floor up 25 steps and there are further split levels, so it's not really suitable for disabled visitors. There are also steps to the loos.

P ▣

Leeds Castle Near Maidstone, Kent (Maidstone (0622) 65400). An interesting place to visit. The setting is lovely and the owners have gone to some trouble to improve accessibility. We found the staff most helpful. Large CP outside the main entrance, about 400m from the castle. There's transport provided but this involves 4 steps and a narrow entrance and is not easy for (w)—it's probably easier to wheel down the tarmac road.

The castle Go across the Inner Bailey and, for (w), enter through the **exit** door. Ask one of the guides, as this route cuts out a considerable number of steps. The guide will take you to the tour starting point. The GF has been made accessible by the use of a **platform chair lift**. The upper floor is accessible only up stairs but there's quite a lot to see on the GF. At the end of the tour a guide can open a door to give **flat access** to the final four rooms and the exit.

The grounds There are **occasional steps and slopes**. The Duckery has an artificial lake with a wooden walkway. The shop and restaurant are about 150m from the drawbridge up a slope. There is **flat access to the shop and the restaurant**, in both cases through an exit. There are tables and chairs outside the restaurant as well, and **(w) loos** just past the restaurant.

P 🖂 D A ⬛ N ♿ 80% ♿wc ♿X

Mapledurham House Mapledurham, near Reading, Berks (Reading (0734) 723350). CP by watermill some 300m from the house. Disabled visitors can drive up to the house if they ask permission. **The entrance has 1+3+2 steps.** GF is accessible but the two upper floors are up about 24 steps each. Chapel is −2 steps from the GF. Loos with ordinary cubicles: Ladies' 1+5 steps; Gents' 1+5+14 steps. The watermill has **flat access to the GF** area (rather rough surface) but the 13 steps inside are very steep. Disabled visitors may use the 'down only' exit stairs for access to the 1st floor, as they are somewhat easier.

The estate also has a number of holiday cottages, two of which have GF facilities and are suitable for families with disabled members.

P 🖂 ⬛ E6 ♿ 40%

Runnymede Windsor Rd, Old Windsor, Berks. The area of meadow down by the River Thames where King John signed the Magna Carta, which became the foundation of our liberties, in 1215. There's a CP on the river side of the meadows and a café in one of the lodge gates. Although there are 4 steps into the café, the management plan to have a (rather steep) temporary ramp available. There are adapted cubicles in the loos round the back of the café.

The Commonwealth Air Forces Memorial is towards the top of Coopers Hill, overlooking Runnymede. A visit can be memorable because of the cool simplicity of the architecture and the beauty of the setting. There's a CP and then about 400m along level roadway to the memorial. Vehicles with orange badges may park near the memorial itself but the road is quite narrow. Access is via 2 steps (although a ramp can be provided if you ring Egham (87) 33329 first). There are spiral staircases leading up to the tower. There are ordinary loos only, with 1 step, near the CP.

P 🖂 H D ♿

St Albans Cathedral St Albans, Herts (St Albans (56) 52120). The abbey church can be approached from three directions. One, for pedestrians only, is via the Waxhouse gate which is off the High St opposite the clock tower. This route brings you by a gentle slope over a paved path to the north side; (w) then go to the left (east) around the end of the abbey to the large cedar tree, where there is **flat access. Should the door be locked, ring the bell.** Just inside the door there are normally two wheelchairs that can be used by (s) if needed. The second way in is from Holywell Hill into Sumpters Yd, where there is limited parking; this brings you close to the cedar tree and the (w) entrance. The third route is by way of George St and

Romeland, where there is a small CP. This way leads to the west entrance, where there are 2+5 steps.

The south side of the abbey has **ramps** for all levels except to the west doorway. Chairs are movable to give room for wheelchairs to pass from south to north. There is 1 step from the Choir to the base of the Tower. The shop area has 2 steps. There is **wheelchair access** to the Saints Chapel. If you ask, a guide will be very pleased to take you around and give you all the history of the various parts of the abbey.

The nearest (w) loos are about 200m from the abbey by the lakes in the park at the south side of the abbey, but there will be one in the abbey shortly.

P ◨ E7 Ⓐ ♿ 80% U

Stratfield Saye House Between Reading and Basingstoke off A33 (Basingstoke (0256) 882882). Parking outside the house. **Flat almost everywhere**. About 200m to go all round. There is a **(w) loo** (no handrails when surveyed) near the pay kiosk. There is also a *wildlife sanctuary* nearby, but this involves quite a walk/push over gravel and grass. Basically accessible and the staff were helpful, and the Wellington exhibition, RNLI exhibition and snack bar near the house are all accessible. **Recommended.**

P E0 ♿   ♿ wc

Thorpe Park On the A320 Staines/Chertsey alongside the M3 (Chertsey (09328) 62633). A wide variety of activities in a recreational park and amusements area built around a lake. There's entertainment galore for children—models, round-abouts, exhibitions, aircraft, boating—but a visit is not cheap. The whole complex is large, covering some 200 hectares. There are maps available. There is a CP just off the A320. **The area is flat** and most of the paths are tarmac'd. The majority of the facilities are accessible and the staff are helpful wherever possible. **There are two unisex (w) loos** at opposite ends of the park, one near Thorpe Farm and the other in the Mountbatten Pavilion.

P D ♿   ♿ wc

Verulamium St Albans, Herts (St Albans (56) 54659). The Verulamium site is **very large but basically flat/ramped**. It is reached by car via George St and Fishpool St, or about a 20-minute walk along the lake from the cathedral (*see above*). The footpath is well signposted and there is a CP about 50m from the site. There is a **ramped entrance** to the museum, which can be opened if you ask. Inside there are really no obstructions and all the exhibits can be seen easily.

P ♿

The Vyne Sherborne St John, near Basingstoke, Hants (Basingstoke (0256) 881337). CP 100m, but cars can be taken to the entrance by prior arrangement. There are **2 steps** to the main part of the GF and a further 25 to the upstairs rooms. **A wheelchair is available for use.** Refreshments in the Old Brew House, 120m away along a gravelled path—difficult for (w). Flat access. Ordinary loos adjacent to the tea rooms.

P ◨ E2N25 ♿ 50% U

Whipsnade Zoo Whipsnade, Herts (Whipsnade (0582) 872171). Whipsnade is enormous, covering an area of about 2.5 sq km. Because of its size, the paddocks and cages are much larger than those at London Zoo or Chessington, and the whole feeling is more relaxed. On the other hand, there's considerably further to drive, walk or wheel in order to see things. The zoo is on the edge of the Chiltern Hills and there are magnificent views. The entrance fee is not cheap, so it's worth making it a whole day's outing.

There's a big CP opposite the main entrance but if you wish **you can take your car in and drive around** the main circuit (about 3km). There are places to stop and park inside and if you go off-peak it will obviously be easier. Many of the animals can be seen from the road or tarmac paths. There are a few rough and hilly paths, difficult if it's just been raining; to get to some places (w) would need a strong pusher. Also, there are no handrails to help (s). It's a good idea to get a map of the site and a guide book.

Children's zoo is fairly accessible.
Cloisters cafeteria has 1 step and movable chairs.
The first aid post has oddly poor access: 2 steps one way, 3 the other.
Loos There's a **(w) loo** in both the Ladies' and Gents' near the main entrance. Other toilets with ordinary cubicles are marked on the maps available.
The shop by the main entrance has 1 step.
The train has coaches with narrow 50cm doors and so is unsuitable for (w). There is, however, a special coach which can take three (w) if booked in advance.
The Tree Cathedral is about 1km away on the other side of the common. It's a National Trust property with access up level but roughish tracks and paths. The layout is that of a conventional cathedral but it consists entirely of grass and trees. There is a Christmas Chapel with fir trees, Easter Chapel with trees that flower at that time of year, and so on.

P H D ♿ 80% ♿ WC

Windsor Castle Windsor, Berks (Windsor (95) 68286). A great 'out of London' draw for visitors. By car it is some 50km from London. Alternatively you can take a Southern Region BR train to Windsor Riverside, a station with flat access but situated at the bottom of Castle Hill (and it is a hill); or take a Western Region train to Windsor Central, which is higher up the hill and nearer to the castle, but you have to change at Slough. For minimum effort, travel by fast train to Slough, cross the platform for the Windsor train, see Windsor—ending up by the river—and take the Southern Region train back to Waterloo. 'A Disabled Person's Guide to Windsor', prepared by the Bracknell Action Group for the Physically Handicapped, is available from Windsor tourist office.

Parking in the vicinity of the castle is very difficult, but **access is generally fairly good although it is hilly**. To see most of it you have to go about 400/500m from the top of Castle Hill. There is a stretch of cobbles by the main gate, but most of the paths are then tarmac'd.

The Albert Memorial Chapel can be approached from the main path, on the level. There are two pairs of steps inside; avoid them by ignoring the one-way system.
Bookstalls Access to the one by the main gate is poor, but there is another one just past the Round Tower, where there is only 1 step.
Loos There is a **(w) loo** in Engine Ct—the key is available at the side door opposite—and another in the new King Edward shopping centre, opposite Waitrose by the entrance to the CP on the upper level. The latter is open only during *normal shopping hours*. There is an unusual system of a tall turnstile to get into the toilets but there is a bell outside that you can use to call an attendant.

St George's Chapel is up 2+1 steps and there is a movable turnstile or **flat access** from the north entrance. Inside, the Nave is flat but there are 2+1 steps to the Chancel and 3+1 to the Ambulatory.

State Apartments Access is difficult for (w) but there is a **small lift** inside the building near the Round Tower, up 3 steps. Once on the 1st floor, access is flat but (w) are admitted at the discretion of the head warder, so try to arrive at an off-peak time. The normal entrances to the State Apartments, the Dolls House and the Old Masters Paintings involve about 30 steps.

Eton College Chapel is nearby (about 1km on foot, but considerably further by car). Gravelled or cobbled access to the front entrance, where there is a stairway with 5+7+5+2 17cm steps and a handrail. After that, only 1 step in the main body of the chapel. Parking in the road, followed by about a 200m walk. The general area of Eton College School is flat, and this is well worth a visit. Visiting is curtailed during the school term, though, and there are some rough surfaces.

Royalty & Railways is a new Madame Tussauds exhibition in Windsor Central station. **Accessible throughout**; wardens will show you the way. A steep temporary ramp gets you into the theatre, where there is a good audio-visual show, and there's a (w) **loo**. The refreshment area in the BR station is flat.

E0 ⬛ ⬛ wc ⬛ ✕

Windsor Safari Park Windsor, Berks (Windsor (95) 69841). About 3km out of the town on the B3022. You can drive through the wild animal reserves—with your windows tightly closed! In the middle is a steep hill but there is parking at the top near the Dolphinarium and refreshment facilities. There are (w) **loos** in the Safari Lodge restaurant and also behind the Dolphinarium.

H D ⬛ 80% ⬛ wc

Wisley Gardens 40km from London off A3 near Ripley, Surrey (Ripley (048643) 2163—information—or 2235—office). CP with reserved spaces for (w) near the entrance. The loos in the CP have (w) cubicles but sideways transfer is not quite possible. **There are wheelchairs to be borrowed** (16 with small back wheels and two with large) and four Batricars (electric buggies). It's advisable to book to ensure they're available. The Batricars are an excellent idea and it would be great to see this provision elsewhere.

Over half the gardens are readily (w) accessible and a map is available to be used in conjunction with the 'Wisley Guide', showing (w) routes. The map is essential to supplement the signs. There's a special Garden for Disabled People and (w) **loos** nearby. There is a variety of surfaces to cope with; broadly speaking, the northern part of the gardens is fairly flat while the southern part is hilly. Most (w) will need a pusher. It's not a bad idea to do the hilly bit first and then trundle gently down towards the restaurant.

Café Steep ramp and 2 steps, but you can use the verandah outside.
Glasshouses A longish push up but flat access in.
Restaurant Steep ramp and 1 step.

P H D E0 ⬛ 60% U

Tailpiece

This Guide has been written in order to make it easier for people to get around in London and we hope that it will be useful in doing that. We've tried to be constructive and have, in fact, played down some of the comments and criticisms made by the various survey teams. For the disabled person, knowing that he or she wants to go somewhere or do something and can surmount the barriers (be they minor or major), it is immensely frustrating to find that he or she is in fact excluded from that activity.

The barriers to access fall into two general categories. First, there are the geographical and historical barriers and second, there are those associated with people's perceptions and attitudes. We readily recognise that London is a big place, that most of its buildings and services were built long before the needs of either (w) or (s) were thought of, let alone taken into account, and that it is a busy and congested place. We also recognise that on a personal and individual basis and sometimes on an organisational basis, people can be helpful and sensitive and sensible. However our surveyors often encountered patronising attitudes and all too often the 'Does He Take Sugar?' syndrome. We also found an over-zealous attention to safety, which on the surface no doubt seemed perfectly reasonable to the committee or individual responsible. Unfortunately, it is all too easy to be unresponsive to individual needs and rights and any committee or organisation responsible for public safety is likely to have as a first priority the need to 'cover themselves' in the event of any aberration or disaster, however unlikely.

It is important that there is a wide understanding of the whole concept of risk. Of course there should be regulations about fire exits and so forth, since these are in everyone's interests. However, all activities involve risk, including cooking, working and crossing the road. The question is simply what is an acceptable degree of risk. On the whole, disabled people have to accept a higher level of risk than their (ab) counterparts and, in order to enable them to live a normal life, the able-bodied population must accept a slight increase in the levels of both inconvenience and risk. Acceptance of the implications of this is coming, slowly. Disabled people know that safety is important, but a new approach is needed. What is necessary is that disabled people should be encouraged to make their own decisions about the risks they take, as everyone else does. Oddly enough, both disabled people and their friends are basically quite sensible.

The authors and survey teams would like to make a strong plea to those responsible for all kinds of facilities and buildings that:

- Modifications are made where sensibly possible to facilitate access by the independent (w) or (s).
- If visitors can get in without assistance from the staff (ie a disabled person with friends) and without causing inordinate obstruction to others, they should be allowed in.

There is no logic in excluding (by regulation) a (w) with a couple of strong friends who can get anywhere, in or out, speedily and easily and allowing in an epileptic, a

161

person with a chronically weak heart or someone weighing 25 stone who can only move very slowly. The problem is simply that the (w) can be identified and categorised. Authorities can righteously ensure that public safety is being looked after, when in fact some decisions are unfairly discriminatory against (w) and do not recognise their right to participate in every aspect of life, even if this does involve a slightly higher element of risk for everyone.

We would like to make some constructive suggestions about improvements, all of which arise from the survey carried out in London. In the diagram we have highlighted some of the criteria which should be used in order to take the needs of disabled people into account. The dimensions of an average wheelchair and things like eyeline and reach are indicated. The figures given are generalised ones, but the principles involved are important. The basic requirements of kerb ramping and of ramps are detailed, also the necessary corridor width for (s). Clearly, there are many other factors to be taken into account and Selwyn Goldsmith's 'Designing for the Disabled' is one of the best books available on the subject. There was considerable progress during IYDP (The International Year of the Disabled Person) in 1981 and our survey highlighted some of the progress made as a result of efforts to publicise needs. Many modifications have been made to old buildings to ease and facilitate access and the attitude towards disabled people has undoubtedly changed dramatically over the past ten years or so. Much, however, remains to be done.

In terms of London, the things that we believe to be most important for disabled people are:

- The provision of many, many more ramped kerbs; we also welcome the project testing ramped kerbs with a textured surface to help visually handicapped people.
- The provision of unisex (w) loos available in the evening near the key tourist/visitor areas like Westminster, Leicester Sq and Oxford St and near restaurant areas, since virtually no restaurants or pubs have loos that are even remotely accessible.
- An improvement in the signposting of facilities. Too often, good facilities weren't properly indicated.
- The acceptance of the principle that if you can manage without help, or with the help you bring with you, you'll be allowed in anywhere.
- Modifications to existing buildings to facilitate access. Often these are relatively minor and inexpensive.
- The extension of Dial-a-Ride schemes and subsidised taxi fares, and the development of an integrated transport and parking facility for both disabled residents and visitors.
- The development of the RADAR National Key Scheme for (w) loos.
- The provision of (w) spaces in more theatres and cinemas by making a small block of seats removable.
- The availability at information desks, box offices and similar enquiry points of a leaflet giving basic access details such as local parking, distances, the number of steps, details of toilets, lift sizes and the like. At the moment, the amount of misinformation is frightening.
- Good planning: all new developments and modifications to existing buildings should include good access facilities for disabled visitors and users.

It should be noted that there is limited grant aid available from various sources to help with adaptations and alterations to buildings. For example, if you have a disabled employee, you can get funding for modifications to toilets and other facilities and for the provision of ramps and handrails if needed. Facilities for an

Design Criteria

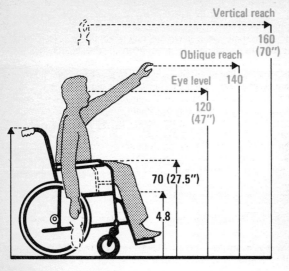

Vertical reach
160 (70")

Oblique reach
140

Eye level

120 (47")

70 (27.5")

4.8

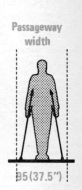

Passageway
width

95 (37.5")

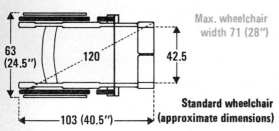

Max. wheelchair
width 71 (28")

63 (24.5")

120

42.5

103 (40.5")

Standard wheelchair (approximate dimensions)

Dimensions in
cm and (inches)

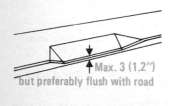

Max. 3 (1.2")
but preferably flush with road

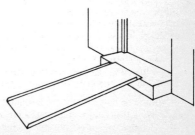

Ramped kerbs and ramps
Max. gradient for short ramps 1:8. Longer ramps 1:12 to 1:20.

employee can frequently be used also by a visitor. In addition, there is a limited amount of grant aid available for the tourist and leisure industries; for example, to make modifications for disabled people in serviced accommodation. The level of grant here would be currently in the range of 20%–30% of the capital cost. Further details from The Manager, Resource Development, English Tourist Board (730-3450 ext 234). No doubt, as time goes by there may be other sources of help; organisations such as GLAD, RADAR and the LTB should be able to advise.

In the Disabled Persons Act 1981 Section 6, the Government strengthened the provisions of earlier legislation, making it a requirement that developers make 'adequate provision' for the needs of disabled people. It is important that the implementation of this Act be encouraged and both CEH and RADAR will be interested to hear from people about whether it has been effective in improving facilities, provisions and ease of access.

We have already started the survey work for the second edition. We are all too aware of the fact that some information needs further checking, that some sections need to be expanded and that things will change. We will survey more music venues and pubs, for example, and will continue the search for cheap and accessible hotels. If you have comments or ideas and more particularly if you would like to send us accurate and comprehensive survey data for inclusion next time, we'll be delighted to hear from you. Survey data must cover parking, access barriers such as bumpy surfaces, steps, provision of handrails, lift and loo sizes. Sketches showing the location and layout of the building, and of the loos, are invaluable. Measurements must be accurate. Long distances should be paced out or measured on a map. Wrong or inaccurate information is worse than useless. A check list is given below; the main thing is to bear in mind people's various disabilities.

Survey checklist

- Date.
- Name and address of surveyor(s).
- Name, address and telephone number of building or site (attach location map if possible).
- Parking facilities/possibilities.
- Are there steps at the main entrance? How many? Handrails? If steps, is there an alternative flat/lift entrance into the building? If so, give details.
- Once in, is there flat/ramped/lift access? To what proportion of the building? 100% (ie everywhere)? If not, estimate percentage.
- Lift? Where is it? Where does it go? How big is it? (Measurements are important.)
- Are there steps inside the building? Define.
- Loos? Where are they? How big? Is there a (w) loo allowing for sideways transfer?
- Are there narrow doors or gaps?
- Are there bumpy/rough surfaces?
- Are wheelchairs available for use?
- Is the signposting of facilities good, both inside and outside the building?
- Please comment on the suitability of the site/place for electric (w), self-propelled (w), (s), elderly persons who can't walk far, the partially sighted and those who are partially or totally deaf.

Please send survey information to Pauline Hephaistos Survey Projects, 39 Bradley Gdns W13.

Symbols & abbreviations
Symbole & Abkürzungen
Symboles & abréviations

English

Symbols

P	Off-street parking attached to the building or very nearby
▭	Bumpy/rough surface(s)
H	Hilly
D	Long distances involved
▣	Steps
E	Entrance. E3 or E1+1 etc indicate the number of steps at the main entrance. If there are two or more entrances, they are indicated like this: E2/5
E0	Flat main entrance
Ⓐ	There is an alternative flat/ramped/lift entrance
N	Inside. Where numbers are added, they indicate the number of steps upwards or downwards from the GF
♿	Flat/ramped/lift access almost everywhere, after surmounting any steps at the entrance
♿	Flat/ramped/lift access to part of the building or area after surmounting any steps at the entrance. The percentage figure, where used, indicates to how much of it
↑↓	Lift. Dimensions are normally given in the text
♿ wc	(w) loo (ie special toilet provision, normally meaning that sideways transfer is possible)
♿)	Telephone at a suitable height for (w)
♿ X	Café or restaurant accessible to (w)
▐▌	Narrow doors or gaps, eg between displays
(?)	Special facilities for the hard of hearing, eg induction loop
◉	Special facilities and/or exhibitions for the partially sighted
🦮	Guide dogs accepted
U	Wheelchair(s) available

NB Steps indicated by a number alone or with a plus sign (+) run upwards; those indicated by a number with a minus sign (−) run downwards; thus 2+3 indicates 2 steps upwards, a gap, then 3 more steps upwards.

In the chapters on theatres and cinemas, the letters A, B and C are used to indicate who may be admitted, following the GLC categorisation:

A is for (s) or those (w) who can walk a little (ie into the auditorium);

B is for (w) who cannot be transferred to an ordinary seat, and who therefore need to stay in the chair during the performance;

C is for (w) who can transfer or be transferred to an ordinary seat, so that the wheelchair can be taken out of the auditorium.

Throughout the guide an indication of price is given by the following signs:

£	Inexpensive
££	Moderately priced
£££	Quite expensive
££££	Very expensive

Abbreviations

(ab)	Able-bodied person	**M**	Manager/management
BO	Box office	**m**	metres
cm	Centimetres	**MSCP**	Multi-storey car park
CP	Car park	**NCP**	National Car Park(s)
cub	Cubicle	**RHS**	Right-hand side
D	Door (usually of a lift)	**(s)**	Stick user(s) or handicapped walker(s)
eg	For example		
ext	Extension number	**SAE**	Stamped self-addressed envelope
GF	Ground floor		
GFB	Ground-floor bedroom	**UGCP**	Underground car park
km	Kilometres	**W**	Width (usually of a lift)
L	Length (usually of a lift)	**(w)**	Wheelchair user(s)
LHS	Left-hand side		

Deutsch

Um Ihnen die Möglichkeit zu geben, sich schnell und exakt einen Überblick über das vorhandene Angebot zu verschaffen, haben wir in diesem Führer Symbole benutzt, die nachstehend genau erklärt werden. Wir hoffen, daß diese Symbole bald auch in herkömmlichen Führern verwendet werden.

Die Zeichenerklärungen wurden für acht Kapitel angewandt. Im Kapitel 'Übernachtungsmöglichkeiten' ('*Accommodation*') erleichtert die tabellarische Übersicht ein schnelles Zurechtfinden.

Als Ergänzung zu diesem Führer bieten wir noch einen speziellen Führer für Behinderte an, '*The Disabled Travellers' Phrasebook*', der nützliche Wörter und Redewendungen in sechs europäischen Sprachen enthält. Er kann für ungefähr £1.00 von Disability Press Ltd, 60 Greenhayes Av, Banstead, Surrey, England bezogen werden.

Symbole

P	Parkmöglichkeiten auf dem Gelände oder in der Nähe
⊡	Unebener/holperiger Bodenbelag
H	Hügelig
D	Mit langen Wegen ist zu rechnen
▟	Stufen
E	Eingang. E3 oder E1+1 etc bezeichnet die Anzahl der Stufen am Haupteingang. Wenn es zwei Eingänge gibt, sind sie folgendermaßen gekennzeichnet: E5/2
E0	Haupteingang ohne Stufen
A	Es gibt einen alternativ-Eingang mit ebenem/Rampen-/Lift-Zugang
N	Innen. Wenn Nummern hinzukommen, bezeichnen sie die Anzahl der Stufen, meistens vom Erdgeschoß nach oben oder unten
♿	Nach der Eingangstreppe fast überall ebenem/Rampen-/Lift-Zugang
♿	Nach der Eingangstreppe, zu einem Teil des Gebäudes oder des Geländes ebenem/Rampen-/Lift-Zugang; wenn das Prozentzeichen (%) benutzt wird, gibt es an, zu wieviel Prozent
⇕	Lift. Angaben über die Größe werden normalerweise im Text gegeben
♿ WC	(w) Toilette. Das heißt, spezielle Toilettenvorrichtungen, die seitliches Umsteigen ermöglichen
♿)	Telefon in erreichbarer Höhe für (w)
♿ ✕	Café oder Restaurant für (w) zugänglich
⊶	Enge Türen oder Öffnungen, zB zwischen Ausstellungen
(?)	Spezielle Einrichtungen für Gehörgeschädigte, zB Induktionsschleife
◉	Spezielle Einrichtungen oder Ausstellungen für Sehbehinderte
⊠	Blindenhunde haben Zugang
U	Rollstühle vorhanden

NB Stufen, die entweder nur mit einer Nummer oder mit einem Pluszeichen (+) versehen sind, führen nach oben; solche, die mit einem Minuszeichen (−) versehen sind, führen nach unten: 2+3 bedeutet 2 Stufen nach oben, Abstand, dann noch einmal 3 Stufen nach oben.

Im Theater-/Kinoteil geben die Buchstaben A, B und C an, wer zugelassen ist, und zwar nach der Einteilung des Londoner Stadtrats (GLC):
A steht für (s) oder solche (w), die zwar gehbehindert, aber selbst bis in den Vorführraum kommen;
B steht für solche (w), die sich nicht auf einen normalen Sitzplatz setzen können und die deshalb während der Vorstellung in ihren Rollstühlen bleiben mussen;
C steht für solche (w), die sich auf einen normalen Sitzplatz setzen können oder gesetzt werden können, so daß man die Rollstühle aus dem Vorführraum entfernen kann.

Für Preisangaben werden die nachfolgenden Symbole verwendet:

£   Billig
££   Preiswert
£££   Ziemlich teuer
££££   Sehr teuer

Abkürzungen

(ab)	Nichtbehinderte	M	Direktor/Direktion
BO	Theater- oder Kinokasse	m	Meter
cm	Zentimeter	MSCP	Parkhaus
CP	Parkmöglichkeit	NCP	Öffentliches Parkhaus
cub	Kabine, Einzeltoilette	RHS	Rechte Seite
D	Tür, meistens eines Lifts	(s)	Stockbenutzer oder behinderter
eg	Zum Beispiel		Fußgänger
ext	Nebenstellennummer	SAE	An sich adressierter, frankierter
GF	Erdgeschoß		Umschlag
GFB	Schlafzimmer im Erdgeschoß	UGCP	Parkmöglichkeit im Tiefgeschoß
km	Kilometer	W	Breite, meistens eines Lifts
L	Länge, meistens eines Lifts	(w)	Rollstuhlfahrer
LHS	Linke Seite	YHA	Jugendherbergs-Organisation
loo	Toilette, WC		Englands

Français

Un certain nombre de symboles ont été utilisés dans ce guide pour accentuer certains renseignements simplifiés sur les moyens d'accès. Une légende s'ensuit à l'intention des lecteurs français. Nous espèrons que ces symboles ou d'autres similaires seront bientôt utilisés couramment dans les guides touristiques conventionels pour résumer les renseignements importants sur les moyens d'accès.

Les symboles expliqués ci-dessous sont utilisés dans huit chapîtres de ce guide. De plus, les renseignements donnés dans le chapître sur hébergement ('*Accommodation*') sont présentés sous forme de tableaux, qui, à condition que vous compreniez les grands tîtres et quelques mots-clés, devraient être faciles à déchiffrer.

'*The Disabled Traveller's Phrase Book*' (le Lexique du Voyageur Handicappé) pourrait également vous rendre service. Vous y trouverez des mots et phrases utiles en six langues Européennes. Vous pouvez l'obtenir pour £1.00 environ auprès de Disability Press Ltd, 60 Greenhayes Av, Banstead, Surrey, Angleterre.

Symboles

P   Parking privé rattaché à l'établissement ou très proche

▭   Surface(s) inégales/défoncées

H   Montagneux/accidenté

D   Longs trajets

▦   Escalier

E	Entrée. E3 ou E1+1 etc indique le nombre de marches à l'entrée principale. S'il y a deux ou plusieurs entrées, elles sont marquées comme suit: E2/5
E0	Entrée principale de plain pied
A	Choix d'entrée de plain pied/avec rampe d'accès/avec ascenseur
N	Intérieur. Lorsque des chiffres sont ajoutés, ils indiquent le nombre de marches montant ou descendant du rez-de-chaussée
⬤	Facilité d'accès de plain pied/avec rampe d'accès/avec ascenseur pratiquement partout, après les marches à l'entrée
⬤	Facilité d'accès de plain pied/avec rampe d'accès/avec ascenseur dans une partie de l'établissement ou de la surface, après les marches à l'entrée. Le pourcentage, lorsqu'il est utilisé, indique la quantité du bâtiment qu'est accessible
⬆⬇	Ascenseur. Les dimensions sont généralement données dans le texte
♿ wc	(w) toilette (à laquelle il est généralement possible d'accéder à la cuvette de biais)
♿ ☎	Téléphone à une hauteur accessible pour (w)
♿ ✗	Café ou restaurant accessible pour (w)
⬌	Portes ou passages étroits, par exemple entre les comptoirs
(?)	Aménagement pour les sourds, par exemple boucles d'induction
👁	Aménagement et/ou expositions pour personnes à vision restreinte
🐕	Chiens d'aveugle acceptés
U	Fauteuils roulants disponibles

NB Les marches qui sont indiquées par un chiffre seulement ou avec le signe (+) sont ascendantes; celles indiquées par un chiffre et le signe (−) sont descendantes; c'est-à-dire que 2+3 indique 2 marches ascendantes, un palier, et 3 autres marches ascendantes.

Dans les chapîtres sur les théâtres et les cinémas, les lettres A, B et C sont utilisées pour indiquer qui peut être admis dans ces établissements, suivant une catégorisation utilisée par la Ville de Londres (GLC):
A pour les personnes avec une canne ou ceux en fauteuil roulant qui peuvent marcher un peu (c'est-à-dire jusqu'à l'intérieur de la salle);
B pour les personnes en fauteuil roulant qui ne peuvent pas être transférées sur un siège ordinaire et qui par conséquent doivent demeurer dans leur fauteuil roulant pendant la séance;
C pour les personnes en fauteuil roulant qui peuvent être transférées sur un siège ordinaire, et dont le fauteuil roulant peut être sorti de la salle pendant la séance.

Dans tout le guide une idée du coût est indiquée par les symboles suivants:
£	Bon marché
££	Prix moyens
£££	Relativement cher
££££	Très cher

Abréviations

(ab)	Personne valide	**M**	Directeur/Direction
BO	Guichet	**m**	Mètres
cm	Centimètres	**MSCP**	Parking à étages
CP	Parking	**NCP**	Parking officiel
cub	Cabine	**RHS**	A droite
D	Porte (généralement d'un ascenseur)	**(s)**	Personne(s) avec canne ou personne(s) handicapée(s) pouvant marcher
eg	par exemple		
ext	poste téléphonique	**SAE**	Enveloppe timbrée et adressée
GF	Rez-de-chaussée	**UGCP**	Parking souterrain
GFB	Chambre au rez-de-chaussée	**W**	Largeur (généralement d'un ascenseur)
km	Kilomètres		
L	Longueur (généralement d'un ascenseur)	**(w)**	Personne(s) se déplaçant en fauteuil roulant
LHS	A gauche	**YHA**	Association des Auberges de Jeunesse en Grande Bretagne
loo	WC		

Index

Also available from Robert Nicholson Publications Ltd:

London Guide	**Tourist London**
London Streetfinder	**London Night Life**
Visitor's London	**London Restaurant Guide**
In London	**London Pub Guide**
London Arts Guide	**Guide to the River Thames**

Other Access guides to:

Paris	**Israel**
Brittany	**Jersey**
The Loire Valley	**The Channel Ports**

can be obtained from:

Pauline Hephaistos Survey Projects
39 Bradley Gdns
West Ealing
London W13

Access guides to other towns and areas in the UK
can be obtained from:

RADAR
25 Mortimer St
London W1

and there is an **International Directory of Access Guides**
available from:

Rehabilitation World
20 West 40th St
New York 10018
USA